NELSON'S
Little Books of
SERIES

LITTLE BOOK OF LAUGHTER

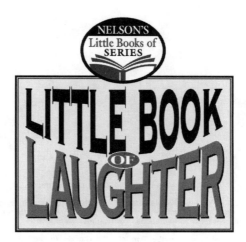

NELSON'S
Little Books of
SERIES

LITTLE BOOK
OF
LAUGHTER

*Hundreds of Smiles
from A to Z*

LOWELL D. STREIKER

THOMAS NELSON PUBLISHERS
Nashville

Published in Nashville, Tennessee, by Thomas Nelson, Inc.

ART CREDITS: Illustrations in this collection are from the following sources, and are used by permission: Corel Corp., BCM Graphics, and Grin Graphics. (BCM Graphics and Grin Graphics are distributed by Lowell Streiker, 3309 El Camino Dr., Cottonwood, CA 96022.)

Library of Congress Cataloging-in-Publication Data

Nelson's little book of laughter A to Z / [compiled by] Lowell Streiker.
   p. cm.
   ISBN 0-7852-4706-8
   1. Quotations, English. 2. Wit and humor. I. Streiker, Lowell.
II. Title.
PN6084.H8 N45 2000
082'02'07—dc21
                                          99–056226
                                             CIP

Printed in the United States of America
1 2 3 4 5 — 05 04 03 02 01

Acknowledgments

THANKS TO:

Eric Petritsch, Access guru extraordinaire, for database guidance.

Ron Dentinger. One of the great aphorists of our time, Ron Dentinger is a corporate comedian. From his home in Dodgeville, Wisconsin, he travels coast-to-coast on the banquet circuit. Various jokes in this book are from his book, *Down Time,* published by Kendall/Hunt, and are used with his permission or from his columns (also titled, "Down Time") in *The Dodgeville* [Wisconsin] *Chronicle*. Ron may be reached by phone at (606) 935-2417.

James "Doc" Blakely, CSP, CPAE, professional humorist/speaker for permission to use material from the book, *How the Platform Professionals Keep 'em Laughin'*. Doc may be contacted at 3404 Fairway Drive, Wharton, TX 77488.

Mel Gibbon and Make 'em Laugh, Ltd. for permission to use selections from their 1000-cartoon collection. They may be contacted by calling (800) 874-3668 or by e-mail at ussales@makemlaugh.com.

Gabe Martin for his *Borderline* cartoons.

Max Hengeveld and Gospel Communications for permission to use Rev. Fun cartoons. Max may be reached at max@gospelcom.net, (616) 773-3361, ext. 247, P.O. Box 455, Muskegon, MI 49443; http://www.gospelcom.net/ max.

Agnes Stogdell. My wife's "Aunt Aggie" helped in the selection of material from many, many sources. She proofread and offered advice (as well as lemon meringue and pecan pies).

Connie Streiker—my wife, who laughed and/or moaned and groaned as I tried out anecdotes on her, often interrupting her reading or TV viewing. No one could have been more supportive!

Charles T. Miles of Grin Graphics and Gary Cooper for their clever artwork.

And my thanks to Teri Wilhelms, editorial director at Thomas Nelson, for her attention to detail and sense of humor. And thanks to John Adams and Jennifer Zimmerman of ProtoType Graphics, Nashville, Tennessee, for their diligence in turning my files into this readable book.

He Who Laughs, Lasts!

An essay on humor by Lowell D. Streiker

Mark Twain observed that humans are the only animals that blush—or need to. And Samuel Butler notes, "Man is the only animal that laughs and has a state legislature." We laugh because we sense the contradiction between the way things are and the way they ought to be. The same impulse that makes us religious also makes us humorous. As a minister, I have found humor a valuable resource as I have sought to communicate spiritual truths to church audiences on Sunday mornings. Sometimes the truth contained in a humorous story or quip gains attention while the same truth in its usual prosaic form is ignored or taken for granted.

Sometimes, to quote actor Woody Harrelson, "the only way to get a serious message across is through comedy." Also the humorous illustrations in a talk, a lecture, or a sermon are remembered long after the other content of the address is forgotten. As Isaac Asimov, author of hundreds of books and lifetime collector of humorous anecdotes, once related, "Jokes of the proper kind, properly told, can do more to enlighten questions of politics, philosophy, and literature than any number of dull arguments." Actor-comedian John Cleese maintains, "If I can get you to laugh with me, you like me better, which makes you more open to my ideas. And if I can persuade you to laugh at the particular point I make, by laughing at it you acknowledge its truth." And Joel Goodman remarks, "Mirth can be a major tool for insight, changing 'ha-ha' to 'aha.'"

This is a collection of some of my all-time favorite anecdotes, jokes, quips, and witty comments. I trust that they will be of value to you as you meet and communicate with others—whatever your vocation may be. Laughter is a powerful force and it is yours to use whether you are a public speaker, a minister, a teacher, a salesman, an office worker, a psychologist, or a plumber!

The laughter encouraged by this collection is supportive of human dignity. It is life-affirming and life-giving. And it is, to borrow a word from religion, prophetic. It comforts the afflicted and afflicts the comfortable. It ennobles our spirits and extends our love to others.

I believe that God is a fantastic humorist and we are all his jokes. God fills each of our lives with more irony and coincidence than a Shakespearean comedy or an afternoon soap opera.

Did you know that Jesus was a fabulous comedian? It is hard to read his parables without laughing. They are filled with irony, wit, and surprise endings. His teachings are replete with hyperbole and exaggeration: "If your eye offends you, pluck it out . . . Don't be so concerned about the speck in your brother's eye. Take care of the rafter in your own." He puts the pretentious and pompous in their place. He celebrates the triumph of little people. If only we could see the smile on his face, we might understand him much better. If I had to summarize his teachings in a single sentence, that sentence would be: "The first shall be last and the laughs shall be first."

Many observers claim that a sense of humor is essential to mental well-being and good physical health. When struggling to overcome a painful and debilitating disease, Norman Cousins discovered, "Ten minutes of genuine belly laughter had an anesthetic effect and would give me at least two hours of pain-free sleep." As Anne Wilson Schaef recognizes, "A chuckle a day may not keep the doctor away, but it sure does make those times in life's waiting room a little more bearable." Mahatma Gandhi confessed, "If I had no sense of humor, I should long ago have committed suicide."

"Laughter," says an anonymous commentator, "is like changing a baby's diaper—it doesn't permanently solve any problems, but it makes things more acceptable for a while."

Psychologist Rollo May explains, "Humor is the healthy way of feeling 'distance' between one's self and the problem, a way of standing off and looking at one's problems with perspective." And to quote Anne Wilson Schaef again, "I realize that humor isn't for everyone. It's only for people who want to have fun, enjoy life, and feel alive."

I have read that Saint Theresa of Àvila "always looked for novices who knew how to laugh, eat, and sleep. She was sure that if they ate heartily they were healthy, if they slept well they were more likely free of serious sin, and if they laughed they had the necessary disposition to survive a difficult life."

As serious a person as Billy Graham recognizes the value of humor. He writes: "A keen sense of humor helps us to overlook the unbecoming, understand the unconventional, tolerate the unpleasant, overcome the unexpected, and outlast the unbearable."

Laughter, of course, can be helpful or harmful. It can be derisive. It can ridicule whatever and whomever we fear, we misunderstand, we resent. Hence, there are racial and ethnic jokes, in-law jokes, sexist jokes, etc. Archie Bunker is never far away in American humor.

In this collection, I have sought to avoid being unnecessarily offensive—which means that at times I may have been a bit rough on someone in order to make a point. Remember what I said about "afflicting the comfortable." Pompous, self-important, insensitive people are always fair game to the humorist. Even so, I have attempted not to be mean-spirited. All humor walks this fine line.

And I have selected "good, clean" anecdotes and jokes. If I could not tell a story from the pulpit or when speaking on television, it is not in this collection.

But let me do more than tell you about this collection and how it can be of value to you. Let me show you exactly what the laughter evoked by a good story can do. (All of the following anecdotes are taken from the body of this collection.)

Laughter sets things in their proper perspective. I am reminded of the college student who wrote to her parents as follows:

> "Dear Mom and Dad, I'm sorry to be so long in writing, but all my writing paper was lost the night the dormitory burned down. I'm out of the hospital now, and the doctor says my eyesight should be back to normal sooner or later. The wonderful boy, Bill, who rescued me from the fire, kindly offered to share his little apartment with me until the dorm is rebuilt. He comes from a good family, so you won't be surprised when I tell you we are going to be married. In fact you always wanted a grandchild, so you will be glad to know you will be grandparents early next year." Then she added this postscript: "Please disregard the above practice in English composition. There was no fire. I haven't been in the hospital. I'm not pregnant. And I don't have a steady boyfriend. But I did get a 'D' in French and an 'F' in chemistry, and I wanted to be sure you received the news in proper perspective. Love, Mary."

Laughter is the great leveler:

> Three burly fellows on huge motorcycles pulled up to a highway cafe where a truck driver, just a little guy, was perched on a stool quietly eating his lunch. As the three fellows came in, they spotted him, grabbed his food away from him and laughed in his face. The truck driver said nothing. He got up, paid for his food and walked out. One of the three cyclists, unhappy that they hadn't succeeded in provoking the little [guy] into a fight commented to the waitress: "Boy, he sure wasn't much of a man, was he?" The waitress replied, "Well, I guess not." Then looking out the window, she added, "I guess he's not much of a truck driver, either. He just ran over three motorcycles."

Laughter keeps us from taking ourselves too seriously:

> I was once invited to speak at a local Rotary club. I felt
> flattered by the invitation until the master of ceremonies
> rose to introduce me. "Unfortunately," he said, "our origi-
> nal choice to be today's speaker is unable to attend." Then,
> in a clumsy attempt at humor, he pointed to a broken
> window pane which had been covered over with a piece
> of cardboard. "Our speaker," he said, "is like that piece of
> cardboard in the window. He's a substitute." Being some-
> what taken aback by the ungraceful introduction, I de-
> cided to show them: Substitute or not I would knock their
> socks off. And I did! When I finished the speech, I received
> a standing ovation. But when the emcee returned to the
> lectern, his attempt to thank me was even more awkward
> than his introduction. "Reverend," he said, "we want you
> to know that you were not at all like a cardboard substi-
> tute. You were a real pane!"
>
>   That humiliation was nothing compared to what hap-
> pened later. After the meeting, the club president gave me
> a check for $100. I gave it back and told him to use it for
> his club's favorite charity. He said, "Oh, good, we can put
> it in our 'special fund,' the one we use to pay for really
> good speakers!"

Actually neither incident really happened to me. They are
anecdotes which I applied to myself so that my audience
could have a laugh at my expense. And since I am in a profession that is notorious for taking itself too seriously, such
self-deflating humor is of enormous value.

Lenoard I. Sweet, President of United Theological Seminary in Dayton, Ohio, gives a vivid illustration from his own
career.

> It was my first "stewardship campaign." I had been ap-
> pointed by the bishop to the missionary church in a small-
> college community in New York's Genessee Valley. The
> first year had been a nervous one for both me, a young,

not-dry-behind-the-ears pastor and wetback Ph.D., and the congregation which was comprised of an odd and unconsummated coupling of rural folk and "academic types." But there was significant enough progress to warrant the belief that we could double the budget after my first year there. If only we had a slogan . . . some catchy motto or jingle around which to design our development campaign.

Or so I thought. The weekend before the "Stewardship Sunday" kickoff, I sought some solitary confinement in Toronto, Canada. There I hit first on a slogan and then an idea: Why not have T-shirts made up for those "every-member canvassers" who could then call on parishioners emblazoned with my newly brainstormed stewardship theme: It seemed the perfect plan.

During the "Community Concerns" time of the morning worship the next Sunday, the chair of the campaign, Doug Klapper, did an outstanding job of making the committee's case for our controversial financial leap forward. As soon as he finished, I bolted to the front, prevented him from returning to his seat, and presented him with a "surprise gift" that I announced confidently would give our campaign focus and force.

The color of Doug's face when he unwrapped his "surprise gift" should have alerted me to what was to come. His embarrassed refusal ("You do it," he giggled) to hold up the T-shirt for the congregation to see was another missed warning signal. But it was not until the moment that I held up that T-shirt and announced that there were enough of these "surprise gifts" for every one of our canvassers to wear that I realized exactly what I had done. Our stewardship slogan would be, I proudly read,

I Upped My Pledge.

Up Yours

I had lost it. At first a trickling tickle, then a torrent of laughter. I tried to preach. But convulsions of laughter drowned out my sermon at unpredictable moments, ebbing and flowing like a moonshine tide. But that moment of my greatest embarrassment and mistake, a moment from which that worship service never fully recovered, was the moment of my ministry's recovery in that community. For suddenly this upstart preacher and hotshot Ph.D. became human, and could do something so outrageously stupid and foolish that it redeemed all his jarring strangeness. From that Sunday on, I became their pastor and was bonded to them for life. And for the next seven years, as I walked the streets of the village, I would find myself greeted with the query, "Are you the 'up-yours' preacher?"

As a pastor, Dr. Sweet was no longer affected by that debilitating disease of preachers, terminal seriousness. In the eyes of his congregation, he was no longer a stranger, he was a human being who—just like them—could "do something . . . outrageously stupid and foolish." As humor writer Larry Wilde proclaims, "If you are willing to make yourself the butt of a joke, you become one of the guys, a human being, and people are more willing to listen to what you have to say."

A story that punctures the pomposity of experts in general and ministers in particular is told about:

. . . an engineer, a psychologist, and a theologian [who] were hunting in the wilds of northern Canada. [Suddenly, the temperature dropped and a snowstorm descended, lashing them with its fury. As they trudged on, they] . . . came across an isolated cabin, far removed from any town. Because friendly hospitality is a virtue practiced by those who live in the wilderness, the hunters knocked on the door to ask permission to rest.

No one answered their knocks, but, discovering the cabin was unlocked, they entered. It was a simple place—two rooms with a minimum of furniture and household equipment. Nothing was surprising about the cabin except the stove. It was large, potbellied, and made of cast iron.

What was unusual was its location: it was suspended in midair by wires attached to the ceiling beams.

"Fascinating," said the psychologist [, stroking his beard]. "It is obvious that this lonely trapper, isolated from humanity, has elevated his stove so he can curl up under it and vicariously experience a return to the womb."

"Nonsense!" replied the engineer [as he scratched some calculations in the dust on the cabin floor]. "The man is practicing the laws of thermodynamics. By elevating his stove, he has discovered a way to distribute heat more evenly throughout the cabin."

"With all due respect," interrupted the theologian, [folding his hands in a gesture of piety,] "I'm sure that hanging his stove from the ceiling has religious meaning. Fire LIFTED UP has been a religious symbol for centuries."

The three debated the point for several hours without resolving the issue. When the trapper finally returned, they immediately asked him why he had hung his heavy potbellied stove from the ceiling.

His answer was succinct: "Had plenty of wire, not much stove pipe!"

Humor, notes Southern folklorist Loyal Jones, "helps us keep objective, reminds us that we are fallible, that we are not the center of the unvierse, and that there is a whole lot that we do not know and still more that we don't understand. Humor puts us in our place just as the teachings of Jesus do. Humor reiterates what he said: The one who exalts himself shall be humbled and the one who humbles himself shall be exalted.

But humor does more than encourage humility.

Laughter makes pain palatable:

A group of high school students went to New York for their senior trip. They had reserved rooms in one of the finest hotels. When they arrived in the city they went to the hotel and registered. A bellhop led them to their rooms, which were on the 30th floor. After getting settled in their rooms they went out to see the sights. They went to Rocke-feller Center, the United Nations Plaza, the Guggenheim Museum, the Empire State Building, the Statue of Liberty, etc. Finally they came back to their hotel, utterly exhausted. They went to the desk and asked for the keys to their rooms.

The clerk said, "I am sorry, the elevators are not running. You will have to walk up or wait until the elevators are repaired."

They were so weary that all they could think of were the comfortable beds in their rooms. Tired as they were, they decided they would climb the thirty flights of stairs. One of them had an idea. He said, "On the way up, each of us will tell the funniest story we know." The others agreed and they started the climb. When they reached the tenth floor they were still going strong.

When they reached the twentieth floor their legs were like lead and they were panting for breath. The steps got longer and longer but they trudged on. The one whose turn it was to tell the next funny story said, "I'm sorry, I'm just too exhausted to laugh."

They trudged on in silence. When they reached the 29th floor, one of them began to laugh. He sat down on the steps and almost had hysterics. Finally, he said, "I have just thought of one of the funniest things I have ever heard of in my life."

The others said, "What is it? Tell us!"

He said, "Our room keys—we left them in the lobby!"

Laughter is therapeutic.

It can mend anything from a broken heart to the crack of dawn. From Alison Crane, executive director of the American Association for Therapeutic Humor, comes a story originally told to her by a middle-aged pastor:

I had a very serious accident a few years ago; it was amazing I survived. And, of course, I was in the hospital for a very long time recuperating.

Because I was there for so long, I became rather nonchalant with the nurses about the procedures they subjected me to—you can't keep decorum up for very long with no clothes on. I was also having trouble finding a relatively painless spot to put yet another injection of pain medication.

One time I rang for the nurse, and when she came on the intercom, I told her I needed another pain shot. I knew it would take just about as long for her to draw up the medication as it would for me to gather the strength to roll over and find a spot for her to inject it. I had succeeded in rolling over, facing away from the door, when I heard her come in. "I think this area here isn't too bad," I said, pointing to an exposed area of my rear. But there was an awful silence after I said that. My face paled as I rolled over slowly to see who had actually come in—it was one of my twenty-two-year-old parishioners. I apologized and tried to chat with her, but she left shortly thereafter, horribly embarrassed.

Well, about thirty seconds after she left, the impact of the situation hit me and I started to laugh. It hurt like you can't imagine, but I laughed and laughed. Tears were rolling down my face and I was gasping when my nurse finally came in. She asked what had happened. I tried to tell her, but couldn't say more than a word or two before convulsing into laughing fits again. Amused, she told me she would give me a few minutes to calm down and she'd be back to give me my shot.

I had just started to regain my composure when my nurse reappeared and asked again what had happened. I started to tell her, but got to laughing again, and she started to laugh just from watching me, which made it worse. Finally, she left again, promising to try back in fifteen more minutes. This scenario repeated itself a couple of more times, and by the time I could tell her what had happened, I felt absolutely no pain. None. I didn't need medication for three more hours. And I know it was an emotional turning point in my recovery.

As an editorial writer for the *Chicago Tribune* declared about the therapeutic power of humor:

Jokes are no laughing matter to the brain. They are a type of release valve that enables us to think the unthinkable, accept the unacceptable, discover new relationships, adjust better and maintain our mental health. They are also funny. Without them we probably would be a dull, dimwitted society, trapped in a harsh world too serious to bear.

And finally,

Laughter reminds us how poorly we communicate with others and how readily we misunderstand those who communicate with us:

There was a nice lady, a minister's widow, who was a little old-fashioned. She was planning a week's vacation in California at Skylake Yosemite campground (Bass Lake, to the uninitiated), but she wanted to make sure of the accommodations first. Uppermost in her mind were bathroom facilities, but she couldn't bring herself to write "toilet" in a letter. After considerable deliberation, she settled on "bathroom commode," but when she wrote that down, it still sounded too forward, so, after the first page of her letter, she referred to the bathroom commode as "BC." "Does the cabin where I will be staying have its own 'BC'? If not, where is the 'BC' located?" is what she actually wrote.

The campground owner took the first page of the letter and the lady's check and gave it to his secretary. He put the remainder of the letter on the desk of the senior member of his staff without noticing that the staffer would have no way of knowing what "BC" meant. Then the owner went off to town to run some errands.

The staff member came in after lunch, found the letter, and was baffled by the euphemism, so he showed the letter around to several counselors, but they couldn't decipher it either. The staff member's wife, who knew that the lady was the widow of a famous Baptist preacher, was sure that it must be a question about the local Baptist Church. "Of course," the first staffer exclaimed, "'BC' stands for 'Baptist Church.'" And he sat down and wrote:

Dear Madam,

I regret very much the delay in answering your letter, but I now take the pleasure in informing you that the BC is located nine miles north of the campground and is capable of seating 250 people at one time. I admit it is quite a distance away if you are in the habit of going regularly, but no doubt you will be pleased to know that a great number of people take their lunches along and make a day of it. They usually arrive early and stay late.

The last time my wife and I went was six years ago, and it was so crowded we had to stand up the whole time we were there. It may interest you to know that right now there is a supper planned to raise money to buy more seats. They are going to hold it in the basement of the "BC."

I would like to say that it pains me very much not to be able to go more regularly, but it is surely not lack of desire on my part. As we grow older, it seems to be more of an effort, particularly in cold weather.

If you decide to come down to our campground, perhaps I could go with you the first time, sit with you, and introduce you to all the folks. Remember, this is a friendly community.

Well, the particular local church each of us attends is also a friendly community, and a community that knows there is a time for laughter. We know that God cares, that he takes away our sorrows and turns them into delight. We know that God weeps with us when we weep and laughs with us when we laugh.

So here is Dr. Lowell's prescription for being happy and spreading happiness: take two jokes before you go to bed and call in the morning—or whenever you have a laugh to spare. And the next time you see someone on the street who appears to have no happiness in him, not even a smile to share, give him one of yours.

Finally, always remember: laughter is an expression of confidence—in God, in yourself, in the future. Laugh and you will endure. Laugh and you will triumph. Laugh and you will overcome adversity. In simplest terms: He who laughs, LASTS!

ACCIDENTS

A kindhearted farmer came upon a young boy who had just lost a load of hay along the side of the road, and suggested that the boy come home with him and have dinner before reloading the wagon. The boy said he didn't think his father would like that, but the farmer persisted, and finally the boy agreed. After eating dinner and relaxing a bit, the farmer drove the boy back to the scene of the accident, and started to help him put the hay back on the wagon. "By the way," the farmer said, "you're awfully young to be pitching this hay yourself. Where's your father?" "He's under this hay," the boy replied.

—*How the Platform Professionals Keep 'em Laughin'*

In filling out an application for a factory job, a man was puzzled for a long time over this question: "Person to notify in case of accident." Finally he wrote: "Anybody in sight."

A man was hit by a car, and as he lay in the street waiting for an ambulance, an onlooker covered him with a jacket and propped his head on a pillow. "Are you comfortable?" the helper asked. The injured man replied, "I make a living."

ACTORS

Dustin Farnum, a talented but conceited actor, once droned on to his dinner host, writer Oliver Herford, about a play he was doing at the time. "Why, yesterday," boasted Farnum, "I had the audience glued to their seats." To which Herford replied, "How clever of you to think of it!"

My old drama coach used to say, "Don't just do something, stand there."   —Clint Eastwood

A Broadway producer hired a talented young actor whose ego became more inflated with each hit. After another successful opening night, the actor strutted haughtily off the stage. Just as he disappeared into the wings, there was a

loud explosion in the street. "By golly," the producer gasped, "his head's burst."
— Joe Martinez

A young actor was cast in a performance of *Julius Caesar*. One evening, at the height of the dramatic scene portraying Caesar's brutal stabbing, an offstage phone suddenly rang. Without missing a beat, the actor lifted his head and said, "What do we tell them if it's for Caesar?"
— Terrence Currier, WETA-FM

An actress was belittling the late Marie Dressler's comedy. "What dignity is there in making people laugh?" she squeaked. "I make them cry." Miss Dressler retorted: "Any onion can do that. Show me a vegetable that can make people laugh."

ADS

A New Zealand publication carried an intriguing advertisement of a tested and proven method for cutting household bills in half. It offered prospective customers the opportunity to get in on the secret for only $3. How could the promoters guarantee such fantastic results? That was what the police wanted to know. They found that the advertisers planned to send each customer a cheap pair of scissors. — King Duncan

A TV commercial I saw while staying in Seattle had an interesting claim near the end: "Pepsi products now contain 25 percent recycled plastic." I wonder if Coke paid for the ad?

An ad in a British newspaper: Circumstances force me to sell 1979 Volvo 144, good condition, will accept smaller car in part exchange for wife.

Personal ad in local paper: "David G. Contact me soon! Bring three rings: Engagement, wedding and teething. Have news. — Debbie."

I, my wife and children regret to announce the opening of my office all day Saturday for the convenience of working mothers and fathers who have found it impossible to accommodate my previous office hours. Please don't invite me to any more Friday night parties.

— Notice from a dentist in the Ocean County, N.J., *Times-Observer*

I find some amazing things in the newspapers. These are actual classified ads:

- From the Saginaw, Michigan, *News:* For Sale—Eight puppies from a German Shepherd and an Alaskan Hussy.
- From the Roanoke, Illinois, *Review:* Hope chest—brand new, half price, long story.
- From the Help Wanted ads in a Michigan paper: Adult or mature teenager to baby-sit. One dollar an hour—plus fridge benefits.
- From the Los Altos, California, *Town Crier:* Lost: Gray and white female cat. Answers to electric can opener.
- Midwest newspaper ad: Idaho bachelor wants wife. Must be interested in farming and own tractor. Please enclose picture of tractor.
- From the *New York Times:* Young man, Democrat, would like to meet young lady, Republican. Object: third party.
- Notice: to the person or persons who took the large pumpkin on Highway 87 near Southridge storage: please return the pumpkin and be checked. Pumpkin may be radioactive. All other plants in vicinity are dead.
- Tired of working for only $9.75 per hour? We offer profit sharing and flexible hours. Starting pay: $7–$9 per hour.
- Help Wanted: Busy lawyer seeks alert young woman to serve as deceptionist.
- For Rent: One-bedroom apt. Adults, no pets. Well, maybe a cat.
- Help wanted: Saleslady for cosmetic counter in department store. Must like people part or full time.
- Help wanted: Secretary wants job; no bad habits; willing to learn.

- From a display ad for an automotive dealership in Cleveland, Tenn.: "Why go anywhere else and get cheated when you can come here!"

FOR SALE:

- 1 man, 7 woman hot tub—$850/offer
- Snow blower . . . only used on snowy days.
- Free puppies . . . part German Shepherd—part dog
- 2 wire mesh butchering gloves: 1 5-finger, 1 3-finger, pair: $15
- '83 Toyota hunchback—$2000
- Star Wars job of the hut—$15
- Free puppies: ½ Cocker Spaniel—½ sneaky neighbor's dog
- Free Yorkshire Terrier. 8 years old. Unpleasant little dog.
- German Shepherd 85 lbs. Neutered. Speaks German. Free.
- Free 1 can of pork and beans with purchase of 3 br 2 bath home.
- For sale: Lee Majors (6 Million Dollar Man)—$50
- Nordic Track $300 hardly used. Call Chubbie
- Shakespeare's Pizza—free chopsticks
- Hummels—largest selection ever. If it's in stock, we have it!
- Free: farm kittens. Ready to eat.
- American flag—60 stars—pole included $100
- Exercise equipment: queen size mattress and box springs—$175.
- Joining nudist colony! Must sell washer and dryer $300.
- Ground beast: 99 cents lb.
- Open house—Body Shapers Toning Salon—free coffee and donuts.
- Fully cooked boneless smoked man—$2.09 lb.
- Puppies for sale. Mother registered AKC St. Bernard. Father, a VERY REMARKABLE beagle.
- 100-year-old brass bed. Perfect for antique lovers.

- Amana washer $100. Owned by clean bachelor who seldom washed.
- Complete set of *Encyclopedia Britannica*. 45 volumes. Excellent condition. $1,000.00 or best offer. No longer needed. Got married last weekend. Wife knows everything.
- Monster! John Deere, 38", front-end, snow blower. Hurls snow from your drive well onto neighbor's property. (I did, he got mad, that's why I'm selling.)
- We put up the loot; daughter won't toot. First $175 takes the flute.

ADULTS

Adults are obsolete children.   —Dr. Seuss

When childhood dies, its corpses are called adults.
    —Brian Aldiss

Here I am, fifty-eight, and I still don't know what I want to be when I grow up.   —Peter Drucker

Adults are always asking kids what they want to be when they grow up because they are looking for ideas.
    —Paula Poundstone

ADVERTISING

There is truth in advertising. I saw that junker car I used to drive. It's on the dealer's lot, and it has a great big sign on it that reads: "TODAY ONLY—$499—THIS ONE WON'T LAST LONG."   —Ron Dentinger

Many a small thing has been made large by the right kind of advertising.   —Mark Twain

Running a business without advertising is like winking at a girl in the dark. You know what you're doing, but she doesn't.

In the late 1600's the finest musical instruments came from three rural families whose workshops were side by side in the Italian village of Cremona. Outside the shop of the Arnatis hung a sign which read, "The Best Violins In All Italy." Not to be outdone, their next-door neighbors, the Guarnieris, hung a sign proclaiming "The Best Violins In All The World!" At the end of the street was the workshop of Anton Stradivarius, and on his front door was a simple notice which read, "The Best Violins On The Block."

One advertising-agency copywriter to another: "Hi! What's new and improved?"
— Tony Zarro

ADVICE

A woman called the utility company and complained that her electricity was out. What should she do? The voice on the other end advised, "Open your freezer and eat the ice cream."

Always stay in with the outs.   — David Halberstam

Be yourself is about the worst advice you can give some people.   — Jeff Marder

General Mark Clark was asked what was the best advice he ever had. The general thought for awhile then replied, "Well, the best advice I ever had was to marry the girl I did." And then the young officer that asked Mark Clark that question said, "Well, sir, who gave you that advice?" And General Clark replied, "She did."

Two quick ways to disaster:
1) Take nobody's advice.
2) Take everybody's advice.   — Ralph Cansler

The trouble with most sound advice is that it's 99 percent sound and one percent advice.   — Peter F. Cullip

Accept good advice gracefully—as long as it doesn't interfere with what you intended to do in the first place.

AGE

Two women in their 20s on a lunch break at the City Market, were chatting about a new boyfriend, a man in his 50s. "Well, he's very nice," said one, "but he is a bit old for you, don't you think?" To which the young woman with the new boyfriend replied: "Well, he may be a bit old, but he's very immature."

— *Quote*

A very wealthy 72-year-old man who married a shapely 21-year-old blonde was asked, How did a 72-year-old codger like you manage to marry such a young, beautiful woman? "I told her I was 90," he replied.

It's not that she's too old. But she's got beautiful antique jewelry . . . and she bought it when it was new.

An elderly gentleman was overheard complaining to a friend: "You know the worst thing about getting old? I'll tell you— it's having to listen to advice from your children."

AGING

During his presidency, Ronald Reagan told the following story at a White House reception. "It seems that an 80-year-old man's golf game was hampered by poor eyesight. He could hit the ball well but he couldn't see where it went. So his doctor teamed him up with a 90-year-old man who had perfect eyesight and was willing to go along to serve as a spotter. The 80-year-old man hit the first ball and asked his companion if he saw where it landed. 'Yep,' said the 90-year-old. 'Where did it go?' the 80-year-old demanded. The 90-year-old replied, 'I don't remember.'"

Old people shouldn't eat health foods. They need all the preservatives they can get. —Robert Orben

You know you're getting older when the only thing you want for your birthday is not to be reminded of it. —Jeff Rovin

Uncle Leo reports: "When the doctor asked what I did for exercise, I said pushing ninety is exercise enough!"

Sad but true: By the time some men learn to watch their step, they are too old to go anywhere.

Louise Adams recently reached her one hundredth birthday. She was honored at a lavish catered birthday celebration arranged for her by her four daughters. She was asked if she felt that old. She perused the crowd for a moment and then gave her answer. "I really don't feel this old, except that I look around the room and see these white-haired ladies and realize they are all my daughters!"

"I'm doing what I can," the doctor explained, "but I can't make you any younger, you know." "The heck with that," said the patient. "I'm not interested in getting younger, I just want to get older."
—Joey Adams

It's an awful thing to grow old alone. My wife hasn't had a birthday in six years.

What's the best thing about turning sixty-five? No more calls from life insurance salesmen.

My parents live in Cape Coral, Florida, a haven for the elderly. My folks are a mere 84-years-old each. Once my dad went to a local service club meeting. I asked him the age of the members. "They were old," he commented. "In fact," he added after a moment's thought, "I would say that their average age was deceased."

The older I grow the more I distrust the familiar doctrine that age brings wisdom.
—H. L. Mencken

If a man has to get old, he might as well get as old as he can.
—Ansel Adams

At age fifty, every man has the face he deserves.
—George Orwell

It's not your age that matters, it's how your matter ages.
—Martin A. Ragaway

My wife's Aunt Aggie claims: "There are four advantages to getting old and forgetful: One, you meet new friends every day; two, every joke you hear is new; three, you can hide your own Easter eggs; and I forget the fourth thing."

Several years ago, a retrospective showing of Pablo Picasso's works was held at the Museum of Modern Art in New York City. Nearly a thousand of Picasso's works were displayed in chronological order, beginning when he was a very young boy. The early works were traditional landscapes and still-lifes. Then, as the artist advanced in age, brilliant colors began to emerge, and the still-lifes were no longer very still. Finally, of course, the works turned into the kind of bold, zesty abstractions for which Picasso is best known. One art critic who saw the show recalled that once, when Picasso was eighty-five, he was asked the reason why his earlier works were so solemn and his later works so ecstatic and exciting. "How do you explain it?" asked the interviewer. "Easily," Picasso responded, his eyes sparkling. "It takes a long time to become young!"

In America, the young are always ready to give to those who are older than themselves the full benefit of their inexperience.   —Oscar Wilde

When I was younger I could remember anything, whether it had happened or not; but my faculties are decaying now and soon I shall be so I cannot remember any but the things that never happened. It is sad to go to pieces like this but we all have to do it.   —Mark Twain

An elderly woman in a nursing home declined her pastor's suggestion that she get a hearing aid. "At 91, I've heard enough," she said.   —Catherine Hall

Old age is a time when you complain that your grown-up children don't visit enough; but when they do visit, you can't wait for them to leave.

Ron Cichowicz observes,"When you're over the hill, you tend to repeat yourself. When you're over the hill, you tend to repeat yourself."

Forty is the old age of youth; fifty is the youth of old age.
— Victor Hugo

The error of youth is to believe that intelligence is a substitute for experience, while the error of age is to believe that experience is a substitute for intelligence. —Lyman Bryson

My grandmother has always led a very busy life. Recently, she celebrated her 90th birthday. "Granny," I said, "it's remarkable how young you look. How do you do it?" "It takes time to grow old, Robert," she answered, "and I've never had any."   —Msgr. Arthur Tonne, *Jokes Priests Can Tell*, vol. 7

Old-timer to neighbor: "I've reached the age where the happy hour is a nap."

It take about ten years to get used to how old you are.

My minister told me that at my age I should be giving some thought to what he called "the hereafter." I told him that I think about it many times a day. "That's very wise," he said. I explained that it's not a matter of wisdom. It's when I open a drawer or a closet and ask myself, "What am I here after?"

AIR TRAVEL

An old-timer who had never flown was taking out some insurance prior to a flight across Lake Michigan. On the application, one of the questions was: "Who should we notify in case of emergency?" The old gent put down: "The Coast Guard."

— Ron Dentinger

YOU KNOW IT'S A NO-FRILLS AIRLINE WHEN . . .

- They don't sell tickets, they sell chances.
- All the insurance machines in the terminal are sold out.
- Before the flight, the passengers get together and elect a pilot.
- If you kiss the wing for luck before boarding, it kisses you back.
- You cannot board the plane unless you have the exact change.
- Before you take off, the stewardess tells you to fasten your Velcro.
- The Captain asks all the passengers to chip in a little for gas.
- When they pull the steps away, the plane starts rocking.
- The Captain yells at the ground crew to get the cows off the runway.
- You ask the Captain how often their planes crash and he replies, "Just once."
- No movie. Don't need one. Your life keeps flashing before your eyes.
- You see a man with a gun, but he's demanding to be let off the plane.
- All the planes have both a bathroom and a chapel.

Tower: "Flight 1234, for noise abatement turn right 45 degrees." Pilot: "Roger, but we are at 35,000 feet. How much noise can we make up here?" Tower: "Sir, have you ever heard the noise a 707 makes when it hits a 727?"

Question: How can you tell when an airplane is about to experience turbulence? Answer: The flight attendant is serving coffee.

—Joey Adams

AIRPLANES

You know you're in trouble when you go to the airline desk to complain about losing your luggage and the guy behind the counter is wearing your clothes.

Pastor Harold saw a member of the flock off at the airport yesterday: "May God and your luggage go with you."

Pilot to passengers on a commuter flight: I've got some good news and bad news. The bad news is that we're lost. But the good news is that we've got a strong tail wind.

Everybody's cutting back. Instead of movies, one airline asks passengers to just pass around pictures of their children.

In South America, scientists have found strange, ancient lost airstrips. They've also found strange, ancient lost luggage.

ALIMONY

I know a couple that got remarried. He missed two alimony payments and she repossessed him.   —Bill Barner

Banks have long printed checks in a wide spectrum of colors; some have offered checks with floral or scenic backgrounds. The modest-sized Bank of Marin in Marin County, California, has gone one step further. A customer can simply bring in a personal photograph or drawing and have it printed onto a standard check form. Undeterred by the higher cost, more than five hundred customers signed for the illustrated checks. But perhaps the most imaginative and vindictive customer is the one who ordered special checks to be used solely for making his alimony payments. They show him kissing his new—and beautiful—wife.

AMERICA

I went to the movies last night. Incredible! Cars crashing, buildings burning, people fighting with guns and knives. And that was just on my way home.

Autumn is a wonderful time of the year even in Los Angeles. You can sit for hours in the smog and watch the birds change colors and fall out of the trees.

Americans love healthy, outdoor sports—especially if they are played indoors.

America is the land where half our salary goes to buy food and the other half to lose weight.

Talking to the suntanned New Mexican about the weather in Albuquerque, the tourist asked, "Doesn't it ever rain here?" The native replied, "Mister, do you remember the story of Noah and the Ark, and how it rained forty days and forty nights?" "Of course I do," the man answered. "Well," drawled the southwesterner, "we got half an inch that time."

Our daughter came from New York to visit us in the small town of Douglas, Ariz., about a hundred miles southeast of Tucson on the Mexican border. As we drove home from the airport, there were lone stretches where nothing could be seen but cactus and cattle. I asked what she thought of Arizona scenery. "I'm impressed; I've never seen so much of nothing so well-fenced."
                    —Francis C. Gaudet in *Arizona Highways*

Of course, America had often been discovered before Columbus, but it had always been hushed up.   —Oscar Wilde

ANCESTORS/ANCESTRY

"Yes," said the boastful young man, "my family can trace its ancestry back to William the Conqueror." "I suppose," remarked his friend, "you'll be telling us that your ancestors were in the Ark with Noah?" "Certainly not," said the other. "My people had a boat of their own."
                              —*Retired Teachers Journal*

ANIMALS

In Minnesota three pastors got together for coffee one day and found all their churches had bat-infestation problems.

"I got so mad," said Pastor Johnson, "I took a shotgun and fired at them. It made holes in the ceiling, but did nothing to the bats." "I tried trapping them alive," said Pastor Linquist. "Then I drove 50 miles before releasing them, but they returned." "I haven't had any more problems," said Pastor Stephens. "What did you do?" asked the others amazed. "I simply baptized and confirmed them," he replied. "I haven't seen them since."

A man had a gopher in his yard. He wanted to get rid of it, and asked an exterminator for his opinion. "I suggest the four-day process," the exterminator said. "How does it work?" "Simple," the exterminator said. "For three mornings you drop an apple and a cookie down the gopher's hole. On the fourth morning you drop in an apple. Then you wait 10 minutes." "And?" "And," the exterminator explained, "when the gopher pokes his head up and says, 'Where's the cookie?' you clobber him."
                                                                —*Capper's Weekly*

Penguins mate for life. That doesn't surprise me much, because they all look alike. It's not like they're going to meet a better-looking penguin someday.
                —*Ellen Degeneres*

A panda walks into a restaurant, sits down and orders a sandwich. He eats the sandwich, pulls out a gun and shoots the waiter dead. As the panda stands up to go, the manager shouts, "Hey! Where are you going? You just shot my waiter and you didn't pay for your sandwich!" The panda yells back at the manager, "Hey man, I'm a PANDA! Look it up!" The manager opens his dictionary and sees the following definition for panda: "A tree dwelling marsupial of Asian origin, characterized by distinct black and white coloring. Eats shoots and leaves."

Did you know that dolphins are so intelligent that within only a few weeks of captivity, they can train Americans to stand at the very edge of the pool and throw them fish?

I live in a semi-rural area. We recently had a new neighbor call the local township administrative office to request the removal of the Deer Crossing sign on our road. The reason: Many deer were being hit by cars and he no longer wanted them to cross there.

It's a sunny morning in the Big Forest and the Bear family are just waking up. Baby Bear goes downstairs and sits in his small chair at the table. He looks into his small bowl and it's empty! "Who's been eating my porridge?" he squeaks. Daddy Bear arrives at the table and sits in his big chair. He looks into his big bowl and it is also empty! "Who's been eating my porridge!?" he roars. Mommy Bear puts her head through the serving hatch from the kitchen and screams, "For crying out loud, how many times do we have to go through this?! I haven't made the porridge yet!"

ANTIQUES

Antiques have become so popular, right now there are 15 million Americans who have things that are old, funny-looking, don't work, and are only kept around for sentimental purposes. Some of these are called antiques—and the rest are called husbands.

—Robert Orben, *2500 Jokes To Start 'Em Laughing*

APATHY

Ronald Reagan was speaking in Seattle of those people who continued to criticize his efforts. He said, "They sort of remind me of the fellow who was asked which was worse, ignorance or apathy, and he said, 'I don't know and I don't care.'"

I've been feeling really apathetic lately. Like today—Jimmy cracked corn, but I don't care.   —Howie Mandell

APPEARANCE

If I were two-faced, would I be wearing this one?
—Abraham Lincoln

A four-hundred-dollar suit on him would look like socks on a rooster.
—Earl Long

He must have had a magnificent build before his stomach went in for a career of its own.
—Margaret Halsey

His face was filled with broken commandments.
—John Masefield

She got her good looks from her father. He's a plastic surgeon.
—Groucho Marx

APPROVAL

We can secure other people's approval, if we do right and try hard but our own is worth a hundred of it, and no way has been found of securing that.
—Mark Twain

ART/ARTISTS

The artist is nothing without the gift, but the gift is nothing without work.
—Emile Zola

Abstract art? A product of the untalented, sold by the unprincipled to the utterly bewildered.
—Al Capp

At an art museum: "There was a time when the artist had to suffer—now it's the viewer."
—Bernhardt in *Mature Living*

ATHEISTS

They have Dial-a-Prayer for atheists now. You can call up and it rings and rings but nobody answers.

Most people past college age are not atheists. It's too hard to be one in our society, for one thing . . . you don't get any days off. And if you're an agnostic you don't know whether you get them off or not.
    —Mort Sahl

AUTOMOBILES

When he was in high school, our son Matt loved fast cars and was thrilled to land a summer job with the local Alfa-Romeo service center. "Gee, Mr. Vespucci," he gushed, grabbing a wrench, "I can't wait to learn all the ins and outs of fixing up these babies." So he was startled when Mr. Vespucci told him to put down his tools and listen up. "The first thing you gotta learn how to do," he instructed the kid, "is to open the hood, stand back, and shake your head very, very sadly."

The sports-car owner was taking his friend for his first ride in his new low-slung car. The friend appeared to be puzzled, so the driver asked him what was wrong. "I can't figure out where we are. What's that long wall we've been passing?" "That's no wall," snapped the driver. "That's the curb."
    —*How the Platform Professionals Keep 'em Laughin'*

Man with car trouble on a country road: "How far is it to the next town?" Farmer: "Two miles as the crow flies." Man: "How far is it if the crow has to walk and roll a flat tire?"

A teenager had an old car he wanted to sell and put this sign on it: "FOR SALE: $4,000. Rebate: $3,500!"

Uncle Sid's wife bawled him out for taking so long to choose a new car. "You married me only one week after you met me," she yelled. "Yeah," he replied defensively, "but buying a new car is serious."

Auto repairman to customer: "If you want, we can freeze your car until future mechanics discover a way to repair it."
    —Stan Fine in *Medical Economics*

When an auto mechanic tells you the repair job will run a certain amount—give or take a few dollars—you know right then who will give and who will take. —Arnold H. Glasow

One winter morning, the man heard his neighbor trying unsuccessfully to start her car. He went outside and asked: "Did you try choking it?" "No," she said, gritting her teeth, "but I sure felt like it." —Catholic Workman

A motorist brought his car in for its 1,500 mile inspection. "Is there anything the matter with it?" the service manager asked. "Well, there's only one part of it that doesn't make a noise," the customer replied, "and that's the horn." —Grit

——————————— B ———————————

BABIES

My parents put us to sleep by tossing us up in the air. Of course, you have to have low ceilings for this method to work.

A baby is an inestimable blessing and bother.—Mark Twain

A mother had just brought her newborn triplets home from the hospital. Her older boy, a four-year-old, took his first doubtful look at the new babies and said, "We'd better start calling folks. They're going to be a lot harder to get rid of than kittens."

Second grader Stepaniee came home from school and said to her mother, "Mom, guess what? We learned how to make babies today." The mother, more than a little surprised, tried to keep her cool. "That's interesting," she said. "How do you make babies?" "It's simple," replied the girl. "You just change 'y' to 'i' and add 'es.'"

Taking care of your baby is easy, as long as you don't have anything else to do.

All a newborn baby really needs is food, warmth and love.
Pretty much like a hamster, only with fewer signs of intelli-
gence.
—Dave Barry

A man finds out what is meant by a spitting image when he
tries to feed cereal to his infant.
—Imogene Fey

Babies are nature's way of showing people what the world
looks like at 2 A.M.
—*Parts Pups*

A FEW INSTRUCTIONS FOR FIRST-TIME FATHERS

- Given the choice, it's always better to use a bib than to
  Scotch Guard your baby.
- Many babies look alike. Marking yours with a colorful sticker
  will keep it from being mixed up in a group.
- A bouncing baby boy doesn't actually mean it bounces.
- You may not return your baby—even if you still have the
  receipt.
- Bouncing a well-fed baby may be hazardous to your
  clothes.
- A cat carrier should never be substituted for a car seat.
- Baby-sitting does not involve actually sitting on the baby.
- Baby formula, when properly mixed, does not produce a
  new baby.
- Godzilla is not basically the same as Barney.
- Generally, a hunk of cheese is not a good pacifier.
- Newspapers are not basically the same as diapers.
- Avoid dusting your baby with a vacuum cleaner.
- Never leave your baby where it may be stepped on by a
  cow.

Arriving for a visit, Joan Ludwig asked her small granddaughter, "Angela, how do you like your new baby brother?"
"Oh, he's all right," the child shrugged. "But there were a lot
of things we needed worse."

BABYSITTERS

We used to terrorize our babysitters when we were little, except for my great-grandfather, because he used to read to us—from his will. —Brian Kiley

Babysitter: A teenager who must behave like an adult so that the adults who are out can behave like teenagers.
—John R. Fox

Babysitter to parents: "By the way, I promised Amy that if she'd go to bed without any fuss, you'd buy her a pony in the morning."

BACHELORS

Bachelors know more about women than married men. If they didn't, they would be married too. —H. L. Mencken

Bachelors should be heavily taxed. It's not fair that some men should be happier than others. —Oscar Wilde

My Uncle Ted, who has never married, claims that a bachelor is a person who believes in life, liberty, and the happiness of pursuit.

BAD NEWS

Never buy a portable TV set on the sidewalk from a man who's out of breath.

Bad news travels fast. Good news takes the scenic route.

BANKS

Ever notice . . . that we trust banks with our money, but they don't trust us with their pens? —*Current Comedy*

My neighbor works in the operations department in the central office of a large bank. Employees in the field call him when they have problems with their computers. One night he got a call from a woman in one of the branch banks who had this question, "I've got smoke coming from the back of my terminal. Do you guys have a fire downtown?"

BARBERS

"Your hair needs cutting badly," remarked the barber. "It does not," exclaimed the customer, sitting down in the chair. "It needs cutting nicely. You cut it badly last time." — *Grit*

BASEBALL

St. Peter and Satan were having an argument one day about baseball. With a beguiling leer, Satan proposed a game (to be played on neutral grounds) between a select team from the heavenly host and his own hand-picked Hades boys. "Very well," the gatekeeper of the Celestial City agreed. "But you realize, I hope, that we have all the good players and the best coaches, too." "I know," said Satan calmly, "but we have all the umpires!"

— *How the Platform Professionals Keep 'em Laughin'*

"While I was playing with the Pirates," writes Joe Garagiola, "I gave a speech to the Pittsburgh Junior Chamber of Commerce. Trying to make the best of a terrible season, I said, 'We may not be high in the standings, and we don't win many ballgames, but you've got to admit we play some interesting baseball.' A voice from the back of the room yelled, 'Why don't you play some dull games and win a few?'"

"Each year I don't play I get better!" said Joe Garagiola. "The first year on the banquet trail I was a former ballplayer, the second year I was great, the third year one of baseball's stars, and just last year I was introduced as one of baseball's immortals. The older I get, the more I realize that the worst break I had was playing." — *Quote*

Don, a minor-league umpire, is used to being heckled by fans. But imagine his surprise when he was rushing to umpire an exhibition game at Coors Field in Denver. After a long search for a place to change clothes, Don finally located a room with a neatly lettered sign: "Dressing Room, Umpires Only." As he was about to go in, however, he inspected the sign more closely. Below the printed legend was the same message . . . written in Braille.

A rookie pitcher was struggling at the mound, so the catcher walked up to have a talk with him. "I've figured out your problem," he told the young southpaw. "You always lose control at the same point in every game." "When is that?" "Right after the National Anthem."   —Jeff MacNelly

A few years back, a reporter asked Mickey Mantle how much he thought he'd be making if he were playing baseball now. "Oh, about $500,000," Mantle said. "But, Mick," replied the surprised reporter, "guys these days are making $7 million." "Yeah," Mantle answered, "but I'm 60 years old."

Rex (Hurricane) Hudler, on being released by the San Francisco Giants after batting .238 in spring training: "I was downgraded from a hurricane to a tropical depression."

BASKETBALL

Old basketball players never die. They just sit in front of you at the movies.

One longtime basketball coach is thinking of becoming a track coach. "It's the easiest job of all," he says. "All you have to do is tell them to turn left and get back as quick as they can."

My neighbor says he'll be hearing any day now whether his son made the starting basketball team at State University, or if the coach intends to play favorites again this year.

The coach of our local community college basketball team, explaining why the team did not pray before games this year:

"We've got so many things to pray for, we'd be penalized for delay of game."

No basketball coach cares about the height of the players as long as their ears pop then they stand up.   —Dick Vitale

A basketball coach reportedly told some friends about a dream he had. "I was walking down the street," he said, "when this Rolls Royce pulled up beside me. Inside, there was a beautiful young woman—blonde, maybe 24 or 25 years old. She asked me to get in. She took me to a fantastic restaurant where we ate and drank and she paid the bill. Then she asked me if I wanted to go home with her. And I said yes. And we did." "Then what happened?" a listener urged. "The best part of all!" the coach drooled. "She introduced me to her four brothers, and all of them were over 7 feet tall!"

BIBLE

Question: Do you know what would have happened if it had been Three Wise Women who came to the stable instead of Three Wise Men?

Answer: They would have asked for directions, arrived on time, helped deliver the baby, cleaned the stable, made a casserole, and brought practical gifts!

The Bible is a very ancient book, yet it is always relevant to our lives. People in it have the same problems we do. Think of Noah . . . it took him forty days to find a place to park.

At Bayside Baptist, Sandra Alexander, the pastor's wife, asked her Sunday school class, "What do we learn from the story of Jonah and the whale?" Ten-year-old Samantha volunteered: "People make whales sick."

Harriett Feneman, the new Sunday school teacher, asked her class, "What do we learn from the story of Jonah?" Robert Ashley, an eight-year-old, put up his hand. "Travel by air," he said.

When I was pastor of the Little Brown Church, I went to visit a family. Before leaving I asked if they would like for me to read from the Bible. The lady of the house said to one of the boys, "Go bring the Big Book we read out of so much!" The boy brought the Sears catalog.

Seven-year-old Keith found an old family Bible and began to look through it. As he was turning the pages, a pressed tree leaf fell out. "Hey," he exclaimed, "this must be where Adam and Eve left their clothes!"

Five-year-old Stephanie asked her seven-year-old brother Paul, "Why does grandmother read her Bible so much?" Replied Paul with all the wisdom of his additional two years, "I guess she must be cramming for her finals."

My daughter-in-law Dalacie was mailing the old family Bible to her brother in a distant city. The postal clerk examined the heavy package carefully and inquired if it contained anything breakable. "Nothing but the Ten Commandments," was her quick reply.

It is illegal to read the Bible in the public schools of Illinois, but a law requires the STATE to provide a Bible for every convict! Don't worry kids, if you can't read the Bible in school, you'll be able to when you get to prison.

—Illinois Baptist Beacon

A little girl returned home from Sunday School. Her mother asked her if she remembered her Bible lesson for the day. The little girl replied, "I sure do! I can even remember the Zip Code—Luke 19:40."   *—Capper's Weekly*

■

THE TOP TEN THINGS SAID BY NOAH

10. Strange! We haven't seen another boat for weeks.
 9. If only I'd brought along more rhino litter!
 8. How many times around this place makes a mile?
 7. I never want to sleep in a waterbed again.

6. I wonder what my friends are doing right now.

5. An outboard motor would have made this more exciting!

4. Fish for supper—again?

3. Does anyone have more Dramamine?

2. What? You don't have film to photograph the rainbow?

1. I should have killed those darn mosquitoes when I had the chance!

Pastor Paul W. Kummer, Grace Lutheran Church, Destin, Florida

BIRDS

Little Jessica was visiting her grandparents' farm. Investigating the chicken lot, she came upon their peacock. She ran quickly to the house, shouting, "Granny, come quick! One of your chickens is in bloom!"

Uncle Irv bought a parrot at an auction after some very spirited bidding. "Now you're sure this bird talks?" he asked the auctioneer. "Talk?" replied the auctioneer. "He's been bidding against you for the past 10 minutes."

BIRTH

Somewhere on this globe, every ten seconds, there is a woman giving birth to a child. She must be found and stopped.   —Sam Levenson

A proud father phoned the newspaper and reported the birth of his twins. The girl at the desk didn't quite catch the message. "Will you repeat that?" she asked. "Not if I can help it," he replied.   —*Quote*

I don't know how old I am because the goat ate the Bible that had my birth certificate in it. The goat lived to be twenty-seven.   —Satchel Paige

BIRTH CONTROL

One of the best responses I've ever heard to a talk show host who tried to nail a guest came when Dick Cavett asked Father Theodore Hesburgh, president of Notre Dame, if he believed birth control was a sin. "I hope not," replied the savvy padre. "I've been practicing it for years."   —Bruce Haney

BLAME

Aunt Edna toured Europe by car with a woman friend. She posed for a souvenir snapshot before the fallen pillars of a historic ruin in Greece. "Don't get the car in the picture," she said, "or my husband will swear I ran into the place!"

There's a new computer out that's so human—when it makes a mistake it blames it on another machine.
      —Mickey Freeman in *Parade*

To err is human; to blame it on somebody else is even more human.   —John Nadeau

BOOKS

This isn't generally known, but Webster is supposed to have written the first dictionary because of a nagging wife. That's right. Every time he opened his mouth, she'd say, "And what's that supposed to mean?"

A man who was very much interested in old books ran into an unbookish acquaintance of his who'd just thrown away an old Bible which had been packed away in the attic of his ancestral home for generations. He happened to mention it. "Who printed it, do you know?" asked the book lover. "Somebody named Guten-something," replied the man with an effort. "Not Gutenberg?" gasped the booklover. "You idiot, you've thrown away one of the first books ever printed. A copy sold at auction recently for over $400,000!" The other man was unmoved. "My copy wouldn't have brought a dime," he announced firmly. "Some fellow named Martin Luther had scribbled all over it."

      —*How the Platform Professionals Keep 'em Laughin'*

BORES

The trouble with people who don't have much to say is that you have to listen so long to find out.

—Quoted by Ann Landers

Some are born great; some achieve greatness; and some just grate upon you.

Bore: Someone who, when you ask him how he is, tells you!

She plunged into a sea of platitudes, and with the powerful breast stroke of a channel swimmer, made her confident way towards the white cliffs of the obvious.

—W. Somerset Maugham

She's so boring you fall asleep halfway through her name.

—Alan Bennett

The trouble with her is that she lacks the power of conversation but not the power of speech. —George Bernard Shaw

Some people can stay longer in an hour than others can in a week. —William Dean Howells

BORING

She's so boring, she can't even entertain a doubt.

—William R. Evans III and Andrew Frothingham

A wingtip personality in a Reebok world. —Al McGill

He is not only dull himself, he is the cause of dullness in others. —Samuel Johnson

BOSSES

Herb and his sales manager stood before a map on which colored pins indicated the representative in each area. "I'm not going to fire you, Uttley," the manager said, "but just to emphasize the insecurity of your position, I'm loosening your pin a little."

It wasn't exactly what the boss expected when he asked his employees to put suggestions in a box as to how the business could be improved. "When I come in each morning, I like to see everyone in his or her place and started on the day's work. Anyone have any suggestions?" The next day he found only one suggestion in the box. It read, "Wear squeaky shoes."

Overheard in a meeting: Please don't think of me as your boss. Think of me as your friend who is never wrong.

—Ron Dentinger

Boss to new employee: "I want you to know that my door is always open. Please walk by quietly."

When he got fired from his last place of employment, the boss told him: "You've been like a son to me—insolent, rude, and ungrateful."

Boss to employee: "We've decided, Sherman, to give you more responsibility. From now on, you'll be responsible for everything that goes wrong."

—Marty Lowe in *The Wall Street Journal*

"How long have you been working here?" "Since the boss threatened to fire me." —Shelby Friedman

For a real quick energy boost, nothing beats having the boss walk in.—Robert Orben, *2500 Jokes To Start 'Em Laughing*

BOXING

George Foreman, champion boxer and grandfather, has this to say about his endurance: "A long time after I die, they're going to dig up my body and search for stuff to explain how I could do what I did. When they examine my DNA, they're going to find a substance called 'cheese' and another substance called 'burger.'"

The sport of boxing has had more than its share of scandals and scoundrels, but this one takes the cake. Two boxers were scheduled to fight each other and each placed a hefty bet against himself, betting he would lose the fight. When the fight started they both danced around the ring, each of them throwing harmless little air-jabs. Neither fighter wanted to land a punch. And then, one of the fighters accidentally brushed the other with his glove. The other fighter saw his chance, and hit the floor. The ref started to count. Realizing he had to do something or he'd win the fight, the fighter who was standing ran over, kicked the fighter on the ground, and was disqualified.

BROTHERS

When I was ten years old, my two-year-old brother Scott and I were out playing in the snow. Suddenly I ran to the front door of the nearest house and yelled to the startled neighbor, "Mrs. Giacomo, Help! Give me a shovel, quick. My brother is stuck in the snow up to his boot tops!" Mrs. Giacomo calmly asked, "Why doesn't he walk out?" My earnest reply, "Because he's in head first."

My brother Scott was great at playing hide-and-seek. He was so good at it, we haven't seen him since 1967!

BUREAUCRATS

My friend Ed was a sheep rancher in Idaho. One day a stranger walked up to him and asked, "If I can guess how many sheep you have may I have one?" Thinking this impossible, Ed agreed. The stranger declared, "You have 1,795 sheep." "Now how did he figure that out?" Ed wondered as the man selected an animal, slung it over his shoulder and turned to leave. "Wait," called the Ed. "If I can guess your occupation can I have that animal back?" "Sure," said the man. "You're a government bureaucrat," said Ed with a grin stretching from ear to ear. "How did you figure that out?" asked the stunned man. "Well," said Ed, "put my dog down and I will tell you."

Paperwork is the embalming fluid of bureaucracy, maintaining an appearance of life where none exists.

—Robert J. Meltzer

An Affirmative Action official of the State of Pennsylvania wrote to a business officer of a company whose policies were being investigated: "Please send to this office a list of all your employees broken down by sex." Some time later, this reply was received: "As far as we can tell, none of our employees is broken down by sex."

BUSINESS

The chief executive officer of an electronics company called in his public relations director. "Listen, Wilson. Someone is trying to buy us out. It's your job to get the price of our stock up so it'll be too expensive for them. I don't care how you do it, just do it!" And he did. When asked how, he replied, "I started a rumor Wall Street obviously liked." "What was that?" "I told them you were resigning."

The shopkeeper was dismayed when a brand new business much like his own opened up next door and erected a huge sign that read: "BEST DEALS." He was horrified when another competitor opened up on his right, and announced its arrival with an even larger sign, reading, "LOWEST PRICES." The shopkeeper was panicked, until he got an idea. He put the biggest sign of all over his own shop—it read, "MAIN ENTRANCE."

The two biggest problems in corporate America are making ends meet and making meetings end.

━━━━━━━━━━━━━━━━━ ■ ━━━━━━━━━━━━━━━━━

The following corporate mergers were announced today, and the new companies will be called . . .

- Fairchild Electronics and Honeywell Computers: New company will be called Fairwell Honeychild

- Polygram Records, Warner Brothers and Keebler: Poly-Warne Cracker
- 3M and Goodyear: MMM Good,
- John Deere and Abitibi-Price: Deere Abi
- Honeywell, Imasco and Home Oil: Honey, I'm Home,
- Denison Mines, Alliance, and Metal Mining: Mine, All Mine,
- 3M, J. C. Penney, and Canadian Opera Company: 3 Penney Opera,
- Knott's Berry Farm and National Organization of Women: Knott NOW!
- Zippo Manufacturing, Audi, Dofasco, NS Dakota Mining: Zip Audi Do-Da.

C

CALIFORNIA

I've been married to the same woman for fourteen years. Which is like eighty-something in LA years.—Robert G. Lee

Nothing is wrong with California that a rise in the ocean level wouldn't cure. —Ross MacDonald

In California, they don't throw their garbage away—they make it into TV shows. —Woody Allen

CATHOLICISM

During a children's sermon, a priest asked the youngsters, "Does anyone know what a bishop does?" A young lad raised his hand. "Moves diagonally."

Father Vazken Movsesian, a Bay area Catholic priest, recalls: "Uplifted by the Papal Mass at San Francisco's Candlestick Park a few years back, I gave my congregation a detailed account of how I was escorted to the 49ers' locker room, where I met with representatives of other Christian churches. I expressed the feeling of warmth that was radiating from the 70,000 faithful that day. Finally, I summarized the inspirational message of Pope John Paul II. At the conclusion of my remarks, I asked for questions. A young voice piped up eagerly, 'Father, did you get to see Joe Montana's locker?' "

CATS

Our new coffee table was hand-carved . . . by the cat.

—Ron Dentinger

Once upon a time, a woman had a wonderful, faithful cat. One day, a man ran over the cat accidentally with his car. So, the man went to the old woman and said, "I'm terribly sorry about your cat. I'd like to replace him." "That so nice of you!" said the old woman, deeply touched. "So how good are you at catching mice?"

Herman: "Well, Jack, I read in the paper that your rich aunt just died."

Jack: "Yeah, I spent the last five years pretending that I loved her cats so she'd remember me in her will."

Herman: "Really? And what did she leave you?"

Jack: "The cats!"

—Msgr. Arthur Tonne, *Jokes Priests Can Tell,* vol. 6

Cats don't caress us—they caress themselves on us. —Rivarol

The real measure of a day's heat is the length of a sleeping cat.

—Charles J. Brady in *Home Life*

The problem with cats is that they get the exact same look on their faces whether they see a moth or an ax murderer. —Paula Poundstone

If Darwin's theory of evolution was correct, cats would be able to operate a can opener by now. —Larry Wright

A 12-year-old girl once wrote to a TV network about a commercial that claimed a rodent poison was more effective than

anything else at killing mice. She asked if cats had been
included in the research.   —Virginia Satkowski
                    in White Plains, N.Y., *Reporter Dispatch*

CELEBRITIES

With profits from his food company, Paul Newman helped
build a camp for critically ill children. It's called the Hole
in the Wall Gang Camp, from Newman's film *Butch Cassidy
and the Sundance Kid*. Newman was sitting at a table one
day with a camper who asked him who he was. The actor
reached for a carton of Newman's Own lemonade and
showed the boy his likeness on the container. "This is me,"
Newman said. Wide-eyed, the camper asked, "Are you lost
or something?"

                    —Quoted in *Yale-New Haven Hospital Magazine*

Unfailingly courteous to fans, Jay Leno always signs auto-
graphs, poses for pictures and somehow finds time to call
many of the people who write to him. "I called one woman,"
says Jay, "and I asked, 'Is Susan there?'" "No, who's this?"
"This is Jay Leno." "Well, this is her mother. Whaddya want?"
"She wrote me a letter," I replied. "Oh, well," she answered.
"She writes to every crackpot on television!"

                                        —Russell Miller

The nice thing about being a celebrity is that when you bore
people they think it's their fault.   —Henry Kissinger

CHARITY

A solicitor from an established charity made a financial appeal to W. C. Fields. Fields responded that he would have to
confer with his lawyer. "And what will you do if your lawyer
says yes?" the solicitor inquired. "Get another lawyer," replied Fields.

CHARM

The wit and charm of Adlai E. Stevenson II made him a
constant target for autograph seekers. Once, as he left the

United Nations Building in New York City and was as usual surrounded by admirers, a small, elderly woman in the crowd finally succeeded in approaching him. "Please, Mr. Ambassador," she said, holding out a piece of paper, "your autograph for a very, very old lady." "Delighted!" Stevenson replied with a smile. "But where is she?"

CHESS

Chess is a game that requires intense concentration and absolute silence. During one game, a player sneezed and his opponent said, "Gesundheit." The first player said, "Did you come here to play or talk?"

—Robert Orben, *2500 Jokes To Start 'Em Laughing*

CHICAGO

Former heavyweight boxer James "Quick" Tillis was a cowboy from Oklahoma who fought out of Chicago in the early 1980s. Years later, he still remembers his first day in the Windy City after his arrival from Tulsa. "I got off the bus with two cardboard suitcases under my arms in downtown Chicago and stopped in front of the Sears Tower. I put my suitcases down and I looked up at the Tower and I said to myself, 'I'm going to conquer Chicago.' When I looked down, the suitcases were gone."

CHILDHOOD

Some childhood! My dad hired another kid to play me in our home movies.   —Ron Dentinger

We had a quicksand box in our backyard. I was an only child, eventually.
—Steven Wright

The imaginary friends I had as a kid dropped me because their friends thought I didn't exist.

—Aaron Machado

"What a childhood I had," says Rodney Dangerfield. "My parents sent me to a child psychiatrist. The kid was no help at all!"

CHILDREN

Helen Wilton, a Sunday school teacher at the Cottonwood Methodist Church, asked her class of preschoolers if they knew where God lives. Stephen Mason, a precocious six-year-old, raised his hand, and the teacher called on him." God lives in my bathroom," the boy confidently answered. "Why do you say that God lives in your bathroom?" inquired the teacher. "Because every morning my dad pounds on the bathroom door and says, 'Good Lord, are you still in there?'"

Kids say the darndest things. Some grade school teachers must agree with that, because they keep journals of amusing things their students have written in papers. Here are a few examples:

- The future tense of I give is I take.
- The parts of speech are lungs and air.
- The inhabitants of Moscow are called Mosquitoes.
- A census taker is man who goes from house to house increasing the population.
- Water is composed of two gins. Oxygin and hydrogin. Oxygin is pure gin. Hydrogin is gin and water.
- (Define H_2O and CO_2.) H_2O is hot water and CO_2 is cold water.
- A virgin forest is a forest where the hand of man has never set foot.
- The general direction of the Alps is straight up.
- A city purifies its water supply by filtering the water then forcing it through an aviator.
- Most of the houses in France are made of plaster of Paris.
- The people who followed the Lord were called the 12 o'possums.

- The spinal column is a long bunch of bones. The head sits on the top and you sit on the bottom.
- We do not raise silk worms in the United States, because we get our silk from rayon. He is a larger worm and gives more silk.
- One of the main causes of dust is janitors.
- A scout obeys all to whom obedience is due and respects all duly constipated authorities.
- One by-product of raising cattle is calves.
- To prevent head colds, use an agonizer to spray into the nose until it drips into the throat.
- The four seasons are salt, pepper, mustard and vinegar.
- The climate is hottest next to the Creator.
- Oliver Cromwell had a large red nose, but under it were deeply religious feelings.
- The word trousers is an uncommon noun because it is singular at the top and plural at the bottom.
- Syntax is all the money collected at the church from sinners.
- The blood circulates through the body by flowing down one leg and up the other.
- In spring, the salmon swim upstream to spoon.
- Iron was discovered because someone smelt it.
- In the middle of the 18th century, all the morons moved to Utah.
- A person should take a bath once in the summer, not so often in the winter.

Ten-year-old Keith Uttley came into the house covered with mud after finishing a rough day at play. "Mom," he shouted at the top of his voice, "if I fell out of a tree, would you rather I broke a leg or tore my pants?" "What a silly question," his mother answered from the next room. "I'd rather you tore your pants!" "Well, I got good news for you then," the boy replied triumphantly. "That's exactly what happened!"

As a kid I used to have a lemonade stand. The sign said, "All you can drink for a dime." So some kid would come up, plunk down the dime, drink a glass, and then say, "Refill it." I'd say, "That'll be another dime." "How come? Your sign says, 'All you can drink for a dime.'" "Well, you had a glass, didn't you?" "Yeah." "Well, that's all you can drink for a dime." —Flip Wilson

The kindergarten class went on a field trip to the local police station where a kindly patrolman showed them around. Stopping in front of a Ten Most Wanted poster, he explained how citizens often help bring about arrests. "Are those pictures of the bad guys?" asked one six year old. The policeman soberly informed him they were indeed. "Well," pursued the kid, "why didn't you hold onto him after you took his picture?"
   —H. Aaron Cohl, *The Friars Club Encyclopedia of Jokes*

You know what's a humbling experience? Whenever I would help the kids with their homework, their grades would go down.   —Ron Dentinger

BATH MAT: A little rug that wet children like to stand next to.   —Ron Dentinger

"I'm really worried," said one teenager to another. "Dad slaves away at his job so I'll never want for anything and so I can go to college. Mom spends every day washing and ironing and cleaning up after me, and she takes care of me when I'm sick." "So what are you worried about?" "I'm afraid they might try to escape!"
   —Jack Moore, Universal Press Syndicate

Once when I was babysitting, my six-year-old grandson refused to eat anything set before him. In exasperation, I asked, "Jonathan, you tell me you don't like meat, you don't like chicken, you don't like fish, you don't like fruit, you don't like vegetables, you don't like milk, you don't like juice. Tell me, what do you like?" Turning his innocent blue eyes on me, he answered, "Why, I like you, Grampa!"

When I was a graduate student, I took my daughter's Montessori school class to a farm near Princeton, New Jersey. Five-year-old Claudia, my daughter's best friend, visiting a farm for the first time, was looking at a fat sow lying in a pen. Said the farmer, "She's mighty big, isn't she?" "She sure is," said Claudia. "I just saw six little piggies blowing her up a few minutes ago."

We had a new teacher and she wanted to know if I had any brothers and sisters, and I told her I was an only child. "What did she say?" my mother asked. She said "Thank goodness!"
—King Duncan

Bill Cell and Ed Woodward, two professors of theology, were walking across the campus of United Theological Seminary when Bill asked Ed, "Do you believe in Original Sin?" Ed answered, "Yes, I do. We have a child." "Do you believe in Total Depravity?" asked Bill. "No, I don't. That is an excess of Calvinistic theology," replied Ed. Bill rejoined, "Just wait until you have two children!"

Two of my grandsons were playing marbles when a pretty little girl walked by. "I'll tell you," said Jake to JD, "when I stop hating girls, that's the one I'm going to stop hating first."

On children: The best way to keep children home is to make the home atmosphere pleasant—and let the air out of the tires.
—Dorothy Parker

Children are a great comfort in one's old age—which one wouldn't reach so quickly if one didn't have children.

Ask your child what he wants for dinner only if he's buying.
—Fran Lebowitz

I take my children everywhere, but they always find their way back home.   —Robert Orben

Never lend your car to anyone to whom you have given birth.
—Erma Bombeck

Tomorrow's kids will probably have to make up something they had to do without.   —Martin A. Ragaway

If God had wanted sex to be fun, He wouldn't have included children as punishment.   —Ed Bluestone

If you want to recapture your youth, cut off his allowance.
—Al Bernstein

Aunt Frieda asked her five-year-old daughter Heather, "Why can't you behave like Tracy next door?" "Because she's a doctor's kid," Heather protested. "What's that got to do with it?" her mother demanded. "The doctor always keeps the best babies for himself," Heather replied.

In 1962, my five-year-old came home from a birthday party and told his mother, "I'm never going to believe another word you say. I was the only kid at the party who didn't know that babies are brought by the stork."

When my son Stephen was a first-grader, he demonstrated how practical children can really be. He slipped in the hall at school and skinned his knee. A gym teacher attempted psychological first aid with, "Remember, big boys don't cry, sonny." Steve replied, "I'm not going to cry—I'm gonna sue!"

Little boy to his mother, "Can I go outside and help Daddy put snow chains on the car? I know all the words."

My boss' son is five years old. He attended his first funeral with his family. I saw him on Sunday and asked him what he thought of it. His answer, "She was already dead when we got there."

A three-year-old went with his dad to see a litter of kittens. On returning home, he breathlessly informed his mother there were 2 boy kittens and 2 girl kittens. "How did you know?" his mother asked. "Daddy picked them up and looked underneath," he replied. "I think it's printed on the bottom."

Another three-year-old put his shoes on by himself. His mother noticed the left shoe was on the right foot. She said, "Son, your shoes are on the wrong feet." He looked up at her with a raised brow and said, "Don't kid me, Mom, I KNOW they're my feet."

On the first day of school, the kindergarten teacher said, "If anyone has to go to the bathroom, hold up two fingers." A little voice from the back of the room asked, "How will that help?"

A mother and her young son returned from the grocery store and began putting away the groceries. The boy opened the box of animal crackers and spread them all over the table. "What are you doing?" his mother asked. "The box says you can't eat them if the seal is broken," the boy explained. "I'm looking for the seal."

Teacher: "Can people predict the future with cards?"
Pupil: "My mother can."
Teacher: "Really?"
Pupil: "Yes, she takes one look at my report card and tells me what will happen when my father gets home."

A four-year-old girl was learning to say the Lord's Prayer. She was reciting it all by herself without help from her mother. She said, "And lead us not into temptation, but deliver us some e-mail. AMEN."

A wife invited some people to dinner. At the table, she turned to their six-year-old daughter and said, "Would you like to say the blessing?" "I wouldn't know what to say," the girl replied. "Just say what you hear Mommy say," the wife answered. The daughter bowed her head and said, "Lord, why on earth did I invite all these people to dinner?"

One day at work, while I was waiting on a customer, my colleague asked the customer's little boy how old he was. "I can't tell you," the child replied. "I have my mittens on."

—*Catholic Digest*

Mort was laying on the discipline and my teenager shot back, "Did I ask to be born?" Mort said, "If you had, the answer would have been no!"

I've got two boys, both of 'em training to be astronauts by correspondence. They're at home taking up space.

One student's definition of a grandmother: "That's someone who comes to visit and keeps your mother from spanking you."

My son keeps a hamster in his room. At first the smell was terrible . . . but the hamster got used to it.

Walking down the street, a man passes a house and notices a child trying to reach the doorbell. No matter how much the little guy stretches, he can't make it. The man calls out "Let me get that for you," and he bounds onto the porch to ring the bell. "Thanks, mister," says the kid. "Now let's run."

A four-year-old boy accompanied his pregnant mother to the gynecologist's office. When mother heaved a sigh and clutched her stomach, her son looked alarmed. "Mommy, what is it?" he asked. "The baby brother you're going to have is kicking," his mother explained. "He's probably getting restless," the youngster decided. "Why don't you swallow a toy?"

The mother of three notoriously unruly youngsters was asked whether or not she'd have children if she had it to do over again. "Sure," she replied, "but not the same ones."

Even though children are deductible, they can also be very taxing.

A pastor adjusted his height and knelt in front of a group of church preschoolers at a special service. He talked to the children about being good and going to heaven. At the end of his talk, the pastor asked, "Where do you want to go?" The little voices shouted out, "Heaven!" "And what must you be to get to heaven?" the pastor asked. "Dead!" a loud chorus yelled. —Msgr. Arthur Tonne

After telling her class the story of God's promise to give His people a land flowing with milk and honey, a Sunday school teacher asked her little ones: "What do you think a land flowing with milk and honey would be like?" "I think it would be pretty sticky," Eric replied. —Msgr. Arthur Tonne

Human beings are the only creatures that allow their children to come home. —Bill Cosby

After Cardinal James Hickey's visit to a parochial school in Maryland, a puzzled youngster asked his teacher, "Why did they keep calling him 'His M&M's'?" —Albert I. Murphy

Ever notice . . . that you can't get your kids to sit still when you want to take their picture, but when you use a video camera, you can't get them to move? —Jay Trachman

THE WISDOM OF CHILDREN

- "Never trust a dog to watch your food." Patrick, age 10
- "When your dad is mad and asks you, 'Do I look stupid?' don't answer." Hannah, 9
- "Never tell your mom her diet's not working." Michael, 14
- "Stay away from prunes." Randy, 9
- "Don't squat with your spurs on." Noronha, 13
- "When your mom is mad at your dad, don't let her brush your hair." Taylia, 11

- "Never allow your three-year-old brother in the same room as your school assignment." Traci, 14
- "Don't sneeze in front of mum when you're eating crackers." Mitchell, 12
- "Puppies still have bad breath even after eating a Tic-Tac." Andrew, 9
- "Never hold a Dust Buster and a cat at the same time." Kyoyo, 9
- "You can't hide a piece of broccoli in a glass of milk." Armir, 9
- "Don't wear polka-dot underwear under white shorts." Kellie, 11
- "If you want a kitten, start out by asking for a horse." Naomi, 15
- "Felt markers are not good to use as lipstick." Lauren, 9
- "Don't pick on your sister when she's holding a baseball bat." Joel, 10
- "When you get a bad grade in school, show it to your mom when she's on the phone." Alyesha, 13
- "Never try to baptize a cat." Eileen, 8

A kindergarten teacher asked, "What is the shape of the earth?" One girl spoke up: "According to my Daddy—terrible!"

Two kids were trying to figure out what game to play. One said, "Let's play doctor." "Good idea," said the other. "You operate, and I'll sue."

A small boy is sent to bed by his father . . . [Five minutes later] "Da-ad . . ." "What?" "I'm thirsty. Can you bring me a drink of water?" "No. You had your chance. Lights out." [Five minutes later] "Da-aaaad . . ." "WHAT?" "I'm THIRSTY . . . Can I have a drink of water??" "I told you NO! If you ask again I'll have to spank you!!" [Five minutes later] "Daaaa-aaaAAAAD . . ." "WHAT??!!" "When you come in to spank me, can you bring me a drink of water?"

One Sunday, I heard two brothers, ages 8 and 4, discussing Adam and Eve. The eight-year-old asked: "How did Adam and Eve die?" And the four-year-old said: "They ate bad fruit."

It is frequently said that children don't know the value of money. This is only partially true. They don't know the value of your money. Their money, they know the value of.
—Judy Markey,
You Only Get Married For the First Time Once

It is not easy to be crafty and winsome at the same time, and few accomplish it after the age of six.   —John W. Gardner
and Francesca Gardner Reese, in
Know or Listen to Those Who Know

The five-year-old had apparently trained her younger sister. For, as the congregation recited the Lord's Prayer at Mass, there came in clear—and loud—young voices from the pew behind me, ". . . And forgive us our trash passes as we forgive those who pass trash against us."   —*Family Digest*

CHOCOLATE

THE LAWS OF CHOCOLATE

- If you get melted chocolate all over your hands, you're eating it too slowly.
- Chocolate-covered raisins, cherries, orange slices and strawberries all count as fruit, so eat as many as you want.
- Problem: How to get two pounds of chocolate home from the store in a hot car. Solution: Eat it in the parking lot.
- Diet tip: Eat a chocolate bar before each meal. It'll take the edge off your appetite and you'll eat less.
- A nice box of chocolates provides your total daily intake of calories in one place. Isn't that handy?
- If you can't eat all your chocolate, it will keep in the freezer. But if you can't eat all your chocolate, it may be a sign of a deeper problem.

C

- If calories are an issue, store your chocolate on top of the fridge. Calories are afraid of heights, and they will jump out of the chocolate to protect themselves.
- Equal amounts of dark chocolate and white chocolate are a balanced diet.
- Two phrases: Money talks. Chocolate sings.
- The preservatives in chocolate make you look younger.
- Question: Why is there no such organization as Chocoholics Anonymous? Answer: Because no one wants to quit.
- If not for chocolate, there would be no need for control-top pantyhose. An entire garment industry would be devastated.
- Put "eat chocolate" at the top of your list of things to do today. That way, at least you'll get one thing done.

CHRISTMAS

I was sitting in my office on the first Saturday of December. Outside in the courtyard of our church the men of the church were in the process of building the stage for a live nativity scene. Since my door was open, I heard two children discussing the process. One asked of the other,  "What is this going to be?" Answered the other, "Oh, they're building a live fertility scene." —Walter Lauster

The children of our parish in Tokyo had been practicing their Christmas play for days and knew all their lines. Right on cue, the innkeeper said, "There is no room. You cannot stay here." No one was prepared, however, for Joseph when he turned to Mary and said, "I told you to make reservations!"
—William Grimm, M.M., *Maryknoll Magazine*

Could I get my husband to address the Christmas cards? I wondered. The family was coming. There was shopping yet to do, gifts to wrap, the tree to decorate, cooking, cleaning. I arranged the cards, stamps, and address book on the table, then hopefully pulled up a chair and said, "Come on, Dear, let's get these out of the way." He glanced at the array on the table, turned away, and went into the den, while I looked daggers at his back. I heard a drawer jerk open and bang shut. He returned with a high stack of cards, stamped, sealed, and addressed. "They're last year's," he said. "I forgot to mail them. Now let's go out to dinner and relax. You've been working too hard." —*Catholic Digest*

The first-grade class presented a nativity play shortly before Christmas. When Joseph came to the inn and asked if there was room at the inn, the little boy playing the innkeeper replied, "You're lucky. We just had a cancellation."
—George Goldtrap

Small boy giving his Christmas gift wish lists to his parents: "Fax this list to Santa Claus, e-mail this one to God, and I want to talk direct to Grandma."

Christmas is the season when people run out of money before they run out of friends. —Larry Wilde

Christmas is a strange time of year. That's when people celebrate the birth of the Prince of Peace by buying toy rockets, submarines, artillery, and hand grenades for their children.

It's a good idea to send the kids to bed early on Christmas Eve. It gives fathers a few more hours to play with their toys.

The cheapest place to meet for the holidays is Grandma's house—unless you're Grandpa.

Banks never seem to get totally into the holiday spirit. My bank sent me a card that said, "Have a Happy Holiday. If You Are Already Having A Happy Holiday, Please Disregard This Notice."

No matter how many Christmas cards you send out, the first one you get is from someone you missed. —*Capper's Weekly*

The nicest things in the world are a Christmas tree when it's first put up—and the living room when you finally take the tree down.   —Lois Reed in *Farm Journal*

Every Christmas we get a visit from the jolly gent with the great big bag over his shoulder. It's my son home from college and the great big bag is laundry.

—Robert Orben, *2500 Jokes To Start 'Em Laughing*

CHURCH BULLETINS

The Sunday bulletin of St. Teresa of Avila parish in Augusta, Ga., listed the sacraments available at the church, including: "Anointing of the Sick. If you are going to be hospitalized for an operation, contact the priest. Celebrated also for those who are seriously sick by request."

EXCERPTS FROM CHURCH BULLETINS:

- The ladies of the church have cast off clothes of every kind and they may be seen in the church basement on Friday afternoon.
- As the maintenance of the church yard is becoming increasingly costly, it would be appreciated if those who are willing would clip the grass around their own graves.
- A note from the pastor: I shall be away from the parish attending the Diocesan Clergy School from April 21–24. It will be convenient if parishioners will abstain from arranging to be buried, or from making other calls on me during this time.
- There is joy in the presence of the angels over one singer who repents.
- All the youth choirs of Our Redeemer have been disbanded for the summer with the thanks of the entire church.
- From the Holy Week bulletin of St. John's Anglican Church, Edmonton, Alberta: Maundy Thursday, April 8, 7 P.M. We will re-enact the Last Supper and journey to the Garden of Gethsemane. We will strip the altar and sanctuary of all

color and symbol. Together, we will leave the church bare and in silence.

- From Lenten bulletin of Zion Lutheran Church, Garretson, South Dakota: 7:30 LENTEN SERVICE. The final Lenten Service theme is: 'Why Doesn't God Do Something?' with Pastor Meidinger.
- In the bulletin of the Westchester (Illinois) Community United Church of Christ: And we give you thanks, O God, for people of many cultures and nations; for the young and old and muddle-aged.
- On March 16th, the prayer group met at the home of Margaret Ressler, who is no longer able to attend church. What a blessing!
- ADULT FORUM. Beginning November 5, Pastor Hodges will lead a six-part series on the book of Genesis. Were Adam and Eve really naked in the Garden? Come and see for yourself.
- From the yearbook of Trinity Lutheran Church, Jeffers, Minnesota: The (correspondence) committee will assist with the mailing of the newsletter and stapling of the Annual Report to congregational members.

From a Sarasota, Florida, church bulletin: "Students will study Matthew 14:22–33, 'Jesus Walks on Walter.'"

From a Lewiston, Idaho, church bulletin: "We need models for our 'Satan and Lace Wedding Party.'"

"Offertory solo: 'O Holy Nighty.'"
　　　—Music listing in Kansas City, Mo., church bulletin

In an Ohio church bulletin: "The Church Board of Bartlett will meet for a few minutes after the school board."

CHURCHES

Johnny Zezas, Wyoming's top wrangler, came up with this dash of whimsy: "Many people have nothing but praise for the church, especially when the collection plate is handed round."

At Mt. Ebal Baptist Church, Melanie Nelson was in charge of promoting the denominational magazine among the members of the congregation. At the Sunday morning service, Pastor Wall gave her a minute to make an appeal to the congregation. "Please, brothers and sisters, if all of us start our subscriptions at the same time, and mail them in before the end of the month, then we'll be able to expire together."

The church today is raising a whole generation of mules. They know how to sweat and to work hard, but they don't know how to reproduce themselves.

The Maywood Community Church once brought in a performing horse. They asked the horse how many Commandments, and he stamped ten times. Then they asked how many apostles, and he stamped twelve times. Some wise guy in the crowd asked, "How many hypocrites are there in this church?" The horse went into a tap-dance on all fours.

Oliver Mendell, Ph.D., the noted scientist, made a careful study of people who fell asleep in church. His conclusion was that if all the sleeping congregants were laid end to end, they would be a lot more comfortable.

When it comes to church leadership, some members rise to the occasion, while others merely hit the ceiling.

My friend Father Miles, a Roman Catholic priest, described the hearing of the confessions of nuns as like being stoned to death with popcorn.

First Baptist Church always has a coffee hour after the Sunday worship service. One Sunday, after Pastor Ed preached much longer than usual, he was enjoying a homemade cookie and the fellowship of his congregation after the service. He was conversing with the Bowmount family and he happened to ask Alex Bowmount, a seven-year-old, if he knew why they served the coffee. "I think," said the boy, "it's to get the people awake before they drive home."

Mrs. Hansen had been a member of First Baptist church for 25 years. As she walked toward the pastor, who stood waiting at the sanctuary door after the service, it was obvious that she had something on her mind. "Reverend, if God were alive today, He would be shocked at the changes in this church!"

A man and his ten-year-old son were on a fishing trip miles from home. At the boy's insistence, they decided to attend the Sunday worship service at a small rural church. As they walked back to their car after the service, the father was filled with complaints. "The service was too long," he lamented. "The sermon was boring, and the singing was off key." Finally the boy said, "Daddy, I thought it was pretty good for a dime."

My home church welcomes all denominations, but really prefers tens and twenties.

On vacation with her family in North Dakota, a mother drove her van past a church in a small town and pointing to it, told the children that it was St. John's Church. "It must be a franchise," her eight-year-old son said. "We've got one of those in our town too."

I don't know why some people change churches—what difference does it make which one you stay home from?

—Rev. Denny Brake

At the Little Brown Church, our Christmas Eve service included a candle-lighting ceremony in which each member of the congregation lit a candle from his neighbor's candle. At the conclusion of the ceremony, the congregation sat hushed, pondering the inspiring beauty of the moment. I rose to announce the concluding hymn and was taken completely by surprise when laughter broke out in response to my invitation: "Now that everyone is lit, let's sing 'Joy to the World.'"

The choir was practicing one Wednesday evening while I worked on my sermon in the church office, just a few feet away. The choir was rehearsing a particularly difficult piece by Mozart when a ferocious thunderstorm burst overhead. Alarmed, I walked into the sanctuary and said to the choir director, "That sounds like hail." "Oh, no," she said reassuringly. "They weren't that bad."

Six-year-old Angie and her four-year-old brother Joel were sitting together in church. Joel giggled, sang, and talked out loud. Finally, his big sister had enough. "You're not supposed to talk out loud in church." "Why? Who's going to stop me?" Joel asked. Angie pointed to the back of the church and said, "See those two men standing by the door? They're hushers."

Gladys attended church services one particular Sunday. The sermon seemed to go on forever, and many in the congregation fell asleep. After the service, to be social, she walked up to a very sleepy looking gentleman, in an attempt to revive him from his stupor, extended her hand in greeting, and said, "Hello, I'm Gladys Dunn." To this the gentleman replied, "You're not the only one!"

CLERGY (See also MINISTERS)

Wanda Watson had asked me to offer the blessing at the women's luncheon being held at her home. But I was delayed by an unforeseen parish emergency. (A snake had appeared in the midst of the preschool playground.) Mrs. Watson was disturbed. She waited as long as she could for me to appear.

Finally, she asked her husband Henry to fill in. Henry hated to speak in public, let alone pray out loud. He was visibly shaken but stood and announced reverently: "As there is no clergyman present, let us thank God."

It happened during a parish supper in the church basement, celebrating the Confirmation ceremony. One of the amateur high school waitresses accidentally bumped the arm of the pastor just as he was taking a sip of coffee. The brown fluid spilled all over his arm and shoulder and on to the tablecloth. With half a smile and half a frown the good padre exclaimed to the parishioners across the table: "Will one of you laymen please say something appropriate?"

— Msgr. Arthur Tonne, *Jokes Priests Can Tell,* vol. 6

The main course at the big civic dinner was baked ham with glazed sweet potatoes. Rabbi Cohen regretfully shook his head when the platter was passed to him. "When," scolded Father Kelly playfully, "are you going to forget that silly rule of yours and eat ham like the rest of us?" "At your wedding reception, Father Kelly," said Rabbi Cohen without skipping a beat.

How do you tell the Episcopal priest at an ecumenical ceremony? She's the one who sends back the wine.

General Ulysses S. Grant once asked Henry Ward Beecher: "Why does a little fault in a clergyman attract more notice than a great fault in a bad man?" Replied Beecher: "Perhaps it is for the same reason that a slight stain on a white garment is more readily noticed than a large stain on a colored one.

CLOTHING

I've got a shirt for every day of the week. It's blue.

— Ron Dentinger

The trouble with fitted shirts is that they were made to fit someone else's body.

Overheard in a women's fitting room: "They don't make large as big as they used to!"

HELPFUL HINT FOR THE HOMEMAKER: You can remove ink stains from a silk dress with ordinary scissors.

—Ron Dentinger

Distrust any enterprise that requires new clothes.

—Henry David Thoreau

COFFEE

Overheard: "I was making $100,000.00 a year, had 75 people under me, a condo in Aspen and was being considered for the Senate—then I switched to decaf."

—Bob Thaves, Newspaper Enterprise Assn

COLLEGE

I learned law so well, the day I graduated I sued the college, won the case, and got my tuition back.   —Fred Allen

The reason that colleges have been described as a place for the accumulation of learning is that freshmen bring some in, and graduating seniors students take none out—so knowledge accumulates.

The father was very proud when his son went off to college. He came to tour the school on Parents' Day, and observed his son hard at work in the chemistry lab. "What are you working on?" he asked. "A universal solvent," explained the son, "a solvent that'll dissolve anything." The father whistled, clearly impressed, then wondered aloud, "What'll you keep it in?"

A physics professor at a state university in Michigan was famous for his animated lectures. He was short and thin with

wild white hair and an excited expression. In lecture he would throw himself from the top of desks and throw frisbees to students in the back row to illustrate various principles. One day in class he was spinning on an office chair holding weights in each hand when he lost his balance and tumbled into the first row. He apologized to his class for going off on a tangent.

"I hear you have a boy in college. Is he going to become a doctor, an engineer, or a lawyer, perhaps?" The slow, quizzical answer was, "That I do not know. Right now the big question is: Is he going to become a sophomore?"   *— Quote*

COLLEGE SENIORS VS. FRESHMEN . . .

Freshmen: Are never in bed past noon.
Seniors: Are never out of bed before noon.

Freshmen: Read the syllabus to find out what classes they can cut.
Seniors: Read the syllabus to find out what classes they need to attend.

Freshmen: Brings a can of soda into a lecture hall.
Seniors: Brings a jumbo hoagie and six-pack of Mountain Dew into a recitation class.

Freshmen: Calls the professor "Professor."
Seniors: Calls the professor "Bob."

Freshmen: Would walk ten miles to get to class.
Seniors: Drives to class if it's farther than three blocks away.

Freshmen: Memorizes the course material to get a good grade.
Seniors: Memorizes the professor's habits to get a good grade.

Freshmen: Knows a book-full of useless trivia about the university.
Seniors: Knows where the next class is. Maybe . . .

C

Freshmen: Shows up at a morning exam clean, perky, and fed.

Seniors: Shows up at a morning exam in sweats with a cap on and a box of Pop Tarts in hand.

Freshmen: Have to ask where the computer labs are.

Seniors: Have 'own' personal workstations.

Freshmen: Use the campus buses to go everywhere.

Seniors: Use the campus buses to run block while crossing the street.

Freshmen: Worry about the last freshman composition essay.

Seniors: Worry about the last GRE essay.

Freshman: Lines up for an hour to buy his textbooks in the first week.

Senior: Starts to think about buying textbooks in October . . . maybe.

Freshman: Looks forward to first classes of the year.

Senior: Looks forward to first party of the year.

Freshman: Is proud of his A+ on Calculus I midterm.

Senior: Is proud of not quite failing his Complex Analysis midterm.

Freshman: Calls his girlfriend back home every other night.

Senior: Calls Domino's every other night.

Freshman: Is appalled at the class size and callousness of Profs.

Senior: Is appalled that the campus "Subway" burned down over the summer.

Freshman: Is excited about the world of possibilities that awaits him, the unlimited vista of educational opportunities, the chance to expand one's horizons and really make a contribution to society.

Senior: Is excited about new dryers in the laundry room.

Freshman: Takes meticulous four-color notes in class.

Senior: Occasionally stays awake for all of class.

A student reported for her university final examination which consisted of "yes/no" type questions. She took her seat in the examination hall, stared at the question paper for five minutes, and then in a fit of inspiration took out her purse, removed a coin, and started tossing the coin and marking the answer sheet—Yes for heads and No for tails. Within half an hour she had completed the exam while the rest of the class was feverishly continuing to work. During the last few minutes, she desperately began throwing the coin, swearing, and sweating. The instructor, alarmed, approached her and asked if there was a problem. "I finished the exam in half an hour," she replied. "Now, I am rechecking my answers."

Wife: "Donald, when was the last time we received a letter from our son?"

Husband: "Just a second, honey, I'll go look in the checkbook." —Die Weltwoche, Switzerland

COMMITTEES

Outside of traffic, there is nothing that has held the country back as much as committees. —Will Rogers

COMMUNICATING

James Schlesinger discovered that in managing the Department of Defense there were many unexpected communications problems. For instance, when the Marines are ordered to secure a building, they form up and assault it. On the other hand, the same instructions will lead the Army to occupy the building with a troop of infantry, and the Navy will characteristically respond by sending a yeoman to assure that the building lights are turned out. When the Air Force acts on these instructions, what results is a three-year lease with an option to purchase.

A young student was trying to earn some money over the summer. He knocked at the door of a rich man's house and asked if there was anything he could do. "Yes, the man replied, you can paint the porch. The paint and brushes are in the garage." Three hours later, the student came back and reported, "Well, it's all painted, but I gotta tell you, that's not a Porsche; it's a Ferrari."

—Eric W. Johnson, *A Treasury of Humor* II

Uncle Herbert from Vermont mailed an order to his butcher in Boston. First he began the note, "Kindly send two gooses." That didn't seem right, so he started over again with "Kindly send two geeses." Still he wasn't satisfied. He settled his dilemma by writing finally, "Kindly send me a goose." Then he signed his name and added a P.S.: "Send another one with it."

Letter to a school principal: "I am annoyed to find out that you branded my child illiterate. It is a dirty lie as I married his father a week before he was born."

—Bob Terrell, *Fun Is Where You Find It*

Two tourists were driving through Louisiana. As they were approaching Natchitoches, they started arguing about the pronunciation of the town. They argued back and forth until they stopped for lunch. As they stood at the counter, one tourist asked the gal at the cash register, "Before we order, could you please settle an argument for us? Would you please pronounce where we are . . . very slowly?" The young woman leaned over the counter and said, "Burrrrrrrr, gerrrrrrr, Kiiiiing."

SOME ENGLISH SIGNS SEEN IN NON-ENGLISH SPEAKING COUNTRIES:

- In a Paris hotel elevator: Please leave your values at the front.
- In a hotel in Athens: Visitors are expected to complain at the office between the hours of 9 and 11 A.M. daily.
- In a Yugoslavian hotel: The flattening of underwear with pleasure is the job of the chambermaid.

- In a Hong Kong supermarket: For your convenience, we recommend courteous, efficient self-service.
- In an East African newspaper: A new swimming pool is rapidly taking shape since the contractors have thrown in the bulk of their workers.
- A sign posted in Germany's Black Forest: It is strictly forbidden on our Black Forest camping site that people of different sex, for instance, men and women, live together in one tent unless they are married with each other for the purpose.
- In an advertisement by a Hong Kong dentist: Teeth extracted by the latest Methodists.
- In a Rome laundry: Ladies, leave your clothes here and spend the afternoon having a good time.
- Detour sign in Kyushi, Japan: Stop: Drive Sideways.
- In a Swiss mountain inn: Special today—no ice cream.
- In a Norwegian cocktail lounge: Ladies are requested not to have children in the bar.
- At a Budapest zoo: Please do not feed the animals. If you have any suitable food, give it to the guard on duty.
- In the office of a Roman doctor: Specialist in women and other diseases.
- In a Tokyo hotel: Is forbitten to steal hotel towels please. If you are not person to do such thing is please not to read notis.
- In a Japanese hotel room: Please to bathe inside the tub.
- In a Bucharest hotel lobby: The lift is being fixed for the next day. During that time we regret that you will be unbearable.
- In a Leipzig elevator: Do not enter the lift backwards, and only when lit up.
- In a Belgrade Hotel Elevator: To move the cabin, push button for wishing floor. If the cabin should enter more persons, each one should press a number of wishing floor. Driving is then going alphabetically by national order.
- In the lobby of a Moscow hotel across from a Russian Orthodox Monastery: You are welcome to visit the cemetery

where famous Russian and Soviet composers, artists, and writers are buried daily except Thursday.

- In an Austrian hotel catering to skiers: Not to perambulate the corridors in the hours of repose in the boots of ascension.
- On the menu of a Swiss restaurant: Our wines leave you nothing to hope for.
- On the menu of a Polish hotel: Salad a firm's own make; limpid red beet soup with cheesy dumplings in the form of a finger; roasted duck let loose; beef rashers beaten up in the country people's fashion.
- Outside a Hong Kong tailor shop: Ladies may have a fit upstairs.
- In a Bangkok dry cleaner's: Drop your trousers here for best results.
- In a Rhodes tailor shop: Order your summers suit. Because is big rush we will execute customers in strict rotation.
- In a Zurich hotel: Because of the impropriety of entertaining guests of the opposite sex in the bedroom, it is suggested that the lobby be used for this purpose.
- In a Vienna hotel: In case of fire, do your utmost to alarm the hotel porter.
- From a brochure of a car rental firm in Tokyo: When passenger of foot heave in sight, tootle the horn. Trumpet him melodiously at first, but if he still obstacles your passage then tootle him with vigor.

Theatre Arts magazine reports a frustrating conversation. It seems a subscriber called "Information" for the magazine's number. "Sorry," drawled the operator, "but there is nobody listed by the name of 'Theodore Arts.'" "It's not a person; it's a publication," insisted the subscriber. "I want *Theatre Arts*." "I told you," repeated the operator in a voice a few decibels higher, "we have no listing for Theodore Arts." "Confound it," hollered the subscriber, "the word is Theatre:

T-H-E-A-T-R-E." "That," replied the operator with crushing finality, "is not the way to spell Theodore."

—Msgr. Arthur Tonne. *Jokes Priests Can Tell*, Volume 8, Multi Business Press, Hillsboro, Kansas, October, 1990.

COMPLAINTS

During a power failure, he complained of having gotten stuck for hours on the escalator.

A commuter sitting on a subway train reading a paperback was so sprawled out in the seat that the woman next to him had very little room. When she asked if he could move a bit, he refused. Just then, a man opposite them yelled, "Why don't you sit like a human being?" "What are you going to do if I don't?" came the reply. "Well, for one thing, I'll tell you how that book ends." —Catherine Romano

A man who lived in Warsaw, Poland, went to the police station to ask for permission to emigrate to Western Europe. "Aren't you happy here?" the police asked. "I have no complaints," said the man. "But are you dissatisfied with your work?" "I have no complaints." "Are you discontented with the living conditions?" "I have no complaints." "Then why do you want to go west?" "Because there I can have complaints." —*Times,* Hong Kong

COMPLIMENTS

My wife rushed into the supermarket to pick up a few items. She headed for the express line where the clerk was talking on the phone with his back turned to her. "Excuse me," she said, "I'm in a hurry. Could you check me out, please?" The clerk turned, stared at her for a second, looked her up and down, smiled and said, "Not bad."

Helen and George, a young married couple, were sitting on a porch swing. Helen asked, "George, do you think my eyes are beautiful?" He answered, "Uh-huh." In a few moments, she asked: "George, do you think my hair is attractive?"

Again he answered, "Uh-huh." A few minutes later, Helen asked, "George, would you say that I have a nice figure?" Once again he answered, "Uh-huh." "Oh, George," she said, "You say the nicest things."

COMPROMISE

Compromise is the art of dividing a cake so that everybody believes he or she got the biggest piece.

—Ludwig Erhard in *The Observer,* London

COMPUTERS

It's supposed to do that.

—Anonymous help-line response, 1982

A bachelor called a computer dating service and listed his specifications: He wanted someone who likes water sports, is gregarious, likes formal dress, and is small. They sent him a penguin.

NEW COMPUTER VIRUSES:

- GOVERNMENT ECONOMIST VIRUS: Nothing works, but all your diagnostic software says everything is fine.
- NEW WORLD ORDER VIRUS: Probably harmless, but it makes a lot of people mad just thinking about it.
- FEDERAL BUREAUCRAT VIRUS: Divides your hard drive into hundreds of little units, each of which do practically nothing, but all of which claim to be the most important part of the computer.
- PAUL REVERE VIRUS: This revolutionary virus does not horse around. It warns you of impending hard disk attack—once if by LAN; twice if by C:\>.
- POLITICALLY CORRECT VIRUS: Never calls itself a virus, but instead refers to itself as an electronic microorganism.
- AT&T VIRUS: Every three minutes it tells you what great service you are getting.

- THE MCI VIRUS: Every three minutes it reminds you that you are paying too much for the AT&T virus.
- TED TURNER VIRUS: Colorizes your monochrome monitor.
- ARNOLD SCHWARZENEGGER VIRUS: Terminates and stays resident. It'll be back to erase your data and say, Hasta la vista, baby!
- GALLUP VIRUS: Sixty percent of the PCs infected will lose 38 percent of their data 14 percent of the time (plus or minus a 3.5 percent margin of error).

There was this fully computer-automated bank in Miami. Seems somebody sent it a card saying, "THIS IS A HOLDUP," and the computer mailed the fellow $200,000 in unmarked bills.

One business executive to another, talking about the office computer: We can't sell it—it knows too much!

Wife, sitting at home computer, excitedly tells husband, "I did it! I broke into the Fitzsimmon's computer and got Edith's recipe for lasagna!"

—*How the Platform Professionals Keep 'em Laughin'*

Thank you for calling the tech-support hotline. If your computer becomes obsolete while you're holding, press 1 to reach our sales department.

HOW TO TELL IF YOU'RE "ADDICTED TO THE INTERNET"

- You find yourself typing "com" after every period when using a word processor.
- You turn off your modem and get this awful empty feeling, like you just pulled the plug on a loved one.

C

- You start introducing yourself as "Jon at I-I-Net.com"
- Your wife drapes a blond wig over your monitor to remind you of what she looks like.
- All of your friends have an @ in their names.
- You can't call your mother . . . she doesn't have a modem.
- Your phone bill comes to your doorstep in a box.
- You laugh at people with 2400 baud modems.
- You move into a new house and decide to Netscape before you landscape.
- You tell the cab driver you live at "http://123.elm.street/house/bluetrim.html".
- Your spouse makes a new rule: "The computer cannot come to bed."
- You ask a plumber how much it would cost to replace the chair in front of your computer with a commode.
- You start tilting your head sideways to smile. :)
- You turn on your computer and turn off your spouse.
- Your spouse says communication is important in a marriage . . . so you buy another computer and install a second phone line so the two of you can chat.
- You begin to wonder how on earth your service provider is allowed to call 200 hours per month "unlimited."
- And the #1 clue that you are addicted to the Internet is . . . Your dog has its own home page.

A man goes into a pet shop to buy a parrot. The shop owner points to three identical looking parrots on a perch and says, "The parrot on the left costs $500." "Why does the parrot cost so much?" asks the first man. The owner says, "Well, the parrot knows how to use a computer." The man then asks about the next parrot to be told that this one costs $1,000 because it can do everything the other parrot can do plus it knows how to use the UNIX operating system. Naturally, the increasingly startled man asks about the third parrot, to be told that it costs $2,000. Needless to say this brings the question "What can it do?" To which the owner replies, "To be honest I have never seen it do a thing, but the other two call him boss!"

Customer to computer salesman. "I would like to return my laptop. My cat is jealous of it."

Compaq is considering changing the command "Press Any Key" to "Press Return Key" because of the flood of calls asking where the "Any" key is.

Part of the inhumanity of the computer is that, once it is competently programmed and working smoothly, it is completely honest.   —Isaac Asimov, *Change!*

CONCEIT

He was so conceited it was beneath his dignity even to talk to himself.   —Sholom Aleichem

CONFIDENCE

Some years ago *Time* magazine reported on a nervous motorist in Lambertville, New Jersey. This man, on being stopped by the police, explained that he had been driving on two hundred and twenty-four consecutive learner's permits over the last twenty-five years. He had flunked his first driver's test and had been unsure of himself ever since.

—George F. Regas

CONGRESS

Jay Leno says, "I saw a Senator on a Sunday-morning talk show who said that the actions of the Senate have created jobs for a lot of citizens." He paused for a moment. "But let's face it," he continued, "you can't make a career out of jury duty."

My dog can bark like a congressman, fetch like an aide, beg like a press secretary and play dead like a receptionist when the phone rings.   —Gerald B. H. Solomon

Senate office hours are from twelve to one, with an hour off
for lunch.   —George S. Kaufman

You know, Congress is a strange place. A man gets up to
speak and says nothing. Nobody listens. And then everybody
disagrees.   —Will Rogers

Software reviewer describing a very slow computer program: . . . it ran with the speed of a congressman getting to
the point.   —Paul Cilwa

There was a fellow who applied for a job as a press aide for
a congressman. Not long after he submitted his application,
he received word from the official's office: "Your resume is
full of exaggerations, distortions, half-truths and lies. Can
you start work Monday?"

CONSCIENCE

Your conscience may not keep you from doing wrong, but it
sure keeps you from enjoying it. A man with a nagging secret
couldn't keep it any longer. In the confessional he admitted
that for years he had been stealing building supplies from
the lumberyard where he worked. "What did you take?" his
parish priest asked. "Enough to build my own home and
enough for my son's house. And houses for our two daughters. And our cottage at the lake." "This is very serious," the
priest said. "I shall have to think of a far-reaching penance.
Have you ever done a retreat?" "No, Father, I haven't," the
man replied. "But if you can get the plans, I can get the
lumber."

CONSUMERS

CONSUMER ALERT: At the top of the list of newly released
products you should not buy are the new inflatable dart
boards.   —Ron Dentinger

COOKING

Couples who cook together stay together. Maybe because
they can't decide who'll get the Cuisinart.   —Erica Jong

Cousin Wendy was very economy minded. During her first month of marriage, she had been preparing ground beef in as many different ways as she knew how — hamburgers, Salisbury steak, tacos, meat loaf, spaghetti and meatballs, etc. On the twelfth straight night, as she served chopped meat, her husband surveyed it and sighed: "How now, ground cow?"

Shortly after they were married, Heather said to Mark, "The two best things I cook are meat loaf and apple dumplings." Mark sheepishly replied, "Um, which one is this?"

The family, knowing how dangerous my cooking is, lets grace last 45 minutes.

There is one thing more exasperating than a wife who can cook and won't and that's a wife who can't cook and will.
—Robert Frost

Ever notice . . . that you can never make the right number of pancakes? —Executive Speechwriter Newsletter

Uncle Sid claims, "My wife's cooking was so bad the flies got together to mend the screens."

'Tis an ill cook that cannot lick his own fingers.
—William Shakespeare

The weary husband was met at the door with sad news. "We'll have to go out for dinner," his wife said cheerily. "I couldn't fix anything because the electricity went off." "Electricity!" growled the husband. "We have a gas range." "I know," the wife went on, "but our can opener is electric."
—Arkansas Baptist

COURTROOM

Carl, an accused debtor, chose to act as his own attorney. He concluded his case with an impassioned plea, "As God is my judge, I do not owe the money!" The judge responded, "He isn't, I am, and you do."

A litigant is a person about to give up his skin for the hope
of retaining his bones.   —Ambrose Bierce

A man, when tried for stealing a pair of boots, said he merely
took the boots as a joke. It was found that he was captured
with them forty yards from the place he had taken them.
The judge said he had carried the joke too far.

Question: "Have you ever been cross-examined before?"
Answer: "Yes, Your Honor, I'm a married man."

It was a lengthy trial. Testimony was heard for six months.
The attorneys took an entire week to present their respective
summations. After a three-hour charge to the jury, the presiding judge finally said: "Are there any other questions before the jury retires?" "Your Honor," said a juror, "please tell
us, what is a plaintiff and what is a defendant?"

Lawyer Ernest Phelps was questioning Theodora Sampson
in a court trial involving slander. "Please repeat the slander-
ous statements you heard, exactly as you heard them," instructed the lawyer. The witness hesitated. "But they were
unfit for any respectable person to hear!" "Then," said the
attorney, "just whisper them to the judge."

Milton Brown, the defense attorney, was cross-examining the
prosecution's main witness, a bus
driver named Jim Samson. "You
say your only meeting with the
defendant was on the municipal
bus you were driving and that he
had been drinking and gambling?" "Yes," replied Samson.
"Did you see him take a drink?"
asked Brown. "No," replied Samson. "Did you see him engage in

any form of gambling?" asked the lawyer. "No," admitted the
bus driver. "Then how do you know," demanded the attorney,

"that the defendant had been drinking and gambling?" "Well," explained Samson, "he gave me a blue chip for his bus fare and told me to keep the change."

Mr. Dewey was briefing his client, who was about to testify in his own defense. "You must swear to tell the complete truth. Do you understand?" The client replied that he did. The lawyer then asked, "Do you know what will happen if you don't tell the truth?" The client looked back and said, "I imagine that our side will win."

Robarts, the defense attorney, was trying to get the prosecution witness to lose her temper. In his line of questioning, he mocked, insulted, and derided her constantly. Despite his tactics, the witness remained calm. Finally, Robarts asked sarcastically: "You say you had no education, but you answered my questions smartly enough." "You don't have to be a Rhodes scholar to answer stupid questions," replied the woman.

The convicted bank robber later admitted, "I think my mistake was yelling 'Hi' to the eyewitnesses as they filed into court."

The lawyer was beginning to grasp at straws during his cross-examination. "You say, Mr. Dyson, that this took exactly five minutes?" The witness replied that he was sure. "I am going to give you a test. I want you to tell me when exactly five minutes has passed, starting . . . now." The lawyer was intently watching a stopwatch taken from his briefcase. At five minutes, to the second, the witness gave the signal. The lawyer told him, "That's quite remarkable. How did you gauge the time so accurately?" Mr. Dyson replied, "I watched the clock on the wall behind you."

The plaintiff and defendant in an action at law, are like two men ducking their heads in a bucket, and daring each other to remain longest under water.   —Samuel Johnson

The reason that there is a penalty for laughing in court is that otherwise the jury would never be able to hear the evidence.
—H. L. Mencken

Defense Attorney to Court: "To save the state the expense of a trial, Your Honor, my client has escaped."   —Chon Day

Treat the bailiff with respect. He has a gun.
—Malcolm Lewis

The plaintiff's medical malpractice attorney was famous for his use of trick questions to gain an advantage over his opponents. He was overheard telling Brubaker, another plaintiff's attorney, of the time a trial judge limited him to a single hypothetical question of the defendant's expert medical witness. My office worked on the question for days. We checked all possible answers against the most authoritative medical opinions, texts and experts. Finally, in court, I took two full hours to ask the question. So?" asked Brubaker. "And then I finished." "Yes?" "The witness asked me. . . ." "Yes, yes?" ". . . if I would mind repeating the question."

From an actual courtroom transcript:

Question: "Were you acquainted with the deceased?"
Answer: "Yes, sir."
Question: "Before or after he died?"

"Weren't you up before me on another drunk driving charge only a few weeks ago?" asked the judge sternly. "I thought you told me you were a recovering alcoholic." "Oh I am," the drunk reassured him sincerely. "I only drink on weekends, and I recover the other five days."

From an actual courtroom transcript:

Question: "What is your name?"
Answer: "Ernestine McDowell."
Question: "And what is your marital status?"
Answer: "Fair."

From an actual courtroom transcript:

Question: "When he went, had you gone and had she, if she wanted to and were able, for the time being excluding all the restraints on her not to go, gone also, would he have brought you, meaning you and she, with him to the station?"

Mr. Brooks: "Objection. That question should be taken out and shot."

The judge says to the plaintiff, "Explain what happened." The plaintiff says, "I was in a phone booth talking to my girlfriend when the defendant opened the door and dragged me out." The defendant says, "The only reason I dragged him out is because he refused to get out, and I needed to make a phone call." The judge asks, "How long were you talking to your girlfriend?" The plaintiff says, "I don't know, Your Honor, but I want to add that he dragged my girlfriend out too."

"Has the jury reached a verdict?" "Yes, Your Honor. We find the defendant . . . dumber than the law allows."

A man was sued by a woman for defamation of character. She charged that he had called her a pig. The man was found guilty and fined. After the trial he asked the judge, "This means that I cannot call Mrs. Johnson a pig?" The judge said that was true. "Does this mean I cannot call a pig Mrs. Johnson?" the man asked. The judge replied that he could indeed call a pig Mrs. Johnson with no fear of legal action. The man looked directly at Mrs. Johnson and said, "Good afternoon, Mrs. Johnson."

The following are things people actually said in court, word for word:

Q: "What gear were you in at the moment of the crash impact?"

A: "Gucci sweats and Reeboks."

Q: "All your responses must be oral, OK? What school did you go to?"
A: "Oral."

Q: "And where was the location of the accident?"
A: "Approximately milepost 499."
Q: "And where is milepost 499?"
A: "Probably between milepost 498 and 500."

Q: "Sir, what is your IQ?"
A: "Well, I can see pretty well, I think."

Q: "Trooper, when you stopped the defendant, were your red and blue lights flashing?"
A: "Yes."
Q: "Did the defendant say anything when she got out of her car?"
A: "Yes, sir."
Q: "What did she say?"
A: "What disco am I at?"

Recently reported in the Massachusetts Bar Association Lawyers journal, the following are questions actually asked of witnesses by attorneys during trials and, in certain cases, the responses given by insightful witnesses:

Q: "Now doctor, isn't it true that when a person dies in his sleep, he doesn't know about it until the next morning?"
Q: "The youngest son, the twenty-year old, how old is he?"
Q: "Were you present when your picture was taken?"
Q: "Was it you or your younger brother who was killed in the war?"
Q: "Did he kill you?"
Q: "How far apart were the vehicles at the time of the collision?"
Q: "You were there until the time you left, is that true?"
Q: "How many times have you committed suicide?"
Q: "Are you qualified to give a urine sample?"

Q: "So the date of conception (of the baby) was August 8th?"

A: "Yes."

Q: "And what were you doing at that time?"

Q: "You say the stairs went down to the basement?"

A: "Yes."

Q: "And these stairs, did they go up also?"

Q: "How was your first marriage terminated?"

A: "By death."

Q: "And by whose death was it terminated?"

And Best of All . . .

Q: "Doctor, how many autopsies have you performed on dead people?"

A: "All my autopsies are performed on dead people."

Q: "Do you recall the time that you examined the body?"

A: "The autopsy started around 8:30 P.M."

Q: "And Mr. Dennington was dead at the time?"

A: "No, he was sitting on the table wondering why I was doing an autopsy."

Q: "Doctor, before you performed the autopsy, did you check for a pulse?"

A: "No."

Q: "Did you check for blood pressure?"

A: "No."

Q: "Did you check for breathing?"

A: "No."

Q: "So, then it is possible that the patient was alive when you began the autopsy?"

A: "No."

Q: "How can you be so sure, Doctor?"

A: "Because his brain was setting on my desk in a jar."

Q: "But could the patient have still been alive nevertheless?"

A: "It is possible that he could have been alive and practicing law in this particular case."

One day Mel Martin stopped by the chambers of a judge with whom he had a lunch appointment. As his friend changed from robe to jacket, Martin noticed a shiny black pistol holstered to the judge's shoulder. The judge was not a firearms enthusiast, so Martin asked him why he was carrying it. His friend said that because of recent threats he had borrowed the pistol from the repository of confiscated weapons. Holding it up, the judge said, "I chose this one because it's so mean-looking, yet it hardly weighs a thing. I hope I don't need it, because I don't even know how to load it." "It's not hard," Martin said examining it closely. "We can fill it at the water fountain on the way out."   —*ABA Journal*

Judge Gerald Kalina of Burnsville, Minnesota, was asking prospective jurors if any of them had illnesses that might prevent their serving. One candidate raised his hand. "I suffer from narcolepsy," he said, "and I'm worried that if I'm chosen, I might nod off during part of the trial." "We can't have that," Kalina replied. "That's the job of the judge."
—*ABA Journal*

Attorney Peter V. MacDonald tells about a murder trial in Texas, during which the first words of the assistant district attorney's address to the jury were as follows: "Ladies and gentlemen, have any of you ever been the victim of a homicide?"   —*Sunday Star,* Toronto

The following testimony is from a trial of a contest over two wills left by the late Mr. Walter:

Question: "When did you last see Walter?"
Answer: "At the funeral."
Question: "Did he make any comment to you at that time?"
—Jerry Buchmeyer in *Texas Bar Journal*

In a sensational court case, the plaintiff, who was all twisted and bent over, won $3 million from the driver of another car. The defendant knew the "injured party" was faking, so after the trial he followed the guy around everywhere, even trailing him to France. "Where do we go now?" the defendant taunted the plaintiff. "Off to Lourdes! If you watch closely, you'll see one of the greatest miracles of all time!"

—Alex Thien in *Milwaukee Sentinel*

COWBOYS

One Sunday a cowboy went to church. When he entered, he saw that he and the preacher were the only ones present. The preacher asked the cowboy if he wanted him to go ahead and preach. The cowboy said, "I'm not too smart, but if I went to feed my cattle and only one showed up, I'd feed him." So the minister began his sermon. One hour passed, then two hours, then two-and-a-half hours. The preacher finally finished and came down to ask the cowboy how he liked the sermon. The cowboy answered slowly, "Well, I'm not very smart, but if I went to feed my cattle and only one showed up, I sure wouldn't feed him all the hay."

A pastor at a frontier church ended a stirring sermon with, "All those who want to go to heaven, put up your hands!" Everybody enthusiastically raised their hands . . . everybody except a grizzled old cowboy who had been slouching against the doorpost at the back of the room. All heads turned as he sauntered up to the front, spurs jangling and said, "Preacher, that was too easy. How d'ya know if these folks are serious? I c'n gar-an-tee to prove who really means it an' who don't!" Bemused and not a little frightened the preacher said, "OK, stranger, go ahead and put the faith of these good people to the test. Ask them anything you want." At that the cowpoke pulled his twin six-shooters, turned to the audience and said, "All right . . . who wants to go heaven . . . raise your hands!"

A cowboy applied for an insurance policy. "Have you ever had any accidents?" asked the agent. "Nope," replied the applicant, "though a bronc did kick in two of my ribs last summer, and a couple of years ago a rattlesnake bit me on the ankle." "Wouldn't you call those accidents?" replied the puzzled agent. "Naw," the cowboy said, "they did it on purpose!" *— Our Daily Bread*

C

COWS

When cows laugh, does milk come out of their noses?
—Jeff Marder

A big city lawyer was called in on a case between a farmer and a large railroad company. A farmer noticed that his prize cow was missing from the field through which the railroad passed. He filed suit against the railroad company for the value of the cow. The case was to be tried before the justice of the peace in the back room of the general store. The attorney immediately cornered the farmer and tried to get him to settle out of court. The lawyer did his best selling job, and the farmer finally agreed to take half of what he was claiming to settle the case. After the farmer signed the release and took the check, the young lawyer couldn't help but gloat a little over his success. He said to the farmer, "You know, I hate to tell you this but I put one over on you in there. I couldn't have won the case. The engineer was asleep and the fireman was in the caboose when the train went through your farm that morning. I didn't have one witness to put on the stand." The old farmer replied, "Well, I'll tell you, young feller, I was a little worried about winning that case myself because that durned cow came home this morning!"

CREDIT CARDS

Two guys were chatting at a cocktail party. "Your wife certainly brightens the room," one said to the other. "Her mere presence is electrifying." "It ought to be," the other man replied. "Everything she's wearing is charged."
—Ron Dentinger

I was signing the receipt for my credit card purchase when the clerk noticed that I had never signed my name on the back of the credit card. She informed me that she could not complete the transaction unless the card was signed. When asked why, she explained that it was necessary to compare the signature on the credit card with the signature I just signed on the receipt. So, I signed the credit card in front of her. She carefully compared that signature to the one I signed on the receipt. As luck would have it, they matched.

CRIME

Before we moved, we lived in a town where no one worried about crime in the streets. The criminals make house calls.

An Illinois man pretending to have a gun kidnapped a motorist and forced him to drive to two different automated teller machines. The kidnapper then proceeded to withdraw money from his own bank accounts.

A man walked into a Topeka, Kansas, Kwik Shop, and asked for all the money in the cash drawer. Apparently, the take was too small, so he tied up the store clerk and worked the counter himself for three hours until police showed up and grabbed him.

CRITICS

After church one Sunday at St. Philip's, two members were critiquing Father Thompson's sermon. The first member said, "I thought the sermon was divine. It reminded me of the peace of God. It passed all understanding." The second member observed, "It reminded me of the mercy of God. I thought it would endure forever."

This is not a novel to be tossed aside lightly. It should be thrown with great force.   —Dorothy Parker

One of the shortest music criticisms on record appeared in a Detroit paper: "An amateur string quartet played Brahms here last evening. Brahms lost."

Another pithy review lasted much longer than the play called *Dreadful Night*. The account: "Dreadful night: PRECISELY!"

C

This actor did a one-man show and the critic wrote: "There were too many in the cast."

Heywood Broun on a play: "It opened at 8:30 sharp—and closed at 10:50 dull."

A playwright was having lunch with his friends the night after his new play opened on Broadway. They asked him how it was going. His reply: "The show got divided notices. We liked it, but the critics didn't."

Two shipwrecked critics were drifting for weeks on a raft. The more frightened of the two started seeking forgiveness for his sins. "I've been a louse all my life," he said. "I've been cruel to actors. Too often I went out of my way to hurt them. If I'm spared, I promise" "Just a moment," interrupted the other critic, "don't go too far. I think I see smoke from a ship!"

I saw the show at a disadvantage—the curtain was up.

If there is a hero in this book, he should kill the author.

The show had a cast of ten—buried in one plot.

For years I was my own worst critic, then I got married.
                                        —Ron Dentinger

According to David Frost, what a writer means by constructive criticism is six thousand words of closely reasoned adulation.

James Agee's comment on a film: "Several tons of dynamite are set off in this picture—none of it under the right people."

One mustn't criticize other people on grounds where he can't stand perpendicular himself.   —Mark Twain

From a film review: "It's the kind of movie that grips you by the eyelids and won't let go until you've fallen asleep."
    —Thomas Mallon, *Rocketts and Rodeos and Other Ameri-
                                    can Spectacles*

Movie critic Richard Harrington: "The plot must have been scripted on a napkin over lunch at a fast-food restaurant."
—*Washington Post*

Comment on a film: "Most of the actors came into this project anonymously and that's how they'll leave it, if they're lucky." —Julie Salamon in *The Wall Street Journal*

Comment by a filmgoer: "The movie should have been rated DG for 'Don't Go.'" —Quoted by James Dent in Charleston, W.Va., *Gazette*

Being attacked by him is like being savaged by a dead sheep.
—Dennis Healy

CYNICS

A cynic is a man who, when he smells flowers, looks around for a coffin. —H. L. Mencken

The cynics are right nine times out of ten. —H. L. Mencken

————————————— **D** —————————————

DANCING

You go to the ballet and you see girls dancing on their tiptoes. Why don't they just get taller girls? —Greg Ray

Rumba is a dance where the front of you goes along nice and smooth like a Cadillac and the back of you moves like a Jeep.
—Bob Hope

DARKNESS

It's always darkest right before you stub your toe. —Al Batt

DATING

She was a lovely girl. Our courtship was fast and furious— I was fast and she was furious. —Max Kauffmann

My grandmother's ninety. She's dating. He's ninety-three. They're very happy. They never argue. They can't hear each other. —Cathy Ladman

Ricky was telling his father about his new girlfriend. He said, "Since I met her I can't eat, drink, or sleep." "Why's that?" asked his father. "Because," he said, "I'm broke."

If men acted after marriage as they do during courtship, there would be fewer divorces—and more bankruptcies.

—Frances Rodman

When Barbara and Jim were dating, Barbara became concerned over the lavish amount of money Jim was spending on her. After an expensive dinner date, she asked her mother, "What can I do to stop Jim from spending so much money on me?" Her mother replied simply, "Marry him."

At the girl's college, dates were permitted only on Saturday night. One young man showed up on a Tuesday evening, explaining to an older woman in the lobby of the dorm that it was imperative he see a certain young lady immediately. "I want to surprise her. You see, I'm her brother." "Oh, she'll be surprised, all right," said the woman. "But think of how I feel. I'm her mother." —*Liguorian*

Young woman to friend: "I'm all in from going out."

—Judith A. Mollner

I was on a date recently; we went horseback riding. It was kind of fun, until we ran out of quarters. —Susie Loucks

A middle-aged widower was dating an attractive young woman of 18. When he got inquiries about his new romance, he commented, "I've found myself asking new questions about life, like, 'What kind of wine goes well with peanut butter?'"

—Leo Aikman

DAUGHTERS

Father welcomed his daughter's boyfriend at the door. "She will be right down. Care for a game of chess?"

My daughter-in-law Dalacie asked her daughter Jessica: "Did you say your prayers last night?" Jessica: "Well, I got down on my knees and started to say them and all of a sudden I thought: *I bet God gets awfully tired hearing the same old prayer over and over.* So I crawled into bed and told Him the story of the three bears."

Years ago when my daughter Susan was sixteen, I was apprehensive about the date she was getting ready for, "Are you sure he's a good driver?" Susan's reply: "Oh, yes, Dad. He has to be. If he gets arrested one more time, he loses his license."

DEATH

Death is God's way of telling you not to be such a wise guy.

Mrs. Pulaski was telling me: "I heard about one small child saying, 'Night-night' to a body at the funeral home. It reminded me of our small daughter. We took her to view her great-grandmother, and she asked, 'Why did they put Great-grandma in a jewelry box?'"

DEFINITIONS

Bulldozer: Someone who sleeps through a political address.

Gadget: Any mechanical device that performs a kitchen task in one-twentieth the time it takes to find it.

Taxpayers: A special class of people who don't have to pass civil service examinations in order to work for the government.

Economics: The science of telling you things you've known all your life, but in a language you can't understand.

—Rep. Dick Armey

Ecstasy: Discovering a second layer of chocolates under the first.

Perfectionist: A person who takes great pains—and gives them to others.

Flattery: the power to describe others as they see themselves.
—*The Farmer—Stockman of the Midwest*

Bargain: a transaction in which each party thinks he has cheated the other.   —Los Angeles Times Syndicate

Compromise: an arrangement whereby people who can't get what they want make sure nobody else does either.
—Dick Cavett with Christopher Porterfield, *Eye on Cavett*

Grapevine: The only communications system in no danger of being replaced by electronics.

Diet: A plan for putting off tomorrow what you put on today.
—Ivern Ball

Pessimist: Someone who can look at the land of milk and honey and see only calories and cholesterol.

DENTISTS

A story along similar lines: One day a man walks into a dentist's office and asks how much it will cost to extract wisdom teeth. "Eighty dollars," the dentist says. "That's a ridiculous amount," the man says. "Isn't there a cheaper way?" "Well," the dentist says, "if you don't use an anaesthetic, I can knock it down to $60." "That's still too expensive," the man says. "Okay," says the dentist. "If I save on anesthesia and simply rip the teeth out with a pair of pliers, I could get away with charging $20." "Nope," moans the man, "it's still too much." "Hmm," says the dentist, scratching his head. "If I let one of my students do it for the experience, I suppose I could charge you just $10." "Marvelous," says the man, "book my wife for next Tuesday!"

Patient: "How much to have this tooth pulled?"
Dentist: "Ninety dollars."

Patient: "Ninety dollars for just a few minutes work?"
Dentist: "I can extract it very slowly if you like."

My dentist keeps his prices down by keeping his overhead down. No unnecessary extras. Instead of laughing gas, he tickles you.
—Ron Dentinger

DIETS

I've been on a diet for two weeks and all I've lost is two weeks. —Totie Fields

If I am ever stuck on a respirator or a life-support system, I definitely want to be unplugged—but not till I get down to a size 8.
—Henrietta Mantel

DIET TIPS:

- If no one sees you eat it, it has no calories.
- If you drink a diet soda with a candy bar, they cancel each other out.
- When eating with someone else, calories don't count if you both eat the same thing.
- Food used for medicinal purposes NEVER counts, such as hot chocolate, brandy, toast, and Sara Lee cheesecake.
- If you fatten up everyone else around you, you look thinner.
- Movie-related foods don't count because they are simply part of the entertainment experience and not a part of one's personal fuel, such as Milk Duds, popcorn with butter, and Junior Mints.
- Enjoy your Diet!!!!

Malcolm Kushner, How to Use Humor for Business Success

You can lead a person to cottage cheese, but you can't make him shrink. —*New York Magazine*

If you're thin, don't eat fast; if you're fat, don't eat—fast!
— *Classic Crossword Puzzles*

DISASTERS

D

A young man came home from work and found his bride upset. "I feel terrible," she said. "I was pressing your suit and I burned a big hole in the seat of your trousers." "Forget it," consoled her husband. "Remember that I've got an extra pair of pants for that suit." "Yes," said the woman, cheering up. "And it's lucky you have. I used them to patch the hole."
—Bob Phillips

DIVORCE

My cousin Bill once sent out a thousand perfumed Valentines signed, "You Know Who . . ." He's a divorce lawyer.

A father was driving home late one evening when he suddenly realizes that it is his daughter's birthday and that he hasn't bought her anything. Out the corner of his eye he sees a shopping mall, and pulling his car through three lanes of traffic, finds a parking spot and runs into the mall. After a frantic search he finds a toy store, goes inside and attracts the attention of a salesman. When asked what he would like, he simply says "a Barbie doll." The salesman looks at him in the particularly condescending manner that only salesmen can muster and asks "Which Barbie would that be, sir?" As the would be shopper looked disconcerted the assistant continues, "We have: Barbie Goes to the Gym for $19.95. Barbie Goes to the Ball for $19.95. Barbie Goes Shopping for $19.95. Barbie Goes to the Beach for $19.95. Barbie Goes Night Clubbing for $19.95, and Divorced Barbie for $265.00." The man can't help himself and asks, "Why is Divorced Barbie $265.00 when all the other Barbies are selling for $19.95?" "That's obvious!" says the salesman. "Divorced Barbie comes with Ken's house, Ken's car, Ken's furniture . . ."

DOCTORS (See also MEDICINE)

I try to remember the case of the gentleman who went in for a physical examination and then said to the doctor, "O.K. Give it to me straight. I can take it." And the doctor said, "Let me put it to you this way. Eat the best part of the chicken first."   —Ronald Reagan

Susan Elroy, our congregation's notorious hypochondriac, was so certain that she had an incurable liver condition that she went to the doctor to find out about it. The doctor assured her she was all right. "You wouldn't know if you had this condition, because it causes no discomfort of any kind." "Oh, my goodness," gasped Susan. "Those are my symptoms exactly."

Sid was a nonstop talker. When his wife became ill, the doctor said, "I prescribe absolute quiet for your wife. Here's a bottle of sleeping pills." "When do I give them to her?" asked Sid. "You don't give them to her," said the doctor. "You take them yourself."   —Bennett Cerf

My neighbor was telling me about her toddler Allison: "I took Allison to the doctor for her two-year-old checkup. They had her do coordination tests, like stacking blocks, and they watch and see if they walk properly. And then the doctor said, 'Allison, can you stand on one foot for me?' And she walked over and stood on his foot."

After surgery, the doctor told the patient, you can pay $500 down and $300 a month. "But that's like buying a car," the patient remarked. "That's right, I am," said the doctor.
    —Msgr. Arthur Tonne, *Jokes Priests Can Tell,* vol. 6

My car skidded on wet pavement and struck a light pole. I was stunned and momentarily unable to speak. Several bystanders ran over to help me. A tall, middle-aged woman was the first to reach my car. She started to speak when a burly truck driver rushed in and pushed her back. "Step aside, lady," he shouted. "I've taken a course in first aid." The woman watched him for a few minutes, then tapped his shoulder. "Pardon me," she said. "But when you get to the part about calling a doctor, I'm right here."

Isn't it a bit unnerving that doctors call what they do "practice"?

A true story. After I survived a very serious illness I went to see my doctor. As his nurse was taking my vital signs and checking my weight and height, I discovered that I was only 5 foot 8 instead of my former 5 foot 10. When the doctor entered the examination room, I reported with alarm, "Doctor! I think I'm shrinking!" The doctor calmly responded, "Now, settle down. You'll just have to be a little patient."

I was in the waiting room of my doctor's office the other day when the doctor started yelling, "Typhoid! Tetanus! Measles!" I went up to the nurse and asked her what was going on. She told me that the doctor liked to call the shots.

The grouchy, short-tempered doctor glared at the new patient. "Have you been to a doctor," he asked, "before you came to me?" "No, sir," replied the meek patient. "I went to a pharmacist." "That shows how much sense some people have," the doctor growled. "And what sort of idiotic advice did he give you?" "He told me to come to see you."

—Rotarian

A young surgeon got a call from a colleague who invited him over for a poker foursome. "Going out, dear?" asked the wife sympathetically. "I'm afraid so," was the brave reply. "It's a serious case. There are three doctors there already!"

Patient: "Doc, what I need is something to stir me up, give me energy, put me in fighting spirit. Did you put something like that in the prescription?"

Doctor: "No—you'll find that in the bill." —Hugh Harrison

DOGS

Minnie said to her friend Marge, "Our dog is just like a member of the family." "Which one?" Marge asked.

My husband and I are either going to buy a dog or have a child. We can't decide whether to ruin our carpet or ruin our lives.

—Rita Rudner

There's a guy with a Doberman pinscher and a guy with a Chihuahua. The guy with the Doberman pinscher says to the guy with the Chihuahua, "Let's go over to that restaurant and get something to eat." The guy with the Chihuahua says, "We can't go in there. We've got dogs with us." The guy with the Doberman pinscher says, "Just follow my lead." They walk over to the restaurant, the guy with the Doberman pinscher puts on a pair of dark glasses, and he starts to walk in. A guy at the door says, "Sorry, Mac, no pets allowed." The guy with the Doberman says, "You don't understand. This is my seeing-eye dog." The guy at the door says, "A Doberman pinscher?" He says, "Yes, they're using them now, they're very good." The guy at the door says, "Come on in." The guy with the Chihuahua figures, "What the heck," so he puts on a pair of dark glasses and starts to walk in. The guy at the door says, "Sorry, pal, no pets allowed." The guy with the Chihuahua says, "You don't understand. This is my see-ing-eye dog." The guy at the door says, "A Chihuahua?" He says, "You mean they gave me a Chihuahua?"

One day a letter carrier was greeted by a boy and a huge dog. The mailman said to the boy, "Does your dog bite?" "No," replied the boy. Just then the huge dog bit the mailman on the ankle. The letter carrier yelped, "I thought your dog doesn't bite!" "He doesn't," replied the boy. "This is not my dog!"

A farmer was bitten on the leg by one of his dogs. At the clinic, the nurse asked him if he had put anything on it. "No," replied the puzzled farmer, "the dog liked it just as it was." —Don Bosco in *Salesian Bulletin*

One good thing about a dark skirt is that it's the best thing for removing dog hairs from the sofa.
—Jane Goodsell, Press Associates

The dog has got more fun out of man than man has got out of the dog, for the clearly demonstrable reason that man is the more laughable of the two animals.
—James Thurber, *Thurber's Dogs*

If you think dogs can't count, try putting three dog biscuits in your pocket and then giving Fido only two of them.
—Phil Pastoret, Newspaper Enterprise Assn.

It's not the size of the dog in the fight; it's the size of the fight in the dog. —Mark Twain

The first thing that veterinary doctors learn about treating pit bulls is that you should never try to force a pit bull to open his mouth and say, "Ahhh."

Whoever said you can't buy happiness forgot about puppies.
—Gene Hill

They say animal behavior can warn when an earthquake is coming. Like the night before the last earthquake hit, our family dog took the car keys and drove to Arizona.
—Gene Perret

DREAMS

After she woke up, a woman told her husband, "I just dreamed that you gave me a pearl necklace for Valentine's day. What do you think it means?" "You'll know tonight," he said. That evening, the man came home with a package and gave it to his wife. Delighted, she opened it—to find a book entitled, *The Meaning of Dreams*.

My aunt said to her husband, "Max, last night I dreamed you bought me a fur coat." Her husband said, "In your next dream, wear it in good health."   —*Henny Youngman*

DRIVING

Police arrested 56-year-old Joe Shaw near White River Junction, Vermont, in April after he tried to break through a rolling roadblock on I-89. Shaw, who was charged with DUI and other offenses, said, "I saw it so many times in the movies, I had to try it."

An applicant for driver's license came to the questions: "How many feet are required to stop car traveling 30 mph?" He answered straightforwardly: "Two feet, one for the clutch, one for the brake." He got his license. —*The Railway Clerk*

On the walls of the men's room at a Kansas truck stop were scribbled the words from Romans 8: "If God be for us, who can be against us?" Scrawled beneath someone had added: "The Highway Patrol!"

A car headed out of Calgary was stopped by a Canadian Mountie. He told the driver: "Congratulations, you have just won a $100 prize for the hundredth car passing through here today with all occupants buckled up with seat belts. Now, what are you going to do with the money?" "Well," said the motorist, "I think I'll go and get a driver's license, now that I can afford it."

A motorist whose car was weaving was ordered to pull off the road into a parking lot, and the policeman told the obviously drunk motorist to walk down a straight line painted on the pavement. "I'm sorry, sir, but I will not walk it unless you put a net under it," said the motorist.   —*Ohio Motorist*

A motorist in Washington, D.C., stopped to help a woman driver stalled on one of the main thoroughfares. He found her taking sand out of the trunk of her car and sprinkling it around the front wheels. "It ought to go under the back wheels," he said. Sneering at his stupidity, she replied, "The back wheels go around all right. It's the front wheels that won't turn."   —*Minneapolis Tribune*

E

ECONOMISTS

If all the financial experts in this country were laid end to end, they'd still point in all directions.   —Sam Ewing

A pair of economists went to a restaurant for lunch. "Never mind the food," one said to the waitress. "Just bring us the bill so we can argue about it." —Carol Simpson in *Funny Times*

EDUCATION

Mr. Gray, the professor asked, what three words are used most among college students? The student answered, "I don't know." The professor responded, "Correct."   —*Irish Grit*

Who's going to do all the work in this world when the trend toward longer education meets the trend toward early retirement?   —Don Reber in Reading, Pennsylvania, *Times*

Education is learning what you didn't even know you didn't know. —Daniel J. Boorstin, *Democracy and Its Discontents*

EFFORT

If at first you don't succeed, try, try, a couple of times more. Then quit. There's no sense making a fool of yourself.
                                                        —W. C. Fields

By trying, we can easily learn to endure adversity. Another man's, I mean.   —Mark Twain

EGO

Field Marshall Lord Montgomery was reported to have started his reading of the Gospel at Matins one Sunday with

the words: "'And the Lord said unto Moses,'—and, in my opinion, quite rightly"
— Norman Broadbridge in *Manchester Guardian Weekly*

A very boastful explorer was boring his dinner guests with accounts of a South African trip he had made. "And just as I looked inside my tent when I retired," he boomed, "I saw a ferocious ape."

"What do you suppose I did?" A weary voice replied, "Took the mirror down?"
— *Quote*

You can always recognize an egotist by the gleam in his I.
— Amy Griffin

The nice thing about egotists is that they don't talk about other people.
— Lucille S. Harper

Sir Arthur Eddington, a British astronomer, was once asked: "Is it true, Professor Eddington, that you are one of the three people in the world who understands Einstein's theory of relativity?" The astronomer appeared reluctant to answer. "Forgive me," said his questioner. "I should have realized a man of your modesty would find such a question embarrassing." "Not at all," said Eddington. "I was just trying to think who the third could be."
— *Toastmaster's Quips & Stories and How to Use Them,*
edited by Herbert V. Prochnow

An egotist is someone who is always me-deep in conversation.
— George Goldtrap

E-MAIL

Consider the case of the Illinois man who left the snow-filled streets of Chicago for a vacation in Florida. His wife was on a business trip and was planning to meet him there the next day. When he reached his hotel, he decided to send his wife a quick e-mail. Unable to find the scrap of paper on which he had written her e-mail address, he did his best to type it from memory. Unfortunately, he missed one letter, and his note was directed instead to an elderly preacher's wife, whose husband had passed away only the day before. When the grieving widow checked her e-mail, she took one look at the monitor, let out a piercing scream, and fell to the floor in a dead faint. At the sound, her family rushed into the room and saw this note on the screen: "Dearest Wife, Just got checked in. Everything prepared for your arrival tomorrow. Signed, Your eternally loving husband. PS. Sure is hot down here!"

EMERGENCIES

Nothing seems to bring on an emergency as quickly as putting money aside in case of one.   —Lynne Youdin

ENEMIES

Never interrupt your enemy when he is making a mistake.
                                                      —Napoleon Bonaparte

He made enemies as naturally as soap makes suds.
                                                      —Percival Wilde

ENVY

Mrs. Felton asked the artist to paint a portrait of her covered with jewels. "Then put them on," said the artist. Replies Mrs. Felton, "You don't understand, I don't have any jewels, but if I die and my husband remarries, I want his next wife to go crazy looking for the jewels."

EPITAPHS

Seven wives I've buried with as many a fervent prayer;
If we all should meet in heaven, won't there be trouble there?

Norman Zierold of Long Island, N.Y., *Newsday,* asked many celebrities to write their own epitaphs. What follows is a sampling:

Comedienne Pat Carroll: "Could I leave a wake-up call?"

Baritone Robert Merrill: "One more encore, please."

Mark Russell: "A comedian. It's not the first time he died."

Author James Michener: "Here lies a man who never showed home movies or served vin rosé."

Comic Joan Rivers: "Wait—can we talk?"

ERRORS

Admit your errors before someone else exaggerates them.

—Andrew V. Mason, M.D.

From Father Ferreira's bulletin from Our Lady of Good Council in San Leandro, California, there's this poignant note: "If you find errors, please consider that they appear for the benefit of those readers who always look for them . . . We try to print something for everybody!"

—*The Priest Magazine*

ETERNITY

Eternal rest sounds comforting in the pulpit . . . Well, you try it once, and see how heavy time will hang on your hands.

—Mark Twain

ETHICS

My doctor has ethics. He won't operate unless he really needs money.

—Ron Dentinger

EVIL

If there isn't a devil, there's sure somebody getting his work done for him.

EXAMPLE

Few things are harder to put up with than the annoyance of a good example.

—Mark Twain

EXCELLENCE

If you pursue excellence, happiness sneaks up behind you and touches you on the shoulder. If you pursue mediocrity, you're sure to catch it.

—Kenneth Boulding

EXCUSES

An Prohibition-era story from the South tells about the time a police officer caught a bootlegger with a lot of jugs in his truck. The officer asked what was in them. The bootlegger said, "Water." The police officer did not believe him. So he opened one of the jugs and took a gulp. He said to the bootlegger, "This looks like wine. And it tastes exactly like wine." The bootlegger exclaimed, "Praise the Lord! He's done it again!"

Little Ted was told not to go swimming in a nearby pond. He came home with his hair wet and told his mother he had fallen into the water. "Then why aren't your clothes wet too?" she asked. "Well," he replied, "I had a hunch I might fall in so I took off my clothes and hung them on a limb."

EXERCISE

I'm not working out. My philosophy: No pain, no pain.
                                                —Carol Leifer

Professor in lab: "Researchers have announced that exercise kills germs."
New student: "Sure, sure. But how do you get germs to exercise?"   —*Capper's Weekly*

I developed a great incentive for doing sit-ups. I put M & Ms between my toes.

EXPERIENCE

We should be careful to get out of an experience only the wisdom that was in it—and stop there, lest we be like the cat that sits on a hot stove-lid. She will never sit down on a hot stove-lid again—and that is well, but also she will never sit down on a cold one anymore.   —Mark Twain

EXPERTS

Even more exasperating than the guy who thinks he knows it all is the one who really does.   —Al Bernstein

An expert is someone called in at the last minute to share the blame.   —Sam Ewing in *Mature Living*

FACTS

Fact: 50% of doctors practicing in this country today graduated in the lower half of their class. —Ron Dentinger

FAMILIES

Home, nowadays, is a place where part of the family waits till the rest of the family brings the car back.—Earl Meltzer

Johann Andersen tells me, "We've got so many kids that we wore out four storks."

Lord have mercy, Mrs. Tugwell just had her sixteenth young 'un. She said she had so many young 'uns she'd run out of names—to call her husband. —Minnie Pearl

Nothing in life is fun for the whole family.

The phone rings and, in a whisper, a six-year-old boy says, "Hello." The caller says, "Can I talk to your mother?" The kid whispers, "She's outside." The caller says, "Can I talk to your father?" The kid whispers, "He's outside too." The caller says, "Is there anyone else there?" The kid whispers, "The police are here." The caller says, "The police are at your house?" The kid whispers, "Yea. They're outside." The caller says, "What's everybody doing outside?" The kid whispers, "Looking for me." —Ron Dentinger

A young couple had their first baby. When it was one year old, it hadn't said a word; one and a half years, still not a word. The parents took the baby to a pediatrician, who said, "Everything's perfectly normal. Just be patient." And so it went until the child's 25th month. They were all having breakfast and the kid turned to his mother and said, "This oatmeal is too darn lumpy." The parents were amazed, and so they said, "Why haven't you talked before?" The kid replied, "Up till now, things have gone very well."

—Eric W. Johnson, *A Treasury of Humor II*

The other day my daughter came home from school and asked a question of my wife. My wife said, "Why not wait until your dad comes home and ask him." To which my daughter replied: "But, Mom, I don't want to know that much about it!"   —King Duncan

Agnes and Beverly were discussing their respective families. "Do you mean to tell me that your son and daughter-in-law were married six months ago and you haven't visited them yet?" exclaimed Agnes. "I'm shocked!" "What's there to be shocked about?" demanded Beverly. "I'm waiting until they have their first baby. Everybody knows that a grandma is always more welcome than a mother-in-law."

I never liked hide-and-seek since the time I hid in the closet and my family moved.

Having a family is like having a bowling alley installed in your brain.   —Martin Mull

A mother asked her son why he didn't take his little sister along as he left to go fishing, and he said, "Because the last time I took her I didn't catch a thing." Mother said, "I'm sure she'll be quiet if you explain to her." "Oh, it wasn't the noise," the boy replied. "She ate the bait."

The rich aunt was hurt and said to her nephew, "I'm sorry you don't like your gift. I had asked you if you preferred a large check or a small check." "I know, Auntie," the nephew said contritely, "but I didn't know you were talking about neckties."   —*Irish Grit*

The bride brought her new husband up to meet Granny at the family picnic. The old woman looked the young man over carefully and then said to him, "Young man, do you desire to have children?" He was a bit startled by her candid approach, but finally came out with, "Well, yes, as a matter of fact, I do." She looked at him scornfully and then surveyed the very large clan gathered around a half-dozen picnic tables and said, "Well, try to control it."

It's hard to say when one generation ends and the next begins—but it's somewhere around nine or ten at night.
—Charles Ruffing in *Family Weekly*

I was admittedly miffed when my children failed to stop by the house for weeks. Finally a visit was arranged, and my sons and their families were due to arrive. "Now don't say anything to them about not visiting when they get here," my husband admonished. I didn't say a word. I just had them fill out name tags as they came in the door.
—Angie Papadakis

Leigh, my five-year-old brother, was listening as my mother and I argued. When Mom told me that I was just going to have to live with the consequences, Leigh piped up, "If Dory is going to live with consequences, can I have her room?"
—Dory Smith in *Woman's Day*

A journey of a hundred miles starts with an argument over how to load the car.

FANATICS

A fanatic is one who is sure the Almighty would agree with him, if only the Almighty had all the facts.
—Rev. Robert E. Harris, *Laugh with the Circuit Rider*

FARMERS

The city man bought a farm and was visited by his new neighbor. He asked him, "Can you tell me where the property line runs between our farms?" The farmer looked him over and asked, "Are you talking owning or mowing?"

An Amish Farmer and his son, traveling by horse and buggy up a narrow lane, met a motorist going the other way. There was no room to pass for two miles in either direction. The motorist, in a hurry, honked his horn. "If you don't back up," said the Amish man, rolling up his sleeves, "I won't like what I'm going to have to do." The surprised driver put his car in reverse and backed up two miles, allowing the horse and buggy to go by. "What was it you wouldn't have liked to have done back there?" asked the Amish man's son. "Back up two miles," replied the farmer.   —AP

A farmer came to a restaurant and bought four hamburgers and had them put into a bag and left the store. He was soon back and bought eight more. As he started out the door the restaurant owner asked him what he was doing with the sandwiches. "Oh," said the farmer, "I sell them down on the corner for twenty-five cents a piece." "My gosh," said the restaurant man. "I charge you fifty cents each. You are taking a 25 cent loss." "I know," said the man, "but it sure beats farming."   —Paul Meysing

FATHERS

A college professor congratulated a man on his daughter's brilliant paper on the influence of science on the principles of government. The father exclaimed, "Good! Next I want her to begin to work on the influence of the vacuum cleaner on the modern carpet!"

I knew I was taking too many business trips away from home when my kids started calling me Uncle.

My father used to tell me, "When Abraham Lincoln was your age, Abraham Lincoln had a job. When Abraham Lincoln was your age, he walked twelve miles to get to school." I said, "Dad, when Abraham Lincoln was your age, he was President, okay?"   —Andy Andrews

The Wall Street attorney sent his only son to his alma mater law school, promising him a gift of $10,000 if he would make the Law Review in one year. At the end of the son's first year, the law student called his father and told him that he had wonderful news for him. "Dad! I've saved you $10,000!"

Two explorers met in the heart of the jungle. "I'm here," declared one, "to commune with nature in the raw, to contemplate the eternal verities and to widen my horizons. And you, sir?" "I," sighed the second explorer, "came because my son has begun playing the saxophone."   —King Duncan

What's wrong with kids today? My friend Mort explains: "When we were kids we were very disciplined. My father was very strict, but along came the electric razor and took away the razor strap. Then furnaces took away the woodshed. And along came taxes and the worries of it took away my Dad's hair and with that the old hair brush disappeared. And that's why kids today are running wild, the old man has run out of weapons!"

Then there's the father who laments the fact that three of his children are in graduate school. He's getting poorer by degrees.

Hal Adams, a Kentucky farmer, had an ambitious son who graduated from Princeton University and upon his graduation (magna cum laude), he went to New York to make his fortune. The breaks were against him, however, and he ended up as a bootblack in Grand Central Station. Hal continued to work his farm. Now the father makes hay while the son shines.

My Cousin Victor had just been graduated from Yale but was unable to find a job. So he went to work for his father, my Uncle Hank, at the steel shelving factory my uncle owned. Catching Victor napping in a supply closet, Uncle Hank commanded, "Go out and sweep the sidewalk." "But dad," Victor protested, "I'm a college graduate!" "Oh, I forgot about that," Uncle Hank replied. "I'll come out and show you how."

During his freshman year, my son Steve couldn't get home for Christmas. So he sent me a set of inexpensive cuff links and a note reading: "Dear Dad, This is not much, but it's all you could afford."

F

One little boy defined Father's Day like this: "Father's Day is just like Mother's Day, only you don't spend as much on a present."

One teenage boy to another: "My Dad had a long talk with me about girls last night. He doesn't know anything about them either."

Three boys are in the schoolyard bragging about their fathers. The first boy says, "My Dad scribbles a few words on a piece of paper, he calls it a poem, they give him $50." The second boy says, "That's nothing. My Dad scribbles a few words on a piece of paper, he calls it a song, they give him $100." The third boy says, "I got you both beat. My Dad scribbles a few words on a piece of paper, he calls it a sermon. And it takes eight people to collect all the money!"

A doting father used to sing his little children to sleep until he overheard the four-year-old tell the three-year-old, "If you pretend you're asleep, he stops."

Kevin's father kept bringing home office work just about every night. Finally his first grader son asked why. Daddy explained that he had so much work he couldn't finish it all during the day. Asked Kevin, "In that case, why don't they put you in a slower group?"

Mark Twain's best known remark is always worth repeating: "When I was a boy of fourteen, my father was so ignorant I could hardly stand to have the old man around. But when I got to be twenty-one, I was astonished at how much the old man had learned in seven years."

Comedian Myron Cohen tells about the 80-year-old man, retired in Florida and visited frequently by his son. One night, son shows up to find father watching television. "What are you watching, Pop?" asks son. "Basketball," says old man. "What's the score?" asks son. "Eighty-six to eighty-two," father replies. "Who's winning?" asks son. "Eighty-six," says father. —Phil Pepe in *New York Daily News*

My neighbor Sam was telling me, "My father is a very highly respected accountant—a ledger in his own time."

A man was complaining to his co-worker about the expense of keeping two kids in college. "About all I can afford to put aside for a rainy day," he sighed, "is a pair of dry socks."

Downcast father: "I finally talked my son into getting his hair cut, and I'm so sorry. Now I can see his earrings."
—*Southeastern Oil Review*

Jan Murray informed his children that he was boss, and they were to obey him. After a long silence his small son spoke up and said, "Gosh, Daddy thinks he is Mommy!"   —*Grit*

On my birthday I was cutting the lawn when my teenage son came home from a baseball game. Seeing me behind the mower, he exclaimed, "Oh, Dad, you shouldn't have to mow the lawn on your birthday." Touched, I was about to turn the mower over to him, when he added, "You should wait until tomorrow!"   —Ernest Blevins

FEAR

Common sense gets a lot of credit that belongs to cold feet.
—Arthur Godfrey

FEELINGS

One thing I like is long walks—especially when they're made by people who annoy me.   —Fred Allen

One of the symptoms of an approaching nervous breakdown is the belief that one's work is terribly important.
—Bertrand Russell

FISHING

While sports fishing off the Florida coast in Key West, a tourist capsized his boat. He could swim, but his fear of alligators kept him clinging to the overturned craft. Spotting an old beachcomber walking on the shore, the tourist shouted, "There wouldn't by chance be any alligators in these waters?!" "No," the old man hollered back, "haven't been any for years!" Feeling relieved, the tourist started swimming leisurely toward the shore. About halfway toward shore he asked the old man, "Say, how'd you get rid of the gators, anyway?" "We didn't do anything," the old man said. "The sharks got 'em."
—H. Aaron Cohl, *The Friars Club Encyclopedia of Jokes*

CORRECTION: In last week's paper we ran a story about a local man who injured himself while fishing. This was an error. We have since learned that it didn't happen while he was fishing. He dislocated his shoulders the next day, while describing a fish that got away.   —Ron Dentinger

My Aunt Edna tells me: "As we were preparing for a fishing trip, I noticed my husband looking at me lovingly. 'What's on your mind?' I asked. 'Oh,' he replied, 'I was just thinking what great lures your earrings would make.'"

The young wife on her first fishing trip was working busily over her line. Finally her husband asked her what she was doing. "I'm changing corks, dear," she replied sweetly. "This one keeps sinking."   —*Quote*

The main reason that comparatively few females go fishing is that women have more important things to lie about.

Give a man a fish and he eats for a day. Teach him how to fish and you get rid of him for the whole weekend.

—Zenna Schaffer

A stranger stopped his car to watch the odd behavior of a fisherman on a river bank. First, he hooked a big pike, but threw it back. Then he landed a beautiful large trout, but threw it back, too. Finally, he reeled in a tiny perch, and with a grunt of satisfaction, deposited it in his bag. The stranger couldn't resist calling out, "Why on earth did you throw those two big ones back and keep this tiny one?" The fisherman explained tersely, "Small frying pan."—Hugh Harrison

After fishing for walleye all day and not getting so much as a bite, the fisherman went back to shore, loaded up his boat and began driving home. He stopped at a fish market. "Throw me six of the biggest fish you have," he said to the proprietor. "Throw them? Why?" "Because I'm going to catch them. I may be a lousy fisherman, but I'm not a liar."

—Ohio Motorist

FOOD

I'm not against using some preservatives in food. What I'm against is any loaf of bread that has a life expectancy greater than my own.   —Orben's Current Comedy

Don't fight a good breakfast. Go with the grain.

—"Graffiti"

Garlic: It may build you up physically, but it shoots you down socially.

Never eat any product on which the listed ingredients cover more than one-third of the package.

FOOLS

He's nobody's fool. On the other hand, maybe someone will adopt him.

—Ron Dentinger

Let us be thankful for the fools. But for them the rest of us could not succeed.

—Mark Twain

Only a fool tests the depth of the water with both feet.

—African proverb

Foolproof systems don't take into account the ingenuity of fools.

—Gene Brown in Danbury, Conn., *News-Times*

Wise men make proverbs, but fools repeat them.   —Samuel Palmer

Everyone is a damn fool for at least five minutes every day. Wisdom consists in not exceeding the limit.   —Elbert Hubbard

King Arthur: "What is an unemployed jester?"
Merlin: "Nobody's fool."   —Edward Tecklin in *Boys' Life*

FOOTBALL

The wife is complaining to her husband, "You seem to know every single football statistic, but you can't remember our wedding anniversary or the year that we got married." He says, "I can too. It was the same year that the Packers traded Williams for a first round draft choice."   —Ron Dentinger

Army doctor to recruit: "Did this injury occur when you were on the football team?"
Recruit: "No, Sir. It happened when the football team was on me."   —*Liguorian*

Football coach, on job security: "I have a lifetime contract. That means I can't be fired during the third quarter if we're ahead and moving the ball."

Following a 34-27 loss to Cleveland, the Tampa Bay coach was asked about what he thought of his team's execution: "I think it's a good idea."

A minister stopped John McKay, coach of the Tampa Bay Buccaneers, and said sternly, "Sir, don't you know that it is a sin to play football on Sunday?" "Well," said McKay glumly, "the way the Bucs are playing, it sure is."

Two armchair quarterbacks were discussing how much their football watching on TV irritated their wives. "My wife won't say much if I watch just one game on Sunday, but if I watch two, she hits the ceiling!" said one guy. "Mine, too! Say, what's her hang time?"

　—How the Platform Professionals Keep 'em Laughin'

A ticket scalper was trying to buy a ticket off a guy who had two 50-yard-line seats. The scalper asked, "Is your wife with you?" "Oh, no," was the reply. "Well, listen. I'll give you $150 for that extra ticket of yours." "No way," the guy said, "I'm gonna go to that game and I'm gonna have a few drinks and I'm gonna yell a lot. And then I'm gonna have a few more drinks. And then I'm probably gonna get into a fight. And then they're gonna come and get me and throw me out of the stadium. And then I'm gonna need this extra ticket to get back in."　　　　　　　　　　　　　　　*—James Dent*

The shivering wife was sitting in the stands with the screaming football maniacs all around her. "Tell me again how much fun we're having," she said to her husband. "I keep forgetting."

I heard two high school superintendents from different school systems talking recently. One asked the other how their football season turned out. The superintendent replied: "We had a 5 and 5 season. We lost 5 at home and 5 on the road."　　　　　　　　　　　　　　　　　*—Doc Blakely*

Joe Montana, on the disabled list with a hand injury, was having lunch with his wife and children at a hotel on Maui. "You poor thing!" the waitress gushed. "How did it happen?" "I broke it playing football," Montana explained. "Really?" replied the waitress. "Aren't you a little old to be playing football?"

After some striking failures in his attempt to pick winning football teams, a columnist for the Dallas *Morning News* suggested last fall that a monkey at the zoo could probably do better and pick at least half the games right. So a year-old gorilla named Kanda was given a chance. A zookeeper wrote the names of the opposing teams on slips of paper and held one in each hand. The hand Kanda slapped was Kanda's choice. For the first week the gorilla's record was 10-3-1. The newspaper was so impressed that it added Kanda to its six-man selection panel. By the end of the third week, the gorilla's record was 27-14-1, giving him a .642 winning percentage as compared with the panel's lackluster .464. — UPI

We didn't lose the game; we just ran out of time.

           —Vince Lombardi

John Brodie, former San Francisco 49er, was asked by a fan, "How come a great quarterback like you has to hold the ball for kickers?" Replied Brodie, "Because if I don't, it would fall over."

Several years ago, a dejected football coach entered a telephone booth just after his team had lost the big game of the season. When he discovered that he didn't have the necessary dime, he called to a passing student, "Oh, Roger! Will you lend me a dime so I can call a friend?" The student grinned sourly and reached in his pocket. "Here's two dimes, coach," he replied. "Call all your friends."

FORGIVENESS

Quite often it's easier to get forgiveness than to get permission.   —Ron Dentinger

Forget and forgive. This is not difficult, when properly understood. It means that you are to forget inconvenient duties, and forgive yourself for forgetting. In time, by rigid practice and stern determination, it comes easy.

           —Mark Twain

Heinrich Heine (1797–1856), a great German poet, was famous for his barbed wit. About religion, he wrote: "I love to sin. God loves to forgive sin. Really, this world is admirably arranged."

FREEDOM

It is by the goodness of God that in our country we have those three unspeakably precious things: freedom of speech, freedom of conscience, and the prudence never to practice either of them. —Mark Twain

People demand freedom of speech to make up for the freedom of thought which they avoid. —Soren Kierkegaard

FRIENDS

There is nothing so disturbing to one's well-being and judgment as to see a friend get rich. —Charles P. Kindleberger

He's really a wonderful guy. Why, if I asked him to, he'd give me the shirt off his back. After all, it's mine.

It takes your enemy and your friend, working together, to hurt you to the heart: one to slander you and the other to get the news to you. —Mark Twain

Lots of people want to ride with you in the limo, but what you want is someone who will take the bus with you when the limo breaks down. —Oprah Winfrey

In the end, we will remember not the words of our enemies, but the silence of our friends. —Martin Luther King Jr.

She is such a good friend that she would throw all her acquaintances into the water for the pleasure of fishing them out again. —Charles Talleyrand

Before you borrow money from a friend, decide which you need more. —Gene Brown in Danbury, Conn., *News-Times*

The surest way to lose a friend is to tell him something for his own good. —Sid Ascher

The holy passion of Friendship is of so sweet and steady and loyal and enduring a nature that it will last through a whole lifetime, if not asked to lend money.　　　—Mark Twain

FRUGALITY

You can always identify the pastor of any parish. He's the one who goes around turning out the lights.

Two young priests were discussing how frugal their senior pastor was. Said one: "When he dies, if he sees light at the end of the tunnel, he'll put it out."　—Msgr. Charles Dollen

FRUSTRATION

Frustration is when the same snow that covers the ski slopes makes the roads to them impassable.
　　　—James Holt McGavran in *The Homesteader*

G

GAMES

"I think it's wrong," says comedian Steven Wright, "that only one company makes the game Monopoly."

GARBAGE

During the garbage workers strike in New York a modern Houdini figured out a way to get rid of his garbage and trash. He gift-wrapped it in several packages and left it in his unlocked car. Every day somebody would steal it.
　　　—Brian O'Hara

GARDENING

I'm glad I didn't throw away my empty seed packages. It turns out they're just the right size for storing my first year's crop!

Excellent gardening advice: "To plant asparagus, dig a ditch three years ago."　　　—E. B. White

One of the worst mistakes you can make as a gardener is to think you're in charge.
—Janet Gillespie, Quoted by Lindsay Bond Totten, Scripps-Howard News Service

A weed is a plant with nine lives. —Arnold H. Glasow

If God had wanted us to plant gardens, he wouldn't have created supermarkets.
—James Dent in Charleston, W.VA, *Gazette*

The one thing every good gardener has is a green thumb. It comes from pulling twenties out of your wallet at the garden supply shop.
—Robert Orben, *2500 Jokes To Start 'Em Laughing*

GENIES

A secretary, a paralegal and a partner in a city law firm are walking through a park on their way to lunch when they find an antique oil lamp. They rub it and a genie comes out in a puff of smoke. The genie says, "I usually only grant three wishes, so I'll give each of you just one." "Me first! Me first!" says the secretary. "I want to be in the Bahamas, driving a speedboat, without a care in the world." Poof! She's gone. In astonishment, "Me next! Me next!" says the paralegal, "I want to be in Hawaii, relaxing on the beach with my personal masseuse, an endless supply of pina coladas and the love of my life." Poof! She's gone. "You're next," the genie says to the partner. The partner says, "I want those two back in the office after lunch."

GENIUS

Everyone is a genius at least once a year; a real genius has his original ideas closer together. —Georg Lichtenberg

GIFTS

At a drugstore, a wife wanted to buy shaving lotion for her mate. "What kind?" asked the clerk. "Well," explained the

wife, "he's seventy years old. Have you got any of that Old Spouse?"
—James Dent

GLORY

Glory is fleeting, but obscurity is forever.

—Napoleon Bonaparte

GOD

If there is no God, who pops up the next Kleenex?

—Art Hoppe

"Gramma, know what you and God have in common?" asked the three-year-old Devon. Mentally polishing her halo and looking as saintly as possible, Gramma waited for the expected compliment. "You're both old," Devon replied.

—*Family Digest*

GOLF

A guy is standing in front of his locker at the country club admiring a golf ball he has in his hand. One of his golfing buddies says to him, "What'd you do, get some new golf balls?" And the guy says, "Would you believe that this is the greatest golf ball ever made. You can't lose it. You hit it into the rough and it whistles. You hit it into the woods and a bell inside goes off. If you drive it into a lake, a big burst of steam shoots up six feet in the air for two minutes." And his friend says, "That's great. Where did you get it?" And the guy says, "I found it."
—Soupy Sales

After a long day on the course, the exasperated golfer turned to his caddie and said, "You must be the absolute worst caddie in the world." "No, I don't think so," said the caddie. "That would be too much of a coincidence."

A golfer swings his club, but misses the ball entirely. He looks at his partner and says, "Boy, this is a tough course."

—Ron Dentinger

If golf had never been invented, how would they measure hail?
                                        —Ron Dentinger

Golfer Tommy Bolt had a terrible temper. Once, after missing six straight putts, generally leaving them teetering on the very edge of the cup, Bolt shook his fist at the heavens and shouted, "Why don't you come down and fight like a man!"

Many men play golf religiously—every Sunday.
                            —Jim Reed, *The Funny Side of Golf*

It's good sportsmanship to pick up lost golf balls while they are still rolling.   —Mark Twain

You can always spot an employee who's playing golf with his boss. He's the fellow who gets a hole in one and says, "Oops!"
                                        —Bob Monkhouse

GOSSIP

Why must the phrase, "It's none of my business," always be followed by the word but?

Neighbor to woman: "I hear your husband is in the hospital. What happened?" The other woman replied, "Knee trouble. I found his secretary sitting on it."

Gossip: The only thing that travels faster than e-mail.
                                        —Angie Papadakis

If you haven't got anything nice to say about anybody, come sit next to me.   —Alice Roosevelt Longworth

Trying to squash a rumor is like trying to un-ring a bell.
                            —Shana Alexander, *Anyone's Daughter*

At a cocktail party: "I never repeat gossip, so I'll say this only once."   —*Selected Cryptograms 5*

GOVERNMENT

A government is the only known vessel that leaks from the top.   —James Reston

A government that robs Peter to pay Paul can always depend upon the support of Paul. —George Bernard Shaw

Crime wouldn't pay if the government ran it!

Harry Truman said that after winning his first election to Washington, he spent six months wondering how he made it to the Senate and the rest of his term wondering how the others made it.

If you laid all our laws end to end, there would be no end.
—Arthur "Bugs" Baer

It's getting harder and harder to support the government in the style to which it has become accustomed.

You can criticize the President, you can criticize the Vice President, you can criticize the Congress. But you have to hand it to the IRS.

A bureaucrat is a man who shoots the bull, passes the buck, and makes seven copies of everything.

The zip code in Washington will be changed to 00000. Nothing there adds up anyhow.

I know a guy who just retired from civil service after 40 years. As a kind of surprise, the government gave him a retirement banquet and told him what his job had been.

When I get a letter in the mail, it makes me grateful to think that 500,000 people have worked for 14 days just to get it to me!

Most problems don't exist until a government agency is created to solve them. —Kirk Kirkpatrick

A member of the Los Angeles County Board of Supervisors welcomed a presidential commission on drug trafficking. "I am sure," he declared, "that this commission will do an infinitesimal amount of good." —*The Baltimore Sun*

Everyone wants to live at the expense of the state. They forget that the state wants to live at the expense of everyone.
—Frederic Bastiat

Justice may be blind, but she has very sophisticated listening devices.   —Edgar Argo in *Funny Times*

Government investigations have always contributed more to our amusement than they have to our knowledge.
—Will Rogers

If the government were to ask to have the paper clip invented today, it would probably have seven moving parts, two batteries, three transistors and require servicing at least twice a year. —Sandy Cooley in New Holstein, Wisconsin, *Reporter*

GRANDCHILDREN

When my grandsons came home from Sunday school during one of our weekend visits to their home, I asked if either of them could tell me where to find the Ten Commandments. Blank stares and silence were finally broken when one of them said, "Have you looked it up in the Yellow Pages?"

I once asked my four-year-old grandson how he liked his Thanksgiving dinner. "I didn't like the turkey much," he replied, "but I sure loved the bread it ate."

A few days ago, I asked my granddaughter which month has 28 days. "Every month has 28 days," she answered, grinning. Guess I ought to rephrase the question.
—*The Milwaukee Journal*

Never have any children, only grandchildren. —Gore Vidal

Elephants and grandchildren never forget. —Andy Rooney

GRANDFATHERS

I was trying to help my grandson with his arithmetic homework. I said to him, "Suppose you reached in your right pocket and found a ten dollar bill, and you reached in your

left pocket and found another one, what would you have?"
My grandson's answer: "Somebody else's pants."

A five-year-old was amazed by his grandfather's false teeth. He watched as Gramps removed his dentures, washed them and put them back in. He asked to see it done again and again. "Okay," said the grandfather, humoring the child. "Anything else?" "Yeah," said the kid, "Now take off your nose."

My seven-year-old niece had gone fishing with her grandpa. After an hour or so, Grandpa asked, "Are you having any luck?" "No!" she replied indignantly. "I don't think my worm is really trying." —Thea Lowell

"Grandpa," the child asked, "what year were you born?" "In 1937," the grandfather replied. "Wow!" exclaimed the grandson. "If you were a baseball card, you would be worth lots of money!" —*The Rotarian*

GRANDMOTHERS

A guy goes to see his grandmother and takes one of his friends with him. While he's talking to his grandmother, his friend starts eating the peanuts that are on the coffee table, and finishes them off. As they're leaving, the friend says, "Thanks for the peanuts." The grandmother says, "Yeah, since I lost my dentures I can only lick the chocolate off of them."

Paul and Marlene Fredericks attended church with their daughter Samantha every Sunday morning. Then the family headed to Paul's parents' home for Sunday dinner. One Sunday after church, Grandmother Fredericks asked six-year-old Samantha, "How was Sunday school?" Samantha replied, "Oh, it was O.K., I guess." The grandmother persisted, "Just O.K.? Who was your teacher?" Samantha answered, "Well, I don't know. She wasn't our regular teacher but she must have been Jesus' grandmother. He was all she talked about."

GRANDPARENTS

When their first grandchild was born, Nancy asked her husband Earl, "Well, Earl, how does it feel to be a grandfather?" Earl replied, "Oh, it feels wonderful, of course, but what feels strange is that I'll have to get used to the idea of sleeping with a grandmother."

It's a good idea to have children while your parents are still young enough to take care of them. —Rita Rudner

The reason grandparents and grandchildren get along so well is that they have a common enemy. —Sam Levenson

The simplest toy, one which even the youngest child can operate, is called a grandparent. —Sam Levenson

GROUCHES

May Tuohy, a seventy-year-old known for her general grouchiness, called the police about her neighbor who was sunbathing in the nude. "I don't see anything," said the police officer, looking out her window. "Of course not," said the woman. "You have to stand on this chair."

My neighbor Eli is a notorious grouch. He spreads good cheer wherever he doesn't go.

GUESTS

Guests will happen even in the best regulated families.

Dinner guest: "We hate to eat and run but we're still hungry." —Ron Dentinger

A poor man had an overnight guest, and as he showed him to his humble bedroom in the hayloft he said, "If there is anything you want, let us know, and we'll come and show you how to get along without it."

I've had a perfectly wonderful evening. But this wasn't it.
—Groucho Marx

HAIR

The man says to his hair stylist, "My hair is falling out. What can I use to keep it in?" The stylist replies, "Might I suggest a shoebox?"

My uncle knows that the Bible says even the hairs on his head are numbered but each year it gets a little easier for the Lord to take inventory.

Men spend thousands on hair transplants and toupees when what is really needed is more women who like bald men.

A bald man took a seat in a beauty shop. "How can I help you?" asked the stylist. "I went for a hair transplant," the guy explained, "but I couldn't stand the pain. If you can make my hair look like yours without causing me any discomfort, I'll pay you $5000." "No problem," said the stylist, and she quickly shaved her head.   —Debbie Costet

HALLOWEEN

Last Halloween was bad for me. I got really beat up. I went to a party dressed as a piñata.   —Jim Samuels

One Halloween night, a neighborhood practical joker decided to frighten the young trick-or-treaters who rang his doorbell. He put on a floor-length black cape, a black hat fitted with devil's horns, and a hideous mask that seemed to combine the most gruesome features of Dracula, Franken-stein, and the Wolf Man. Then he waited. Finally, his doorbell rang. He turned off all the lights and, shining a flashlight on his mask, he opened the door and pierced the night air with an eerie scream. Then he looked down and saw standing before him a tiny, golden-haired five year old, dressed as a dainty fairy. The little tyke stared wide-eyed for a moment. Then she raised her eyes up along the massive black cape, looked straight into the hideous mask, smiled and said, "Is your mommy home?"

HAPPINESS

It's never too late to have a happy childhood.

There are people who can do all fine and heroic things but one; keep from telling their happiness to the unhappy.
—Mark Twain

Action may not always bring happiness, but there is no happiness without action.
—Benjamin Disraeli

The secret of happiness is to count your blessings—not your birthdays.
—Shannon Rose

HATS

Her hat is a creation that will never go out of style. It will look ridiculous year after year.
—Fred Allen

Joan: Whenever I get down in the dumps, I buy myself a new hat. Jack: So that's where you get them!
—Pen

"Isn't it darling?" bubbled the young matron, showing her husband a new lampshade. "Darling or not," said the husband, "wear it to church and you go alone."
—Grit

HEADACHES

The strong man appeared at an agent's office carrying a stone, a big hammer, and a huge suitcase. "This big stone," he explained, "is placed on my head, then my assistant takes the hammer and swings it as hard as he can, and breaks the stone." The agent's head nearly ached just from the description and he was quite enthusiastic. "Sounds wonderful!" he shouted. "But if you need only the hammer and the big stone, why did you bring this suitcase?" The strong man replied, "It's full of aspirin." —*Quote*

HEALTH

I tried Flintstones vitamins. I didn't feel any better but I could stop the car with my feet. —Joan St. Once

It's no longer a question of staying healthy, it's a question of finding a sickness you like. —Jackie Mason

From under a beach umbrella: "Just when I can afford to lie in the sun, they decide it's hazardous to my health."

My allergy tests suggest that I may have been intended for life on some other planet.

Attention to health is life's greatest hindrance.
—Plato (427–347 B.C.)

You have to hand it to the modern-day health clubs. They've learned how to make a fortune at our expense. —*Liguorian*

The U.S. government's High Blood Pressure Information Center uses this carefully calculated address: 120/80 National Institutes of Health, Bethesda, Maryland.
—*The Wall Street Journal*

Life expectancy would grow by leaps and bounds if green vegetables smelled as good as bacon.

HEAVEN (*See also* AFTERLIFE)

A woman died and went to heaven. At the pearly gates, St. Peter was quizzing the new arrivals. "Before you may enter, can you tell me God's first name?" he asked. After thinking a moment, the woman smiled and said, "Andy? Andy?" St. Peter replied. "Where'd you get Andy?" "We sang it in church all the time: 'Andy walks with me, Andy talks with me, Andy tells me I am His own . . .'"

"How's your wife?" the man asked an old friend he hadn't seen for years. "She's in heaven," replied the friend. "Oh, I'm sorry." Then he realized that was not the thing to say, so he added, "I mean, I'm glad." And that was even worse. He finally came out with, "Well, I'm surprised."

HECKLERS

Once, when Al Smith had paused in a speech because a heckler kept interrupting him, the man shouted, "Go ahead, Al, don't let me bother you. Tell 'em all you know. It won't take you long." Smith, always quick on the trigger, replied: "If I tell 'em all we both know it won't take me any longer."

HELL

Hell is a half-filled auditorium. —Robert Frost

HIGH TECH

The Electronic Mail Association estimates that the volume of e-mail will grow by more than half this year, to 6 billion messages. And with my luck, they'll all have my name on them. —Mike Hogan

High tech has gotten out of hand. My grandson has an imaginary playmate that requires batteries.

I once received a fax with a note on the bottom to fax the document back to the sender when I was finished with it, because he needed to keep it.

Jay Leno on Campbell's 19 new kinds of soup: "They're trying to attract a hipper, high-tech customer. The alphabet soup now has spell-check."

Now wristwatches beep. Alarm clocks beep. Typewriters beep. Beepers beep. We have entered the age of electronic nagging. —*Changing Times, The Kiplinger Magazine*

HISTORY

History will be kind to me, for I intend to write it.
—Winston Churchill

In 1991, Rep. Frank Annunzio (D., Ill.) appeared before a House subcommittee to drum up support for legislation authorizing a commemorative coin to honor the 500th anniversary of Columbus's arrival in the New World. Annunzio was questioned by Rep. Al McCandless (D., Calif.), who said his district had a large Scandinavian constituency that believed Leif Ericson discovered America. How would Annunzio respond to them? "Well," Annunzio told McCandless and the audience, "when Columbus discovered America, it stayed discovered."

On his way to a reception held in his honor, Ulysses S. Grant got caught in a shower and offered to share his umbrella with a stranger walking in the same direction. The man said he was going to Grant's reception out of curiosity; he had never seen the general. "I have always thought that Grant was a much overrated man," he said. "That's my view also," Grant replied.   — *The Little, Brown Book of Anecdotes*

HOLIDAYS

Turkeys will be higher this Thanksgiving, except around Washington where there's a surplus.

Americans are putting up Christmas decorations so early, I saw an Easter bunny in a pear tree.

HOME

We have one of those floor lamps with three degrees of brightness: dim, flicker, and out.

Two housekeepers were talking over their problems of work. One said, "This lady I work for says I should warm the plates for our dinner guests, but that's too much work. I just warm hers and she never knows the difference."
        — *How the Platform Professionals Keep 'em Laughin'*

Nothing makes cleaning out the attic such a long job as being able to read.

HONEYMOONS

On their honeymoon, Eric took Louise by the hand and said, "Now that we're married, dear, I hope you won't mind if I mention a few little defects that I've noticed about you." "Not at all," Louise replied sweetly. "It was those little defects that kept me from getting a better husband."

Honeymoon: A short period of doting between dating and debting.

—Ray Bandy

HOSPITALITY

Hospitality is making your guests feel at home, even if you wish they were.

As the Smiths were about to sit down to dinner, they spotted friends coming up the walk. "Oh, dear," Mrs. Smith moaned, "I'll bet they haven't eaten yet." "Quick!" ordered Mr. Smith, "everybody out on the porch with toothpicks."

—Hugh Harrison

HOSPITALS

One of those high-powered executives was checking into the hospital. Barking orders left and right, he had his own way until he reached the desk of a small, mild-mannered lady. She typed the man's name on a slip of paper, stuck the paper into a plastic bracelet, then snapped it on the man's wrist before he could react. "What's this for?" demanded Mr. Big. "That," replied the woman, "is so we won't give you to the wrong mother when you're ready to leave."

—*Rotary Bulletin*

A visitor in Dallas asked, "What's the quickest way to get to the hospital?" "Say something bad about Texas!" came the reply.

Then there was the hospital patient complaining about the cost of some minor surgery. "What this country needs," he griped, "is a good $50 scar."

Statistics disclose that babies are born to every fifth person going into the hospital. If you've already been in four times, be prepared.

Nurse: "Did you drink the carrot juice after the hot bath?"
Patient: "I haven't finished drinking the hot bath yet."

Hospitalized man to wife: "Do you have any idea what it does to somebody to be 'W. J. Hambley, Senior Vice President' one minute and 'the gall bladder in 403' the next?"

When a hospital runs out of maternity nurses they have a midwife crisis.

A small boy swallowed some coins and was taken to a hospital. When his grandmother telephoned to ask how he was, a nurse said, "No change yet."

Why do the nurses at hospitals wear masks when it's the cashiers who should?
        —John Drybred

HOTELS

On a hotel marquee in Commerce, Calif.: "Our towels are so fluffy, it'll be hard to put them in your suitcase."

DESK CLERK TO MAN AT THE COUNTER: "Somebody must have given you the wrong information . . . the Liars Club doesn't meet here."
        —Ron Dentinger

A Professor from Michigan State University arrived at a hotel in Montreal after a long flight and was told that his confirmed reservation couldn't be honored. There were no rooms. "I'll give you three minutes to find me a room," he told the clerk. "After three minutes, I'm going to undress in the lobby, put on my pajamas and go to sleep on one of the sofas." He got a room.

HOUSEWORK

Did you see where someone wants to erect a monument to the Unknown Housewife? Isn't that a great idea? A housewife is someone who spends seven days a week scrubbing the floors, shopping for food, cooking the meals, washing the dishes, watering the lawn, weeding the garden, walking the dog, and being a valet, maid, and chauffeur for the kids. But that isn't what hurts. It's when someone asks her husband, "Does your wife work?" And he says, "No!"
—Robert Orben, *2500 Jokes To Start 'Em Laughing*

The bride was anything but a tidy housekeeper. It bothered her no end, until one evening her husband called from the hall, somewhat dismayed. "Honey," he shouted, "where's the dust on this table? I had a phone number written on it."
—*Indianapolis Sun Star*

HUMANKIND

Human beings, who are almost unique in having the ability to learn from the experience of others, are also remarkable for their apparent disinclination to do so.—Douglas Adams

There are only three kinds of human; those that count, and those that can't.

HUMILIATION

Your worst humiliation is only someone else's momentary entertainment.   —Karen Crockett

HUMILITY

I asked the avid young friar, "Is your monastic order one I might have heard of?" "Well," replied the friar, "we're not famous as the Jesuits are for scholarship or the Trappists for silence and prayer. However, when it comes to humility, we're the tops!"

Don't be humble. You're not that great.   —Golda Meir

HUMOR

Mark my words, when a society has to resort to the rest room for its humor, the writing is on the wall. —Allan Bennett

Humor is an affirmation of dignity, a declaration of man's superiority to all that befalls him.
—Romain Gary, *Promise at Dawn*

Satire is traditionally the weapon of the powerless against the powerful.   —Molly Ivins

Laughter can be heard farther than weeping.
—Yiddish proverb

Humor allows us to step out of the moment, look at it and sum it up with no great reverence. It is a gift nature gives the mature intellect. If a Presidential candidate is lacking in humor, don't vote for him. He lacks the Presidential sensibility, and he'll never succeed with Congress or rally the will of the people.   —Peggy Noonan

HUNTING

Ditsey Baummortal went duck hunting with old Uncle George Tervilliger. A flock of ducks flew overhead and Uncle George took a potshot at them and one fell down on the beach, dead. Ditsey walked over and looked at it. "Hey, Uncle George," he said, "that was a waste of ammunition to shoot that duck. The fall alone would have killed it."
—"Senator" Ed Ford

I ask people why they have deer heads on their walls. They always say because it's such a beautiful animal. I think my mother is attractive, but I have photographs of her.
—Ellen DeGeneres

HURTS

He never bore a grudge against anyone he wronged.

—Simone Signoret

HUSBANDS

Executive overheard talking to a friend: "My wife tells me I don't display enough passion. Imagine! I have a good mind to send her a memo!" —*Speaker's Idea File*

I met my husband at a travel agency. He was looking for a vacation and I was the last resort. —Bessie and Beulah

My husband forgot my birthday and my anniversary. I didn't feel bad. On the contrary. Give me a guilty husband any day. Some of my best outfits come from his guilt!

—Betty Walker

Why is the husband who constantly complains he can't get a word in edgewise always so hoarse? —Peggy Weidman

Husband to wife as he turns on the first football game of the year: "Is there anything you want to say before the season starts?" —Ron Dentinger

I began as a passion and ended as a habit, like all husbands.

—George Bernard Shaw

At Thanksgiving dinner one wife said, "Who wants to carve the turkey? And her father said, "You carve him, you married him."

The man who goes around finding out who is boss in his home might be happier if he didn't know.

Man can climb the highest mountain, swim the widest ocean, fight the strongest tiger, but once he's married, he can barely take out the garbage.

A husband is a man who wishes he had as much fun when he goes on business trips as his wife thinks he does.

—Ann Landers

A man spoke frantically into the phone, "My wife is pregnant and her contractions are only two minutes apart!" "Is this her first child?" the doctor asked. "No, you idiot!" the man shouted. "This is her husband!"

HUSBANDS AND WIVES

TWO GUYS ARE TALKING OVER LUNCH: The first guy says, "My wife and I are very happy, but I often overhear her talking about her first husband." The second guy says, "You're lucky. I keep hearing my wife talk about her next husband."

—Ron Dentinger

Martha: "Look at the old clothes I have to wear. If anyone came to visit they would think I was the cook."

Herb: "Well, they'd change their minds if they stayed for dinner."

A woman returned home from a holiday shopping spree with her arms loaded with packages. Her husband met her at the door and said, "What did you buy? With prices as high as they are, I'll bet you spent a fortune. I hate to think what has happened to our nest egg." "I'll tell you what happened to our nest egg," his wife said defensively as she began to put her packages on the dining room table. "The old hen got tired of sitting on it."   —*Sunshine Magazine*

There are many things these days, that aren't what they used to be. They bothered me so much that I decided to make a list. My wife said, "Don't forget to include yourself."

—Ron Dentinger

My wife is an interior decorator. She wants to get rid of me because I clash with the drapes.   —Morey Amsterdam

Every time I leave the house, my wife tells me to call her in case something goes right.
— Rodney Dangerfield

I told my wife that a husband is like a fine wine—he gets better with age. The next day she locked me in the cellar.

My wife and I have a perfect understanding. I don't try to run her life and I don't try to run mine.

One husband knew that every year on the family's way to their vacation spot, just as they would get about eighty miles out of town, his wife would cry out, "Oh, no! I'm sure I left the iron on." Each year they would return home only to find it unplugged. One year, however, was different the man had anticipated what was coming. When his wife gasped, "We must go back, I just know I left the iron on," he stopped the car, reached under his seat, and handed his wife the iron.
— Allen Klein, *The Healing Power of Humor*

One year my Aunt Aurelia told Uncle Floyd, "Honey, I've bought you an unusual birthday present." "What did you buy me?" he asked her. "A cemetery plot." He agreed with her that it was indeed unusual but thanked her anyway. The next year, she didn't buy him a gift, so he asked her why. "Because," she said, "you didn't use the one I bought you last year."

My husband said he needed more space, so I locked him outside.
— Roseanne

Two onetime neighbors met after not having seen one another for some months. "And how are things with you?" asked one of the women. "Oh," said the other, "I'm managing all right, although I lost my husband several months back." "What happened?" asked the friend. "Well," explained the widow, "I was making dinner and asked him to go out to the garden and pick some corn. After he had been gone a long time, I went to see what the trouble was. There he was dead—a heart attack." "Oh, how awful! What did you do?" "Oh, I had a can of corn in the house, and just used that," said the widow.

My uncle Tim loves art museums. Wherever he travels, he squeezes in a visit to the local art collections. Unfortunately, Aunt Kay is easily bored and tired by them. When Tim and Kay were in Chicago a few years back, Tim dragged Kay to the Art Institute to see the famous Impressionist paintings. After only a few galleries he spotted "Sunday on The Grande Jatte" at the end of the hall. Nearly transported with ecstasy, he danced down the corridor calling: "Kay! Seurat! Seurat!" My aunt shot back, "Whatever will be, will be."

Lawyer to lawyer: "It sure would make things easier if our wives accepted plea bargaining."   —Wilder

The stockbroker's secretary answered his phone one morning. "I'm sorry," she said. "Mr. Bradford's on another line." "This is Mr. Ingram's office," the caller said. "We'd like to know if he's bullish or bearish right now." "He's talking to his wife," the secretary replied. "Right now I'd say he's sheepish."   —John Pizzuto, *The Great Wall Street Joke Book*

Wife to husband: "Overdrawn, overdrawn, always my fault! Has it ever occurred to you that you might be underdeposited?"   —*Ohio Grange*

HUSTLE

Everything comes to he who hustles while he waits.
                                          —Thomas A. Edison

HYPOCHONDRIACS

All my life I've been a hypochondriac. Even as a little boy, I'd eat my M & Ms one at a time with a glass of water.
                                          —Richard Lewis

IDEALISTS

An idealist is one who, on noticing that a rose smells better than a cabbage, concludes that it will also make better soup.

—H. L. Mencken

IDEAS

Good ideas are not adopted automatically. They must be driven into practice with courageous impatience.

—Adm. Hyman G. Rickover

IMAGINATION

You can't depend on your eyes when your imagination is out of focus.

—Mark Twain

Against a diseased imagination demonstration goes for nothing.

—Mark Twain

IMPOSSIBILITY

It is said that many years ago the council of a town in County Cork, Ireland, was having a lot of trouble with criminals, and their jail was overflowing. But the town also had a great shortage of funds. The council dealt with the problem by passing a three-part resolution:

(1) The city shall build a new jail.

(2) The jail shall be built out of materials in the old jail.

(3) The old jail shall be used until the new jail is completed.

—Eric W. Johnson, *A Treasury of Humor*

INCOME

There are few sorrows, however poignant, in which a good income is of no avail.

—L. P. Smith

e. e. cummings once remarked: "I'm living so far beyond my income that we may almost be said to be living apart." I always suspected that e. e. cummings was undercapitalized!

INDIGNATION

Moral indignation is jealousy with a halo.   —H. G. Wells

INDISPENSABLE

The graveyards are full of indispensable men.
—Charles de Gaulle

INFERIORITY COMPLEX

I had an inferiority complex very early. At birth, when the doctor slapped my bottom I didn't cry. I felt I deserved it.
—Gene Perret

IN-LAWS

Her whole family hates me. During the wedding ceremony when they ask, "Is there anyone here who objects to this marriage?" Her side of the family stood up and started forming a double line.   —Ron Dentinger

INSPIRATION

If we expire when we die, shouldn't we inspire while we live?
—George Goldtrap

Inspiration works best when you do.
—Andrew V. Mason, M.D.

INSULTS

A stand-up comic, I was performing at a center for the elderly in the Chelsea section of Manhattan. After my act, a woman, who was probably in her 90s approached me. "Young man," she said, "I want you to know that I saw Milton Berle when he was your age." "That's nice to know," I said. "Yes," she replied. "And he was no good either."   —Bill Gordon

Her face was her chaperone. —Rupert Hughes

Her family is extremely protective of her—they don't let her out on garbage-collection day.

He does the work of three men: Larry, Curley and Moe.
—Ron Dentinger

He was good-natured, obliging and immensely ignorant, and was endowed with a stupidity which by the least little stretch would go around the globe four times and tie.
—Mark Twain

He is useless on top of the ground; he ought to be under it, inspiring the cabbages. —Mark Twain

A mind like Paul Revere's ride—a little light in the belfry.
—Marcus D. Williamson

The only gracious way to accept an insult is to ignore it. If you can't ignore it, top it. If you can't top it, laugh at it. If you can't laugh at it, it's probably deserved.
—Russell Lynes in *Vogue*

She not only kept her lovely figure, she's added so much to it. —Bob Fosse

She was a large woman who seemed not so much dressed as upholstered. —James Matthew Barrie

Why do you sit there looking like an envelope without any address on it? —Mark Twain

He knows so little and knows it so fluently. —Ellen Glasgow

He loves nature in spite of what it did to him.
—Forrest Tucker

He never said a foolish thing nor never did a wise one.
—Earl of Rochester

I would not want to put him in charge of snake control in Ireland. —Eugene McCarthy

If he ever had a bright idea it would be beginner's luck.
—William Lashner

She is a water bug on the surface of life. —Gloria Steinem

You've got the brain of a four-year-old boy, and I bet he was glad to get rid of it.   —Groucho Marx

Greater love hath no man than this, to lay down his friends for his life.   —Jeremy Thorpe

He could never see a belt without hitting below it.
—Margot Asquith

He had delusions of adequacy.   —Walter Kerr

He was about as useful in a crisis as a sheep.
—Dorothy Eden

He's very clever, but sometimes his brains go to his head.
—Margot Asquith

I feel so miserable without you, it's almost like having you here.   —Stephen Bishop

Sometimes I need what only you can provide: your absence.
—Ashleigh Brilliant

George Bernard Shaw sent Winston Churchill two tickets for the first night of his play *Pygmalion* with the note: "Here are a couple of tickets for the first night. Bring a friend—if you have one." Mr. Churchill replied, "Sorry, I cannot come to the first night but will come to the second—if there is one."

INSURANCE

"Do you know the present value of your husband's policy?" the life-insurance salesman asked his client. "What do you mean?" countered the woman. "If you should lose your husband, what would you get?" The woman thought a minute, then brightened up and said, "A poodle!"   —Frank Eames

INTELLIGENCE

AT&T fired President John Walter after nine months, saying, "He lacked intellectual leadership." He received a $26 million severance package. Perhaps it's not Walter who's lacking intelligence.

INVENTORS

My dad just invented a new microwave television set. He can watch "60 Minutes" in twelve seconds.

Once, when introducing Thomas A. Edison at a dinner, the toastmaster mentioned his many inventions, dwelling at length on the talking machine. The aged inventor then rose to his feet, smiled, and said gently to his audience: "I thank the gentleman for his kind remarks, but I must insist upon a correction. God invented the talking machine. I only invented the first one that can be shut off."   *—Grit*

INVESTING

If you use all this financial information diligently, you may even make money. Especially if the market goes up.
                    —William J. Cook, describing various
                    stock trading and data software, 1984

IRELAND

In some parts of Ireland, the sleep which knows no waking is always followed by a wake which knows no sleeping.
                    —Mary Wilson Little

IRONY

It can be no sufficient compensation to a corpse to know that the dynamite that laid him out was not of as good a quality as it had been supposed to be.   —Mark Twain

IRS

Sign in Internal Revenue Service office: "In God we trust, everyone else we audit."

JOBS

No job is so simple that is can't be done wrong.

JOGGING

The human body has several hundred muscles, mostly to tell us we shouldn't have jogged so far. — *The Idea Treasury*

Jogger: "I can't run today. My headset broke."
— Ralph Dunagin, Tribune Media Services

America is the only country in the world where people jog ten miles a day for exercise and then take elevators up to the mezzanine.
— Robert Orben, *2500 Jokes To Start 'Em Laughing*

JOKES

Sometimes I wish I were Adam. Whatever problems he may have had in days of yore, when he cracked a joke, no one said, "I've heard that one before."

Whenever anything bad happens to me, I write a joke about it. Then it isn't a bad experience, it's a tax deduction.
— Denise Munro

A joke is an epitaph on an emotion.
— Friedrich Nietzsche

If you can't remember a joke, don't dismember it.
— Anthony J. Pettito

When Secretary of State George Shultz sent a cable to Ronald Reagan, he included a joke so he could check whether the President had read it. If the Secretary got back to Washington and Reagan said, "That was a great joke, George. I've been telling it to everybody," then Shultz knew his message got through to the President.

JOURNALISM

The photographers doing the *Sports Illustrated* swimsuit edition are on strike . . . for longer hours. —Ron Dentinger

JUDGES

Insulted by the disrespect shown him by lawyer Harvey Smith, the judge thundered, "What do you suppose that I am on the bench for, Mr. Smith?" Smith replied, "It is not for me to attempt to fathom the inscrutable workings of Providence."

JUNK

The average time between throwing something away and needing it badly is about two weeks. —Norman Bell

JURIES

A jury is a group of twelve men who, having lied to the judge about their hearing, health and business engagements, have failed to fool him. —H. L. Mencken

The judge asked Marty Land, the prospective juror, "Is there any reason why you could not serve as a juror in this case?" "I don't want to be away from my job that long," replied Land. "Can't they get along without you at work?" "I'm sure they can, but I don't want them to realize it."

Reflecting their firm grasp on the facts of the matter, a jury in West Virginia brought in the following verdict in a suit against the Baltimore and Ohio Railroad: "If the train had run as it should have run; if the bell had rung as it should have rung; if the whistle had blowed as it should have blowed, both of which it did neither—the cow would not have been injured when she was killed."

Rev. Winston Jackson, pastor of the First Assembly of God Church, reported for jury duty. The minister asked to be excused. "On what grounds?" asked the judge. "Because I'm prejudiced," replied the preacher. "I hate to admit it," said the cleric, pointing to the man seated in front of the judge, "but I took one look at those shifty eyes, Your Honor, and I knew right away he was just as guilty as sin." "Sit down," barked the judge. "The man you're pointing at happens to be the defendant's lawyer."

We have a criminal jury system which is superior to any in the world and its efficiency is only marred by the difficulty of finding twelve men every day who don't know anything and can't read.
—Mark Twain

JUSTICE

Injustice is relatively easy to bear; it is justice that hurts.
—H. L. Mencken

K

--------------------- **K** ---------------------

KIDDING

Reaching the end of a job interview, the Human Resources Person asked a young engineer who was fresh out of MIT, "What starting salary were you thinking about?" The engineer said, "In the neighborhood of $125,000 a year, depending on the benefits package." The interviewer said, "Well, what would you say to a package of 5 weeks vacation, 14 paid holidays, full medical and dental, company matching retirement fund to 50% of salary, and a company car leased every 2 years—say, a red Corvette?" The engineer sat up straight and said, "Wow! Are you kidding?" The interviewer replied, "Yeah, but you started it."

KNEES

When nature designed the male knee, she obviously had neither football nor walking shorts in mind.   —Bill Vaughan

KNOWLEDGE

A wise old sea captain stood on the bridge of his ship day in and day out, opening a box and peeking inside, never letting anyone else see the contents. The day he retired, the crew rushed to the bridge, cut the lock and looked inside the box. Hidden inside was a piece of paper that read, "Left—port. Right—starboard."

L

LANGUAGE

A linguistics professor was lecturing to his class one day. In English, he said, a double negative forms a positive. In some languages though, such as Russian, a double negative is still a negative. However, he pointed out, there is no language wherein a double positive can form a negative. A voice from the back of the room piped up "Yeah, right."

Mastery of the art and spirit of the Germanic language—enables a man to travel all day in one sentence without changing cars.
—Mark Twain

A woman, wanting to impress two old college chums, took them to dinner at an exclusive French restaurant and ordered for all three in flawless French. Handing the menu back to the waiter with a flourish, she asked, "Would you mind reading our order back to me?" "Oui, madame? No. 4, No. 9, No. 16."
—Leadership

Charles Berlitz was asked how a linguist identifies a native tongue. "It probably comes down to what you say when you hit your thumb with a hammer," he replied. "For me, my first reaction is in French."
—Carol Krucoff, Los Angeles Times-Washington Post News Service

LATE

Heard at the bus stop: "Joe's chronically late for everything. His ancestors came over on the Juneflower."
—Shelby Friedman

LAUGHTER

Someone at the Food and Drug Administration was heard to say, "If laughter is the best medicine, shouldn't we be regulating it?"

Blessed are they who can laugh at themselves for they shall never cease to be amused.

LAUNDRY

If you come out of the laundry with an even number of socks, you have somebody else's laundry.

—Laurence J. Peter, *Peter's Almanac*

LAWNS

A midsummer reflection: All you need to grow healthy, vigorous grass is a crack in your sidewalk.

—*The Milwaukee Journal*

A man who admits he is allergic to lawn work says, "I long for the day when anybody caught working in the yard will be arrested for disturbing the ecology."

—Red O'Donnell in *The Nashville Banner*

LAWYERS

When the law is on your side, argue the law. When the facts are on your side, argue the facts. When neither the facts nor the law are on your side, holler!   —Albert Gore, Jr.

"How can I ever thank you?" gushed a woman to Clarence Darrow, after he had solved her legal troubles. "My dear woman," Darrow replied, "ever since the Phoenicians invented money there has been only one answer to that question."

If builders built buildings the way lawyers write laws, the first woodpecker to come along would destroy civilization.

If it wasn't for lawyers, we wouldn't need them.

In 1991, terrorists hijacked a Bar Association charter flight. The terrorists issued a press release. They said that, until their demands were met, they would release one lawyer per hour.

Phil Williams, the trial lawyer, came dragging in after a hard day at work. He said to his concerned wife Hilda, "It was a terrible day in court—I exhibited moral outrage when I meant to show righteous indignation."

Ken Morley, a burly construction worker, watched in horror as the heavy beam fell from the crane and landed on a well-dressed passerby. Morley rushed to the victim, carefully removed the beam, and said, "Hang in there, fellow. Are you badly hurt?" "How should I know?" snapped the victim. "I'm a doctor, not a lawyer."

Ludlow Whittaker went into the Chamber of Commerce in Dickinson, North Dakota. He appeared frazzled and desperate. He asked Flora Iverson, the Chamber's receptionist, "Is there a criminal attorney in town?" Flora replied, "Yes, but we can't prove it yet."

The down-on-his-luck attorney was sitting in the bar, nursing his beer. "How's it going?" asked a colleague. "Terrible. I just was evicted from my office. I wrote up the papers myself. I never would have done it if I hadn't needed the money so bad."

The minute you read something you can't understand, you can almost be sure it was drawn up by a lawyer.
—Will Rogers

When the armies of lawyers get through settling an estate, the friendless beneficiary doesn't have a legacy to stand on.
—Francis Duffy

One lawyer successfully defended a client in a scandalous and highly publicized trial. At a party after the trial ended, he was cornered by an indignant woman. "Is there no client so low, so despicable, so outrageous, that you wouldn't take the case?" she demanded. "It all depends," said the lawyer equably. "What did you do?"

Hell hath no fury like a lawyer of a woman scorned.

Lawyer to young client: "You should have signed a contract. A high-five just isn't binding." —Sidney Harris, *So Sue Me!*

Definition of a prenuptial agreement: Paper a lawyer prepares to protect the party of the first part from the party of the second part should they discover the party's over.
  —Rheta Grimsley Johnson, Scripps Howard News Service

Always read the small print—and that goes for lawyers too. A letter sent out by City Attorneys' Association of Los Angeles County announced that the group's next monthly luncheon would be held at a restaurant on South Flower Street. Price: $10 per legal eagle. "No better bargain exists," the letter said. "Find one and your money is cheerfully refunded." A notation at the bottom of the letter read: "Offer limited to bargains within a 10-foot radius of South Flower Street. Offer may be revoked at any time. Offer is hereby revoked."   —Steve Harvey, *Los Angeles Times*

LEADERSHIP

If you want to lead the orchestra, you must turn your back on the crowd.

Some church members rise to the occasion, while others merely hit the ceiling.

LIBRARIES

Abraham Lincoln once walked 20 miles to borrow a book. Now they close libraries to celebrate his birthday.
                                        —Laura Baker, *Quote*

LIES

The biggest lie in America, according to Norm Chad of *Sports Illustrated* is: "The game's almost over, honey, I'll be there in a minute."

The principal difference between a cat and a lie is that a cat has only nine lives. —Mark Twain

She tells enough white lies to ice a wedding cake.
—Margot Asquith

A minister told his congregation, "Next week I plan to preach about the sin of lying. To help you understand my sermon, I want you all to read Mark 17." The following Sunday, as he prepared to deliver his sermon, the minister asked for a show of hands. He wanted to know how many had read Mark 17. Every hand went up. The minister smiled and said, "Mark has only sixteen chapters. I will now proceed with my sermon on the sin of lying."

LIFE

As Arnot L. Sheppard, Jr. once remarked: "Just when you think you see the whole picture of life clearly, the channel changes."

Life is a public performance on the violin, in which you must learn the instrument as you go along. —E. M. Forester

Among the graffiti on a subway wall: "This life is a test. It is only a test. Had this been an actual life you would have received instructions as to what to do and where to go."

Life is what happens to you while you're busy planning more important things.

Some people just can't enjoy life; the first half of their lives are spent blaming their troubles on their parents and the second half on their children. —Rev. Denis R. Fakes

I try to take one day at a time, but sometimes several days attack me at once. —Ashleigh Brilliant

The first half of life consists of the capacity to enjoy without the chance; the last half consists of the chance without the capacity.
—Mark Twain

Life resembles a novel more often than novels resemble life.
—George Sand

If all the world's a stage, why do only half of us wear makeup?
—Brad Stein

After taking tea with a parishioner, the bishop said, "I am glad to see in what a comfortable way you are living." "Oh, bishop," replied the man, "if you want to know how we really live, you must come when you're not here."
—Helen Howe, *The Gentle Americans*

Life is a lot like a high-school algebra class. Every time you get one problem solved, the teacher is waiting to give you another.

==

A first grade teacher collected old, well-known proverbs. She gave each child in her class the first half of a proverb, and asked them to come up with the rest. Here are some choice replies.

- Ambition is a poor excuse for . . . not having enough sense to be lazy.
- As you shall make your bed so . . . shall you mess it up.
- Better be safe than . . . punch a 5th grader.
- Strike while the . . . bug is close.
- Its always darkest before . . . daylight savings time
- You can lead a horse to water but . . . how?
- Don't bite the hand that . . . looks dirty.
- A miss is as good as a . . . Mr.
- You can't teach an old dog new . . . math.
- It you lie down with the dogs . . . you'll stink in the morning.
- The pen is mightier than the . . . pigs
- An idle mind is . . . the best way to relax.
- Where there's smoke, there's . . . pollution.

- Happy the bride who . . . gets all the presents.
- A penny saved is . . . not much.
- Two's company, three's . . . the musketeers.
- Laugh and the whole world laughs with you, cry and . . .
  you have to blow your nose.
- Children should be seen and not . . . spanked or grounded.
- When the blind leadeth the blind . . . get out of the way.

After I'm dead I'd rather have people ask why I have no
monument than why I have one.
> —Cato the Elder (234–149 B.C., AKA Marcus
> Porcius Cato)

The prime of life is that fleeting time between green and
over-ripe. —Cullen Hightower

LIGHT BULBS

How many pollsters does it take to screw in
a light bulb?
Two. One to hold the ladder and one to turn
the light bulb. Plus or minus 4 percent.
> —Tom Brokaw

How many Stanford researchers does it take
to screw in a light bulb?
Three. One to hold the ladder, one to turn the
bulb, and one to bill the government for the house.

How many executives does it take to change a light bulb?
Five. One to change the bulb, and four to yank the ladder
out from under him.

How many mystery writers does it take to change a light
bulb?
Only one, but it needs a spectacular twist at the end.

How many surrealists does it take to change a light bulb?
Two. One to turn the giraffe and the other to fill the bathtub
with multicolored clocks.

LIMITS

Some of our limits exist only in our own minds. A couple of years ago, during a sports clinic at Princeton High School in Cincinnati, Ohio, Dan Woodruff, the softball coach, lent his office to Dave Redding, the strength coach for the Cleveland Browns. Dave wanted to shower before his scheduled appearance at the clinic. Dan showed Dave the facilities, then left while he was in the shower. When Dave finished showering, he went to leave the office, but found he couldn't open the door! He wrote a note and slipped it under the door, then sat back and waited. When Dan went back to his office about an hour later, he heard someone yelling, "Help, help!" Then he found the card outside his door. He opened the door and found Redding. "What's the problem?" Dan asked. Dave told him that he had been locked inside for over an hour. Dan told him that the door wasn't locked, that he had only to push a button on the handle to make it open. "We laughed about it a lot when we walked down the hall," said Dan. The 230-pound strength coach of a professional football team being trapped behind an unlocked door.

LISTENING

Good listeners are more than just popular. After a while, they know something. —*Executive Speechwriter Newsletter*

LIVING

Let us endeavor so to live that when we come to die even the undertaker will be sorry. —Mark Twain

Live so that you wouldn't be ashamed to sell the family parrot to the town gossip. —Will Rogers

LONELINESS

You know what's a real bummer? When you send your picture to the lonely hearts club and they send it back with a note saying: "We're not that lonely." —Ron Dentinger

LOSERS

The door-to-door salesman reported to his sales manager, I got two orders today—"Get out!" and "Stay out!"

What a loser . . . he's the kind of guy who asks for a wine list at McDonalds.

There are two sorts of losers—the good loser, and the one who can't act.　　　　　　—Laurence J. Peter, *Peter's People*

LOSING

It doesn't matter if you win or lose, until you lose.

LOSS

One man's loss is another man's umbrella.
　　　　　　　　　　　　—Sam Ewing in *Mature Living*

LOVE

I love her for what she is. Wealthy.

Many a man in love with a dimple makes the mistake of marrying the whole girl.　　　　　　—Ring Lardner

Two Laws of Love:

1. You will always fall in love and marry someone with the opposite body temperature.
2. If you can't stand his mother and he can't stand yours then you're bound to get married.

Love conquers all things except poverty and a toothache.
　　　　　　　　　　　　　　　　　—Mae West

Love is like hash. You have to have confidence in it to enjoy it.　　　　　　　　　　　　　　—Bob Hope

Love is insanity with a collaborator.

A woman should marry for love and she should get married until she finds it.

　　　　　　　　　　　　　　　—Elizabeth Taylor

It's easier to love humanity as a whole than to love one's neighbor.
—Eric Hoffer

Love is the triumph of imagination over intelligence.
—H. L. Mencken

Love is staying awake all night with a sick child—or a healthy adult.
—David Frost

Love is a fire. But whether it is going to warm your heart or burn down your house, you can never tell. —Joan Crawford

Love is like a soft mattress: It's easy to fall into, but not so easy to get out of.
—Gladiola Montana and Texas Bix Bender

Love is much nicer to be in than an automobile accident, a tight girdle, a higher tax bracket, or a holding pattern over Philadelphia.
—Judith Viorst

I can see from your utter misery, from your eagerness to misunderstand each other, and from your thoroughly bad temper that this is the real thing.
—Peter Ustinov

Be wary of puppy love; it can lead to a dog's life.
—Gladiola Montana

My true love brought me flowers tonight, and I'm all smiles and song. I guess I'm doing something right—or he's done something wrong!
—Maureen Cannon

I Love You Only Valentine cards: Now available in multipacks.
—Sign on a drug store display

Friendship is love minus sex and plus reason. Love is friendship plus sex and minus reason.
—Mason Cooley

Erotic love begins with separateness, and ends in oneness. Motherly love begins with oneness, and leads to separateness.
—Erich Fromm

There is no sincerer love than the love of food.

—George Bernard Shaw

When I fall in love . . . Falling in love is awfully simple. Falling out of love is simply awful.

LUCK

Man to friend: "With my luck, by the time I build a better mousetrap, mice will be declared an endangered species."

—Al Bernstein

I find that the harder I work, the more luck I seem to have.

—Thomas Jefferson

M

MADNESS

Madness takes its toll. Please have exact change.

A friend of mine told me this story: One day an acquaintance of his family mentioned to his mother: "Does everybody in your family suffer from insanity?" "Not at all, not at all," she smiled, "in fact we all enjoy it."   —Father Mike Malone

MANAGED HEALTH CARE

For ten years, my wife worked for an HMO (Health Maintenance Organization). In her circles, the following story is making the rounds: The scene is heaven, just outside the Pearly Gates, and three distinguished looking men are waiting to request admittance. Finally, St. Peter arrives and asks each man to identify himself and state his greatest contribution to the human race. The first man says, "I am Christian Barnard and I performed the first successful heart transplant. Because of my work, thousands of lives have been saved." St. Peter seems duly impressed and says, "You may enter into your eternal rest." The gates open, celestial music is heard, and Dr. Barnard disappears. The second man states, "I am Jonas Salk and I discovered the polio vaccine which has saved millions of lives." Once again, St. Peters seems impressed and says, "You may enter into your eternal rest." The gates open, celestial music is heard, and Dr. Salk disappears. The third man says, "I am John Nelson and I invented the notion of managed health care. Because of me millions of dollars have been saved." St. Peter strokes his beard and says, "You, too, may enter into your eternal rest—but only for three days."

MANNERS

Clark Clifford was White House counsel in the administration of Harry Truman, and Secretary of Defense in 1968 and 1969. Clifford was once a guest at a Washington dinner party. He politely turned to a woman seated next to him. "Did I get your name correctly?" he asked. "Are you Emily Post?" "Yes," she replied. He said, ". . . the world-renowned authority on manners?" She said, "Yes, why do you ask?" "Because," he said, "you have just eaten my salad."

MARK TWAIN

One of Mark Twain's bad habits was calling on neighbors without his collar or necktie. One afternoon upon his return from a neighborhood visit in the usual degree of undress, his wife scolded him for his negligence. Clemens departed to his study and in a few moments sent a small package back to the neighbor's house. An accompanying note read somewhat as follows: "Just a while ago I visited you minus my collar and tie. The missing articles are enclosed. Will you kindly gaze at them for 30 minutes and then return them to me?"

—Msgr. Arthur Tonne, *Jokes Priests Can Tell*, Vol. 4

MARRIAGE

A man may be a fool and not know it, but not if he is married.

—H. L. Mencken

All of a sudden I noticed she was saying my daughter, my son, my silver, my furniture, my house, and your friends, your troubles, your worries, your problems, and your fault.
—H. Martin

In the old days, men rode chargers. Now they marry them.
—Philip Whlie

It is more blessed to give than to receive—for example, wedding presents.
—H. L. Mencken

Tommy Lee asked Pastor Parkes, "Reverend, am I right in assuming that the Bible says it's wrong to profit from other people's mistakes?" Pastor Parkes replied, "That is substantially correct." Tommy Lee demanded, "In that case, how about refunding the twenty dollars I paid you for marrying us last year?"

Cousin Roberta recalls: "One evening I drove my husband's car to the shopping mall. On my return, I noticed how dusty the outside of his car was and cleaned it up a bit. When I finally entered the house, I called out, 'The woman who loves you the most in the world just cleaned your headlights and windshield.' My husband looked up and said, 'Mom's here?'"

Greg Ladego said to his unmarried daughter's boyfriend, "The man who marries my daughter will get a prize." "Okay," said the young man, "but let me see the prize first."

There is something magical about the fact that success almost always comes faster to the guy your wife almost married.

Marriage means commitment. Of course, so does insanity.

A smart husband buys his wife fine china so she won't trust him to wash it.

I married Miss Right. I just didn't know her first name was Always.

I haven't spoken to my mother-in-law for eighteen months—
I don't like to interrupt her.   —Ken Dodd

The only thing my wife and I have in common is that we got
married on the same day.   —Ron Dentinger

The neighbors seem to have the perfect marriage. He'd rather
play golf than eat, and she'd rather go to auctions than cook.
They are really addicted. In his sleep he often hollers out,
"Fore," and she answers, "Four-fifty."   —Ron Dentinger

Only two things are necessary to keep one's wife happy. The
first is to let her think she's having her own way. The second
is to let her have it.   —Lyndon B. Johnson

Uncle Marty explains: "My wife of twenty years and I have
very little in common. I'm a big city boy; she's a small town
girl. I like spicy food; she doesn't. I dig action and suspense
movies. She goes for romance and comedy. Nothing in common. Yet we are deeply in love. It just goes to show: You
don't get harmony when everybody sings the same note."

I married her for her looks, but not the ones she's been giving
me lately!

My wife and I have an agreement that works . . . she is
responsible for the small decisions, and I am responsible for
the big ones. This means that she decides things like where
to take our next vacation, the color of our next car, and the
construction budget for adding on the new family room. I
decide whether or not the President should extend most fa-
vored nation trading status to China, how high the Federal
Reserve should go with short-term interest rates, and the
timetable for the elimination of CFCs from automobile air
conditioners.

Aunt Marlene had a troubled marriage. She sought the advice of one of those phone-in psychics. The psychic told her,
"Prepare yourself for widowhood. Your husband is about to
die a violent death." Marlene sighed deeply and asked, "Will
I be acquitted?"

Marriage is the only adventure open to the cowardly.
—Voltaire

Marriage is the alliance of two people, one of whom never remembers birthdays and the other who never forgets them.
—Ogden Nash

A college freshman was expounding on her idea of the perfect mate. "The man I marry," she said, "must shine among company, be musical, tell jokes, sing, dance, and stay at home." Her boyfriend replied, "It sounds to me like you don't want a husband. What you want is a television set!"

The formula for a happy marriage? It's the same as the one for living in California: when you find a fault, don't dwell on it.
—Jay Trachman, *One to One*

"Do you know what today is?" asked the wife of her husband who was hurrying off to work. Hesitating only a moment and flashing a smile he replied, "Sure, I remember." He didn't propose being caught again . . . forgetting the date of his wedding anniversary . . . so that night he returned home with some candy, flowers and a gift. His wife was overjoyed! "You see," he said smugly, "I did remember what day this is." She laughed and giggled: "Honey, this is the happiest Groundhog Day of my life."

My mother was the old-fashioned kind who was firmly committed to the sanctity of marriage. Just before I got married, she took me aside and said, "I'm not going to give you a long sermon. Just remember one thing: in every marriage, there are grounds for divorce. What you have to do is to keep finding grounds for marriage."
—Lillian Woods

A middle-aged man was sitting on his porch as falling snow swirled all around him. A passing neighbor called out: "Why in the world are you sitting out there in the snow and cold?" The porch-sitter called back: "I have to." "What do you mean . . . I have to?" "Well," declared the man on the porch,

"my wife is taking singing lessons, and I don't want the neighbors to think I'm beating her."
—Msgr. Arthur Tonne, *Jokes Priests Can Tell,* vol. 6

The concept of two people living together for twenty-five years without a serious dispute suggests a lack of spirit only to be admired in sheep.   —A. P. Herbert

Mr. and Mrs. Ivers were pushing their cart down the aisle at the supermarket when they spotted an elderly pair walking hand in hand. Said Mrs. Ivers: "Now, that looks like a happy married couple." "Don't be too sure, dear," replied Mr. Ivers. "They're probably saying the same thing about us."

One of the oldest human needs is having someone to wonder where you are when you don't come home at night.
—Margaret Mead

Marriage is like a 7-Eleven. Not much variety, but at 3 A.M., it's always there.

M

Man confiding to friend: "My wife and I argued so much that we finally saw a marriage counselor. We still argue, but now we call it sharing."   —Ivern Ball

Man to colleague: "Few things upset my wife. It makes me feel rather special to be one of them."
—*Napa Parts Pups 1992 Joke Book*

Just remember: Every man needs a wife. Because you can't blame everything that goes wrong on the government!

Actress Anne Bancroft, who is married to Mel Brooks, maintains: "The best way to get most husbands to do something is to suggest they are too old for it."

John bought his new colleague, Peter, home for dinner. As they arrived at the door his wife rushed up, threw her arms around John and kissed him passionately. "My goodness," said Peter, "and how long have you been married?" "Twenty-two years," replied John. "You must have a fantastic marriage if your wife greets you like that after all those years." "Don't be fooled! She only does it to make the dog jealous."

Often the difference between a successful marriage and a mediocre one consists of leaving about three things a day unsaid.

A happy marriage is the world's best bargain.

—O. A. Batista

The dear old couple who has been married sixty years were paying a sentimental visit to their home town and paused at one of the street corners. "Isn't it wonderful to remember that we used to meet at this very spot every evening during the first few months we were courting?" the old lady asked, sighing. "I certainly remember, my dear," replied her husband, "but that sign wasn't here then." And he pointed to the notice which read: "DANGEROUS CORNER: Go Slow."

—*Tid-Bits*, London

When the late Mr. and Mrs. Henry Ford celebrated their golden wedding anniversary, a reporter asked them, "To what do you attribute your 50 years of successful married life?" "The formula," said Ford, "is the same formula I have always used in making cars—just stick to one model."

—*Nebraska Smoke Eater*

MARRIAGE COUNSELING

Overheard in a marriage counselor's office: "When I don't praise him, he thinks I don't love him and when I do praise him, he thinks he's too good for me."   —Ron Dentinger

MATH

Back in ancient times a brilliant mathematician came up with the concept of zero. Prior to that there were positive and negative numbers but zero hadn't been used. Knowing that the zero was an important new concept, a dinner was given in honor of the scholar. A banner behind the head table read: "Thanks for nothing."   —Ron Dentinger

The first grade teacher was trying to interest her class in arithmetic. "Jimmy," she asked. "If I had two sandwiches and you had two sandwiches, what would we have?" Jimmy answered without hesitation. "A picnic!"   —Liguorian

Not everything that can be counted counts, and not everything that counts can be counted.   —Albert Einstein

MAXIMS

In my opinion, the only time it's better to give than to receive is if the commodity that's being given is advice.
                    —Ron Dentinger

MEANNESS

He is so mean, he won't let his little baby have more than one measle at a time.   —Eugene Field

MEDIA

The hero reveals the possibilities of human nature; the celebrity reveals the possibilities of the media.
                    —Daniel J. Boorstin, *The Image*

MEDICAL INSURANCE

Insurance is a lot like wearing a hospital gown. You're never covered as much as you think you are.
          —Robert Orben, *2500 Jokes To Start 'Em Laughing*

MEDICINE (See also DOCTORS)

A lady in the waiting room was complaining bitterly about having to wait so long for the doctor. Seems he took so much time with some patients that he was always behind schedule.

"Why don't you change doctors?" another patient asked. "Because," the complainer admitted, "I'm one of the patients he takes so much time with."

He had had much experience of physicians, and said, "The only way to keep your health is to eat what you don't want, drink what you don't like, and do what you'd druther not."
—Mark Twain

If you treat a sick child like an adult and a sick adult like a child, everything usually works out pretty well. —Ruth Carlisle

MEDIOCRITY

Some men are born mediocre, some men achieve mediocrity, and some men have mediocrity thrust upon them.
—Joseph Heller, *Catch-22*

MEETINGS

Belgium's Paul-Henri Spaak was presiding over the first United Nations General Assembly. When it ended, he told his colleagues, "The agenda is exhausted. The secretary-general is exhausted. I am exhausted. At last we have achieved unanimity!"

MEMORY

A group of French Foreign Legionnaires are marching through the desert. One says to another: "I'm trying to forget about a girl, but it's hard! Her name is 'Sandy.'" —S. Gross

What's the best thing about losing your memory as you get older? You never have to watch reruns on television.

Aunt Aggie says, "My memory is starting to go. I locked the keys in my car the other day. Fortunately, I had forgotten to get out first."

My brother Scott's memory is just as bad as mine. We're both convinced we're an only child.

Aunt Aggie went to see her physician. She complained, "Doctor, I don't know what to do. You've got to help me. I just can't remember a thing. I've no memory at all. I hear something one minute, and the next minute I forget it." Tell me, what should I do?" Her doctor replied, "Pay in advance!"

MEN

I'm at the point where I want a man in my life—but not in my house. Just come in, attach the VCR, and get out.

—Joy Behar

Life isn't fair to us men. When we are born, our mothers get all the compliments and the flowers. When we are married, our brides get the presents and the publicity. When we die, our widows get the insurance and the winters in Florida.

—*Viking Vacuum*

If you want to get rid of a man whom you have not been seeing very long, I suggest this: Say, "I love you . . . I want to marry you . . . I want to have your children." Sometimes they leave skid marks.

—Rita Rudner

Writing in 1941, Professor Marjorie Nicholson said, "The fundamental reason that women do not achieve so greatly as men do is that women have no wives."

Anyone who believes that men and women have the same mindset hasn't lived on earth. A man thinks that everything he does is wonderful; a woman has doubts.

—Margo Kaufman

Take care of him. Make him feel important. If you can do that, you'll have a happy and wonderful marriage—like two out of every ten couples.

—Neil Simons, *Barefoot in the Park*

Nellie B. Stull, in *Reader's Digest,* 1935: "A man admires the woman who makes him think, but he keeps away from her.

M

He likes the woman who makes him laugh. He loves the girl who hurts him. But he marries the woman who flatters him."

Very few men care to have the obvious pointed out to them by a woman.

—Margaret Baillie Saunders, *A Shepherd of Kensington*

It's been my experience that men who say they believe in 50/50 relationships are prone to telling half-truths.

Women see differently than men. If you doubt this, I would merely remind you of the last time a male walked into a room that looked as though it had been ransacked by hostile—and profoundly sloppy—foreign agents and innocently uttered the words: "What mess?"

—Dorian Yeager

You can talk to a man about any subject. He won't understand, but you can talk to him.

Whatever women do they must do twice as well as men to be thought half as good. Luckily, this is not difficult.

—Charlotte Whitton

The softer a man's head, the louder his socks.

—Helen Rowland

Blessed is the man who, having nothing to say, abstains from giving in words evidence of the fact.

—George Eliot (Mary Ann Evans)

We were walking down the street. He looked into another girl's eyes, and just fell madly in love. She was wearing mirrored sunglasses.

—Rita Rudner

Question: What's the difference between a man and E.T.?
Answer: E.T. phoned home.

A man finds out what is meant by a spitting image when he tries to feed cereal to his infant.

—Imogene Fey

Men have a much better time of it than women. For one thing, they marry later. For another thing, they die earlier.
—H. L. Mencken

No man is a man until his father tells him he is—I was forty-eight.
—Burt Reynolds

A modern-day example comes from a longtime female resident of Alaska, asked by a new arrival: "What are the chances of finding a good man around here?" There was a pause. Alaska was full of men. But would she recommend any of them? The old-timer replied: "Well, the odds are good, but the goods are odd."
—Dr. Mardy Grothe

I never liked a man I didn't meet.
—Dorothy Parker

If men can run the world, why can't they stop wearing neckties? How intelligent is it to start the day by tying a little noose around your neck?
—Linda Ellerbee

Men build bridges and throw railroads across deserts, and yet they contend successfully that the job of sewing on a button is beyond them.
—Heywood Broun

MEN AND WOMEN

I think—therefore I'm single.
—Liz Winstead

Women are never disarmed by compliments. Men always are.
—Oscar Wilde

Women with pasts interest men because they hope history will repeat itself.
—Mae West

A man is a person who will pay two dollars for a one-dollar item he wants. A woman will pay one dollar for a two-dollar item she doesn't want.
—William Binger

When a man gets up to speak, people listen, then look. When a woman gets up, people look; then if they like what they see, they listen.
—Pauline Frederick

A man has his clothes made to fit him; a woman makes herself fit her clothes. —Edgar Watson Howe

Males seek power to compensate for loss of connection; females seek connection to compensate for loss of power. —Gary Malmon

After a quarrel between a man and a woman the man suffers chiefly from the thought that he has wounded the woman; the woman suffers from the thought that she has not wounded the man enough.
—Friedrich W. Nietzsche

A woman worries about the future until she has a husband, but a man never worries about the future until he has a wife.
—Liselotte Pulver

To a woman the first kiss is the end of the beginning; to a man it is the beginning of the end. —Helen Rowland

You see an awful lot of smart guys with dumb women, but you hardly ever see a smart woman with a dumb guy.
—Clint Eastwood

Over the years statistics revealed that women are safer drivers than men. Now we know why. The reason is: Men drivers constantly place themselves in unsafe situations—by trying to get a better look at the women drivers.

It was true for Cleopatra, and it is true today. Men are at their weakest when some female is telling them how strong they are.

METAPHORS

Carolyn Tinker, public affairs director at the University of New Mexico Medical Center, is also a collector of mixed and mangled metaphors. Some of her gems:

- What finally broke the straw.
- You can't go out there cold turkey with egg on your face.

- Run it up the flagpole and see if it sticks.
- We took the thunder out of his sails.
- He sank to new heights.
- She hitched her star to his wagon.
- He's really rubbing it in our noses.
- I'm still green behind the ears.

Jim Arnholz in Albuquerque, N.M., Journal

MIDDLE AGE

I'm at that age where if I go all out, I end up all in.
                                              —Ron Dentinger

Middle-age is when work is a lot less fun, and fun is a lot more work.   —Milton Berle

My Aunt Flo explains: "Middle age is when broadness of the mind and narrowness of the waist change places."

Middle age begins with the first mortgage and ends when you drop dead.   —Herb Caen

Middle age is . . . when your mind retains nothing, and your waist retains everything.   —Joe Hickman

The really frightening thing about middle age is the knowledge you'll outgrow it.   —Lauren Bacall

You know you are middle-aged when your children tell you that you're driving too slow and your parents tell you that you're driving too fast.

Middle age is when you wish you could have some of the naps you refused to take as a kid.

MILITARY

"Well," snarled the tough old sergeant to the bewildered private. "I suppose after you get discharged from the army you'll be waiting for me to die so you can come and spit on my grave." "Not me, Sarge!" the private replied. "After I get out of the army, I ain't never going to stand in line again!"

After fighting only 24 hours, the British RAF released the following communique. "TODAY WE DOWNED 90 PLANES; 60 DEFINITE, 30 PLEDGED."

At an afternoon tea for officers and their wives, the commanding general of the base delivered a seemingly endless oration. A young second lieutenant, listening with obvious disfavor, grumbled to the woman at his side, "What a pompous and unbearable old windbag that slob is." The woman turned to him, her face red with rage and said, "Lieutenant, do you know who I am?" "No, ma'am." "I am the wife of the man you just called 'an unbearable old windbag.'" "Indeed," said the young lieutenant, looking steadfast and unruffled, "and do you know who I am?" "No, I don't," said the general's wife. "Thank God," said the lieutenant as he disappeared into the crowd.

The sergeant, explaining the routine to the new recruits, said, "There will always be a choice in your meals: You can take them . . . or leave them." —*The Rotarian*

MINDS

Some minds are like concrete, thoroughly mixed up and permanently set. —Rev. Denny J. Brake

MINISTERS (*See also* CLERGY)

A disconcerted minister to his congregation: "Crying babies and disruptive children, like good intentions, should be carried out immediately."

One of the toughest tasks a church faces is choosing a good minister. A member of an official board undergoing this painful process finally lost patience. He'd watched the pastoral relations committee reject applicant after applicant for some fault, alleged or otherwise. It was time for a bit of soul-searching on the part of the committee. So he stood up and read a letter purporting to be from another applicant.

"Gentlemen: Understanding your pulpit is vacant, I should like to apply for the position. I have many qualifications. I've been a preacher with much success and also have had some success as a writer. Some say I'm a good organizer. I've been a leader most places I've been. I'm over 50 years of age. I have never preached in one place for more than three years. In some places, I have left town after my work caused riots and disturbances. I must admit I have been in jail three or four times, but not because of any real wrongdoing. My health is not too good, though I still get a great deal done. The churches I have preached in have been small, though located in several large cities. I've not gotten along well with religious leaders in towns where I have preached. In fact, some have threatened me and even attacked me physically. I am not too good at keeping records. I have been known to forget whom I baptized. However, if you can use me, I shall do my best for you."

The board member looked over at the committee. "Well, what do you think? Shall we call him?"

The good church folk were aghast. Call an unhealthy, trouble-making, absentminded, ex-jailbird? Was the board member crazy? Who signed the application? Who has such colossal nerve?

The board member eyed them all keenly before he answered, "It's signed, the Apostle Paul."

═══

As dessert was served to the visiting pastor, the hostess apologized for not having any cheese to go with the apple pie. Hearing this, her little son slipped down from his chair and left the room for a moment. He returned shortly with a small piece of cheese and shyly placed it on the pastor's plate. "Well, thank you, son," said the guest. "You must have sharp eyes to have seen that piece of cheese when your mother didn't. Where did you find it?" Flushing with pride, the little boy said, "Oh, it was in the mousetrap."

Our pastor was preaching on Proverbs 16:24: "Pleasant words are as a honeycomb, sweet to the soul, and health to the bones." The minister then added, "You can catch more flies with honey than with vinegar." My wife leaned over, put her head on my shoulder and whispered in my ear, "I just love to watch your muscles ripple when you take out the garbage."

 A preacher was making his rounds to his parishioners on a bicycle, when he came upon a little boy trying to sell a lawn mower. "How much do you want for the mower?" asked the preacher. "I just want enough money to go out and buy me a bicycle," said the little boy. After a moment of consideration, the preacher asked, "Will you take my bike in trade for it?" The little boy asked if he could try it out first, and after riding the bike around a little while said, "Mister, you've got yourself a deal." The preacher took the mower and began to try to crank it. He pulled on the string a few times with no response from the mower. The preacher called the little boy over and said, "I can't get this mower to start." The little boy said, "That's because you have to cuss at it to get it started." The preacher said, "I am a minister, and I cannot cuss. It has been so long since I have been saved that I do not even remember how to cuss." The little boy looked at him happily and said, "Just keep pulling on that string. It'll come back to ya!"

To his horror, the pastor discovered during the service that he had forgotten his sermon notes, so he said to the congregation, by way of apology, that this morning he should have to depend upon the Lord for what he might say, but next Sunday he would come better prepared.

Pastors, of course, are not supposed to curse. Instead of cursing, one pastor I know, when he's alone, calls out the names of several members of his congregations—with feeling.
—Rev. Dennis R. Fakes

James Huskins recalls: "While I was the new pastor of a church in rural east Tennessee, I assisted a family of parishioners who owned a feed store. It was their busy season, and they needed someone to help fill 100-pound sacks of corn. As I pulled my first bag off the scale and started to close it, I noticed a look of concern on the face of the store owner. 'When we tie sacks, we use a miller's knot,' he said. 'I don't suppose you can do that.' He didn't know that I had spent ten years farming before entering the ministry. When I easily tied the knot, he was visibly impressed. 'You're the first preacher I ever saw,' he told me, 'who knew anything at all about working.'"

M

Rev. Mel, a local Baptist minister, liked to slip old proverbs into his sermons, but had trouble getting them right. For example, he would remind the congregation not to "kick a gift horse in the mouth" or that "a stitch in line saves time" or "a fool and his money are soon started" or "you can lead a horse to water, but that's a horse of a different color." One Sunday, he was describing how easy some task was to perform and said, "It's just like falling off a log." We all thought he had finally mastered one. Then he added, "Once you learn how, you never forget."

I was attending a conference out-of-town with two deacons from my congregation. The first evening's meeting did not finish until rather late. So we decided to have something to eat before going to bed. Unfortunately, the only place still open was a seedy bar-and-grill with a questionable reputation. After being served, one of the deacons asked me to say grace. "I'd rather not," I replied. "I don't want Him to know I'm here."

REAL LETTERS TO MINISTERS:

Dear Pastor, I know God loves everybody but He never met my sister. Yours sincerely, Arnold. Age 8, Nashville

Dear Pastor, Please say in your sermon that Peter Peterson has been a good boy all week. I am Peter Peterson. Sincerely, Pete. Age 9, Phoenix

Dear Pastor, My father should be a minister. Every day he gives us a sermon about something. Robert, Age 11, Anderson

Dear Pastor, I'm sorry I can't leave more money in the plate, but my father didn't give me a raise in my allowance. Could you have a sermon about a raise in my allowance? Love, Patty. Age 10, New Haven

Dear Pastor, My mother is very religious. She goes to play bingo at church every week even if she has a cold. Yours truly, Annette. Age 9, Albany

Dear Pastor, I would like to go to heaven someday because I know my brother won't be there. Stephen. Age 8, Chicago

Dear Pastor, I think a lot more people would come to your church if you moved it to Disneyland. Loreen. Age 9. Tacoma

Dear Pastor, I liked your sermon where you said that good health is more important than money but I still want a raise in my allowance. Sincerely, Eleanor, Age 12, Sarasota

Dear Pastor, Please pray for all the airline pilots. I am flying to California tomorrow. Laurie. Age 10, New York City

Dear Pastor, I hope to go to heaven some day but later than sooner. Love, Ellen, Age 9. Athens

Dear Pastor, Please say a prayer for our Little League team. We need God's help or a new pitcher. Thank you. Alexander. Age 10, Raleigh

Dear Pastor, My father says I should learn the Ten Commandments. But I don't think I want to because we have enough rules already in my house. Joshua. Age 10, South Pasadena

Dear Pastor, Are there any devils on earth? I think there may be one in my class. Carla. Age 10, Salina

Dear Pastor, I liked your sermon on Sunday. Especially when it was finished. Ralph, Age 11, Akron

Dear Pastor, How does God know the good people from the bad people? Do you tell Him or does He read about it in the newspapers? Sincerely, Marie. Age 9, Lewiston

One of the members of our pastors' study group may have hit on an excellent idea for church-state relations in these difficult economic times. "The greatest thing the federal government could do for the church," he quipped, "is to stop printing $1 bills."

—Rev. Julie A. Hart

The parishioners were gathered at the hall to honor their pastor, who was celebrating his twenty-fifth anniversary in the ministry. He was called on to say a few words and his opening remark went something like this: "I feel like the boy who got F in spelling: words fail me."

MISERS

Not all Scotsmen are penny pinchers—despite their reputation. But one was as frugal as frugal can be. His name is Duffy McDuff. On a visit to New York, he caught a taxi and as it sped along, it was hit by another car. The door flew open and Duffy was thrown to the pavement, bleeding and in great pain. The cab driver jumped out, ran to Duffy, and asked if there was anything he could do for him. "There sure is," Duffy moaned. "Shut off the meter."

There is an old saying: "Misers may not be very much fun to live with, but they make extremely good ancestors."

—Ron Dentinger

McDuffy was standing outside the church after his fifth daughter's wedding ceremony when a reporter came up to him and asked, "McDuffy, this is your fifth daughter's wedding. You must be a very proud man." "Och aye, I'm proud, but the confetti is just getting a wee bit gritty."

My uncle Irv, the family tightwad, expressed himself as highly sympathetic to the viewpoint and aims of the National Anti-Tipping Society, but his enthusiasm waned perceptibly when he heard the annual dues were two dollars a year. "Two dollars," he moaned. "I can save money at that figure by going on tipping, right through the year."

My Uncle Irv is so cheap he sends one Christmas card out each year—in the form of a chain letter.

My tightwad Uncle Irv joined an organization that fights inflation but he was very disappointed. An hour after he joined, they raised the dues.

Duffy McDuff sent an indignant letter to the editor of the newspaper. He said that if any more stories about stingy Scotchmen appeared in the columns, he was going to stop borrowing the paper.

A penny-pinching patron stopped in a garage and asked for a pint of anti-freeze. The man on duty asked: "What kind of car is it for?" "It's not for a car," replied the patron, "I'm going to drink it and save buying myself an overcoat this winter."

—Brian O'Hara

MISTAKES

I made a deal with my wife. I will stop calling her the little woman if she will stop calling me the big mistake.

—Ron Dentinger

During World War II, my uncle Ed, a naval aviator, went into a barber shop to get a shave, and since the manicurist was really beautiful, he asked for a manicure at the same time. He kept looking at her, really taken with her, and finally said, "How about going out with me tonight?" She said, "No, I'm married." He said, "Well, just tell your husband you're busy tonight." "Tell him yourself," she said. "He's shaving you."

We usually call our blunders mistakes, and our friends call our mistakes blunders.　　　　　—Henry Wheatley

Half of our mistakes in life arise from feeling where we ought to think, and thinking where we ought to feel.

　　　　　—John Churton Collins

MODERATION

Flora Lewis, columnist for the New York *Times,* criticizing simplistic, cure-all "solutions" to complex political, economic, national and world problems:" "I am a rock-ribbed, hard-nosed, knee-jerk, bleeding-heart moderate."

MODERN LIFE

Data is flying around, across, and through your systems at speeds the Jetsons could appreciate, but has any of this technology let you go home one minute early? I doubt it.

　　　　　—Richard Santalesa

I never expected to see the day when girls would get sunburned in the places they now do.　　　　　—Will Rogers

They say that people are healthier, they have more money, and better sex lives today. I have no joke about this but, it's important that I remind myself of that fact.　　　—Bill Maher

We live in an age when pizza gets to your home before the police.　　　　　—Jeff Marder

These days the marriages just do not last very long. In fact, any more, if I write a check for a wedding gift, I postdate it.

　　　　　—Ron Dentinger

"In the wilderness, we need to keep learning," Boy Scout leader Bud Wilcox said to his troop as they took off on a long hike. "Remember, fellows, if you become lost in the woods at night, get your bearings from the sky." "How do we do that, especially if it's cloudy?" asked one scout. "Just look," said Wilcox. "A glow will indicate the nearest shopping center."

Census-takers have found that one third of all married couples aren't.

You have to question any period in history in which people are saying that God is dead and Elvis is alive. Robert Orben

The U.S. is the only country where a housewife hires a woman to do her cleaning so she can do volunteer work at the nursery where the cleaning woman leaves her child.
—Helen Bender

The woman who remembers her first kiss now has a daughter who can't even remember her first husband.

It is the old story again: once we had wooden chalices and golden priests, now we have golden chalices and wooden priests. —Ralph Waldo Emerson

"On cable TV, they have a weather channel—24 hours of weather," says comedian Dan Spencer. "We had something like that where I grew up. We called it a window."

The Psychiatric Hotline: "Hello, Welcome to the Psychiatric Hotline. If you are obsessive-compulsive, please press 1 repeatedly. If you are co-dependent, please ask someone to press 2. If you have multiple personalities, please press 3, 4, 5 and 6. If you are paranoid-delusional, we know who you are and what you want. Just stay on the line so we can trace the call. If you are schizophrenic, listen carefully and a little voice will tell you which number to press. If you are manic-depressive, it doesn't matter which number you press. No one will answer."

Man to friend: "Exactly when was 'Have a nice day' replaced with 'Please visit our web site'?" —Mike Shapiro

Dan Schow, a resident of San Francisco's Nob Hill, spent a semi-sleepless night last summer listening to what he calls "the ridiculously self-important sound of a car alarm." Next morning, as he tottered bleary-eyed to work, he was gratified to find this scrawled note on the windshield of the offending BMW: "Thieves! Please break into this car. Disconnect the car alarm and you can have the stereo as a thank-you gift from the neighborhood."   —Herb Caen

The phrase "melting pot" used to mean the United States of America. Now it means you put the wrong container in the microwave.   —Robert Orben

What this country needs is something that outlasts the box it came in.

What this country needs is self-destructing campaign and yard sale posters.

The shipwrecked mariner had spent several years on a deserted island. Then one morning he was thrilled to see a ship offshore and a smaller vessel pulling out toward him. When the boat grounded on the beach, the officer in charge handed the marooned sailor a bundle of newspapers and told him, "With the captain's compliments. He said to read through these and let us know if you still want to be rescued."
                          —Bill Leverette, *On Edgar Bergen's Lap*

About the only thing you can do on a shoestring these days is trip.   —Los Angeles Times Syndicate

One newborn baby in the hospital nursery to another: "You know what's cool? We're all born with an automatic $5000 credit limit."   —Mick Stevens in *USA Weekend*

MONDAYS

If it is bright and sunny after two cold and rainy days, it is probably Monday.
                          —Hugh B. Brous, Jr.

Mondays are the potholes in the road of life.
                          —Tom Wilson

MONEY

Zorba Dukakis, a wealthy art dealer, discovers he has a terminal illness. Zorba calls his three best friends, a doctor, a priest and a lawyer, and gives them $500,000 apiece. He tells them, "I know I can't take it with me, but I want to try. I want your assurances that you will put this $500,000 cash into my casket at my funeral and have it buried with me." A month later, Zorba died and following the funeral, the three friends got together. The doctor said, "I've got to confess, I didn't put the money in the casket. I gave it to the hospital's foundation to build a new children's wing." The priest said, "I've got to confess too. I didn't put that $500,000 in the casket either. I gave it to the Little Sisters of the Poor to build a new treatment center at the nursing home." The lawyer said, "Well, I'm aghast. I just want you to know that he was buried with my personal check for $500,000 in his casket!"

A study of economics usually reveals that the best time to buy anything is last year.   —Marty Allen

A man of some wealth overheard a lady remarking, "Oh, if I only had fifty dollars I would be perfectly content." He thought about that for a few moments. "If the lady only had fifty dollars she would be content." He thought to himself, "Well, I can help her out." So he walked up to her and handed her a fifty dollar bill with his best wishes. She was very overt in her show of gratitude. She really appreciated his gift. As she walked away he heard her mumble under her breath, "Why on earth didn't I say one hundred dollars?"

Inflation is creeping up, a young man said to his friend. "Yesterday I ordered a $25 steak in a restaurant and told them to put it on my Visa . . . and it fit."

Things aren't always what they seem. A million dollar house in Beverly Hills could be a $600,000 house with a $400,000 burglar alarm.   —*Funny Funny World*

An American history teacher, lecturing the class on the Puritans, asked: "What sort of people were punished in the stocks?" To which a small voice from the back of the room responded: "The small investor."

I like the story about Ralph the cab driver who had accumulated $100,000 and was going to retire. As was customary, the company gave him a farewell dinner. At the toast, Ralph said a few words." I owe my retirement in part to my thrifty habits," said Ralph. "Even more, I owe it to the good judgment of my wife. But still more, I owe it to my aunt who died and left me $95,000."

Cecil Rhodes was an enormously wealthy man. One day a newspaperman said to him, "You must be very happy." Rhodes replied, "Happy?! No! I spent my life amassing a fortune only to find I have spent half of it on doctors to keep me out of the grave, and the other half on lawyers to keep me out of jail!"

Billionaire Jean Paul Getty was once asked the secret of his success. Said Getty, "Some people find oil. Others don't."

I saw a new book just this week entitled *How To Be Happy Without Money*. I would have bought it, but it cost $29.95.

Uncle Sid says he buys things on the "lay awake plan." He lays awake each evening trying to figure out how he will pay for it.

I like the sign I saw on the front of one church: "You can't take it with you, but you can send it on ahead."

Money still talks. Usually it says good-bye.

One man was asked, "What would you do if you had all the money in the world?" He replied, "I'd apply it to all my debts as far as it would go."

As Adlai Stevenson once put it, "There was a time when a fool and his money were soon parted, but now it happens to everybody."

The fortune-teller peering into his crystal ball, said: "You will be poor and unhappy until you are 30." The client asked: "And then?" The fortune-teller answered: "Then you'll get used to it."

"Pastor," said Mr. Paulson, "I am a spendthrift. I spend money like a drunken sailor. I throw my money around right and left. In this morning's service I want you to pray that I may be cured of this habit." "Yes, my friend," said the pastor, "I'll be happy to pray for you—right after the offering."

"A millionaire's money is," to quote Mark Twain, "twice tainted—tain't yours and tain't mine."

Money sometimes makes fools of important persons, but it may also make important persons of fools.—Walter Winchell

Woman paying bills, to husband: "Our financial situation definitely is fluid. We're going straight down the drain."
                    —Hoest and Reiner, King Features Syndicate

No one can earn a million dollars honestly.
                    —William Jennings Bryan

It is better to have a permanent income than to be fascinating.   —Oscar Wilde

Behind every great fortune there is a crime.
                    —Honore de Balzac

These days if somebody pays you in cash you get suspicious—you think maybe his credit is no good.   —Joey Adams

To be sure your cash is safe, hide it in an empty beer bottle on your lawn. No one will pick it up there.   —Noel Wical

As was grandma's custom, when Ann, her 5-year-old granddaughter, was about to head for home following an afternoon visit, she handed the child about $1 in change. "Thank you, grandma," Ann said. "But this time I think I'll spend the money instead of putting it into my piggy bank." "Why?"

grandma asked. "Well," replied Ann. "It's turning ma and pa into bank robbers." —*Catholic Digest*

My Uncle Les only carries $50 and $100 bills—for health reasons: Lucre can be filthy literally as well as figuratively, according to a study by two doctors at the University of Louisville. They found that 13% of the coins and 42% of the bills they examined contained potentially disease-producing bacteria. Their advice? Carry only less-handled $50 or $100 bills. —*Today's Health*

MORALITY

The newspaper editor grew weary of the abusive letters he received. Finally, instead of an editorial he simply printed a copy of the Ten Commandments. A few days later he received a letter which said, "Cancel my subscription. You're getting too personal."

M

MOSQUITOES

No sound concentrates so much spitefulness and malice into a very small volume as the pinging of mosquitoes.
—Elspeth Huxley, *The Flame Trees of Thika*

MOTHERS

A young man said to the psychiatrist, "I had a strange dream last night. I dreamed you were my mother. I woke up and couldn't understand it. Why should I dream you were my mother?" The psychiatrist said, "Well, what did you do after having the dream?" "I had this appointment with you first thing in the morning, so I grabbed a cookie and a diet soda for breakfast and rushed out here." The psychiatrist frowned, "A cookie and a diet soda? You call that a breakfast?"

I idolized my mother. I didn't realize she was a lousy cook until I went into the Army.

—Jackie Gayle

Mother's Day perfume is kind of an all-purpose gift. It pleases mothers one day a year—and kills mosquitoes the rest.

Motherhood is full of frustrations and challenges. Eventually, though, they move out.

Mothers all want their sons to grow up to be president, but they don't want them to become politicians in the process.
—John F. Kennedy

Doctor to new mother: "It appears you're not getting enough sleep. If the baby starts to cry in the middle of the night, who gets up?" She says, "The whole neighborhood."
—Ron Dentinger

Mother: "Every time you're naughty I get another gray hair."

Son: "Gee, Mom, you must have been a terror when you were young . . . just look at Grandma."   —King Duncan

A super-cautious mother always wore a gauze mask when coming near her baby and insisted that all visitors do likewise. Several older and wiser women tried to tell her tactfully that she was carrying things too far, but the young mother insisted that most parents were absolutely criminal in their carelessness about a child's health. Then the mother mentioned that she thought the baby was beginning to cut a tooth and she wished she could find out about it in some way. A friend with more experience said, "Why, just put your finger in his mouth and . . ." There was such a horrified expression on the mother's face that the friend quickly added, "Of course, boil your finger first."   —King Duncan

When his pager went off during a council meeting in Knoxville, Tenn., police chief Phil Keith was startled to see that the call was from his mother. Concerned, he rushed to the press table and phoned her. "Phil Keith, are you chewing gum?" asked his mom, who had been watching the council meeting on cable TV. "Yes, ma'am." "Well, it looks awful. Spit it out." Keith dutifully removed the gum and went back to his meeting.   —Knoxville, Tenn., *News Sentinel*.

In 1995 my wife and I bought a new home near the Pacific ocean. When my father learned the price, he asked me how I had come up with the down payment. My reply: "I owe my success to keen investments in the stock market, my wife's thrift, and my mother's failure to throw away my comic book collection."

The harried housewife sprang to the telephone when it rang and listened with relief to the kindly voice in her ear. "How are you, darling?" it said. "What kind of a day are you having?" "Oh, mother," said the housewife, breaking into bitter tears, "I've had such a bad day. The baby won't eat and the washing machine broke down. I haven't had a chance to go shopping, and besides, I've just sprained my ankle and I have to hobble around. On top of that, the house is a mess and I'm supposed to have two couples to dinner tonight." The mother was shocked and was at once all sympathy. "Oh, darling," she said, "sit down, relax, and close your eyes. I'll be over in half an hour. I'll do your shopping, clean up the house, and cook your dinner for you. I'll feed the baby, and I'll call a repairman I know who'll be at your house to fix the washing machine promptly. Now stop crying. I'll do everything. In fact, I'll even call George at the office and tell him he ought to come home and help out for once." "George?" said the housewife. "Who's George?" "Why, George! Your husband! . . . If this 555-1373?" "No, it's 555-1375." "Oh, I'm sorry. I guess I have the wrong number." There was a short pause and the housewife said, "Does this mean you're not coming over?"   —Isaac Asimov, *Asimov Laughs Again*

When my grandson Jonathan was five, he was looking at his parents' wedding pictures in the family album. Matt, his father, described the ceremony and tried to explain its meaning. In a flash, Jonathan understood (or thought he did). He exclaimed, "I think I've got it. That's when Mom came to work for us, right?"

September is when millions of shining, happy faces turn toward school. They belong to mothers.

When my mother moved from Manhattan to a rural area in Connecticut, she missed the Yiddish newspaper, *The Forward,* she had been reading for many years. So my sisters and I decided to give her a subscription as a gift. I phoned *The Forward* and explained to the woman who answered that I wanted to buy a gift subscription for my mother. "We don't do gift subscriptions," she replied crisply. "We'll set up an ordinary subscription for your mother and then you write her a nice letter and tell her it's a gift. She'll love to hear from you."

—Sophie Glazer

One day a man comes home from work to find total mayhem at home. The kids were outside still in their pajamas playing in the mud and muck. There were empty food boxes and wrappers all around. As he proceeded into the house, he found an even bigger mess. Dishes on the counter, dog food spilled on the floor, a broken glass under the table, and a small pile of sand by the back door. The family room was strewn with toys and various items of clothing, and a lamp had been knocked over. He headed up the stairs, stepping over toys, to look for his wife. He was becoming worried that she may be ill, or that something had happened to her. He found her in the bedroom, still in bed with her pajamas on, reading a book. She looked up at him, smiled, and asked how his day went. He looked at her bewildered and asked, "What happened here today?" She again smiled and answered, "You know everyday when you come home from work and ask me what I did today?" "Yes," was his reply. She answered, "Well, today I didn't do it!"

I still hadn't recorded a greeting on my new answering machine. My mother was visiting, so I asked her to tape one. "This is Marcia's mother," my machine announced. "Marcia is an only child; she never writes, she never calls. So why not give me a buzz? I'd be happy to talk to you. My number is . . ." Everyone called my mother. She loved the attention.

My mother said, "You won't amount to anything because you procrastinate." I said, "Just wait."   —Judy Tenuta

A mother need only step into the shower to be instantly reassured she is indispensable to every member of her family."   —Lynn M. Williams

A mother was very much annoyed because a written excuse explaining her little son's absence from school following a heavy snowfall was demanded by his teacher. Whereupon she wrote: "Dear Teacher: My little Eddie's legs are fourteen inches long. The snow was eighteen inches deep. Now maybe you understand why he didn't get to school yesterday."

          —*Nuggets*

Entering the supermarket with her five bouncing, exuberant children, a harassed mother asked the manager, "Isn't there a cereal that will sap their energy?"

The mother was bravely gulping down some of the cake her young daughter had so thoughtfully baked as a "surprise" for her birthday. After somehow managing to convey the idea, between laborious swallows, that she was enjoying herself, the little girl beamed, "I'm so glad you like it, Mommy. There should have been 32 candles on the cake but they were all gone when I took it out of the oven."   —*Family Digest*

A woman who wanted to show off her son's scientific knowledge to members of her bridge club called the youngster in and asked: "Bobby, what does it mean when steam comes out of the spout of the kettle?" "It means," said Bobby, "that you are going to open one of Daddy's letters."

—*Woodside Chain News*

MOTHERS-IN-LAW

Behind every successful man stands an absolutely astounded mother-in-law.

The man who claims that his mother-in-law can't take a joke forgets himself.   —Jeff Rovin

I said to my mother-in-law, "Mi casa, su casa" and last week she sold it.

The cop stopped the speeding motorist and asked, "Where's the fire, buddy?" Replied the anguished man behind the wheel, "In the place my wife's going to give me if I miss the plane her mother's coming in on."   —*Wall Street Journal*

MOVIES

In Hollywood, there are just three ages for women: babe, district attorney, and *Driving Miss Daisy.*

—Olivia Goldsmith, *The First Wives Club*

My three grandsons were on their way to the movies to see a cowboy picture, but one objected to it because he'd heard it had too many kissing scenes. His younger brother said, "That's okay—when the kissing starts, we can close our eyes and pretend he's choking her."

Actor James Garner, when asked if he would ever do a nude scene, replied, "No. I don't do horror films."

They say the movies should be more like life. I think life should be more like the movies.   —Myrna Loy

Hollywood: It's a great place to live, but I wouldn't want to visit there.   —Will Rogers,

Some of my best leading men have been dogs and horses.

—Elizabeth Taylor

A young man, returning a library book about movie stars of the silent-film era, opened it to a photograph of vamp queen Theda Bara. "Was she really a sex symbol in the '20s?" he asked. "Yes, she was," the librarian answered. The teen-ager studied the photograph. "Boy," he said finally, "no wonder you people had a depression.

MULES

Only a fool argues with a skunk, a mule or the cook.
—Harry Oliver

MURDER

If the desire to kill and the opportunity to kill came always together, who would escape hanging?   —Mark Twain

---

MURPHY'S FAMOUS LAW

M

If anything can go wrong, it will—is said to have entered history in 1949 at Edwards Air Force Base, when a malfunctioning strap transducer moved a Captain Murphy to his highest eloquence. Other truths attributed to Murphy are:

- Nothing is ever as simple as it seems.
- Everything takes longer than you expect, and, left to themselves, things always go from bad to worse.

Since Murphy's extraordinary leap into immortality, many imitators have sought in similar manner to plumb the human condition. Perhaps the most successful was British historian C. Northcote Parkinson, who found that work expands to fill the time allotted to it. Next in notoriety is the (Lawrence) Peter Principle, that in every hierarchy each employee tends to rise to his level of incompetence.

Lesser known, but just as penetrating, are all the slippery laws of money. For example, there's Parkinson's Second Law, which states that expenditures rise to meet income. Further refined by Dunn's Discovery—that the shortest measurable interval of time is the time between the moment you put a little extra aside for a sudden emergency and the arrival of that emergency. This state of affairs is summed up in Gumperson's Law: that after a rise in salary you will have less money at the end of each month than you had before. With regard to products, Graditor's Laws: (1) If it can break it will, but only after the warranty expires, and (2) A necessary item only goes on sale after you have purchased it at the regular price. To which you can add Dyer's Discovery: it's easy to tell when you've got a bargain—it doesn't fit. And Herblock's Law: If it's good, they'll stop making it.

Car owners are well acquainted with Hartman Automotive Laws: (1) Nothing minor ever happens to a car on the weekend. (2) Nothing minor ever happens to a car on a trip. (3) Nothing minor ever happens to a car. Which brings me to Goldwyn's Law of Contracts: A verbal contract isn't worth the paper it's written on.

Such "law"-giving actually precedes Murphy by a good many centuries. Samuel Butler knew that all progress is based on the innate desire for every organism to live beyond its income. Josh Billings similarly admonished: Live within your income, even if you have to borrow to do it.

Another great name in the field is Finagle. His unique contributions came in the area of science, but Finagle's Laws on Information apply equally to understanding financial transactions: (1) The information you have is not what you want. (2) The information you want is not what you need. (3) The information you need is not what you can obtain. (4) The information you can obtain costs more than you want to pay.

The difference between rich and poor is sharply caught by Getty's Reminder, that the meek shall inherit the earth but not its mineral rights. Followed by the Golden Rule of Arts and Sciences: Whoever has the gold makes the rules. Donohue's Law says that what's worth doing is worth doing for money. And Goldfarber's Law, that under any system a few sharpies will beat the rest of us.

On pocketbook matters, everyone has to keep his eyes open. It's Gross's Law that when two people meet to decide how to spend a third person's money, fraud will result. As in O'Doyle's

Corollary: No matter how many reporters share a cab, and no matter who pays, each puts the full fare on his own expense account.

Woody Allen said that the lion shall lay down with the lamb, but the lamb won't get much sleep. To which add Clopton's Law: For every credibility gap there's a gullibility fill. The Checkbook Balancer's Law holds that in matters of dispute, the bank's balance is always smaller than yours. But if you think the problem is bad now, Epstein adds, just wait until we've solved it. Then there is Quinn's Law: The reader interest generated by any newspaper column is inversely proportional to the importance of its subject.

In his book, *The Official Rules at Home,* Paul Dickson adds a few new corollaries. Here is a sample of Dickson's laws, rules, observations and maxims:

Ballweg's Discovery: Whenever there is a flat surface, someone will find something to put on it. Rabbe's Rule of the Bedroom: The spouse who snores louder always falls asleep first. Rosenbaum's Rule: The easiest way to find something lost around the house is to buy a replacement. Smith's Fourth Law of Inertia: A body at rest tends to watch television.

M

MUSIC

The Beatles said, "All you need is love." And then they broke up.
—Larry Norman

From a British schoolboy's essay: "Johann Sebastian Bach was a most prolific composer. He was the father of twenty children. In his spare time he practiced in the attic on a spinster."

Too many pieces of music finish too long after the end.
—Igor Stravinsky

Anything that is too stupid to be spoken is sung. —Voltaire

I don't know anything about music. In my line you don't have to. —Elvis Presley

There are some experiences in life which should not be demanded twice from any man, and one of them is listening to the Brahms Requiem. —George Bernard Shaw

Wagner's music is better than it sounds. —Mark Twain

Q:What happens when you play country music backwards?
A:Your wife comes back, you get your truck back, your boss gives you back your job, your momma gets out of jail, the man you shot in Reno survives and drops all charges . . .

Explaining why the keys of his piano were so yellow, Victor Borge insisted that it was not because the piano was old, but because the elephant smoked too much.

During rehearsals and performances of the opera *Thais,* baritone Sherrill Milnes was required to lift leading lady Beverly Sills an aggregate of 30 times and carry her across the stage. At one point she apologized for those weighty artistic duties, but a cheerful Milnes assured her they didn't really bother him. "After all," he said, "I was a farm boy and accustomed to hoisting five-hundred-pound bales of hay." "Somehow," she says, "our love scene that night lacked its usual ardor." —Beverly Sills, *Bubbles, An Encore*

Periodically, the comment is heard that "The Star-Spangled Banner" is too hard to sing. But much of the charm of public gatherings In the United States is the suspense over whether the soloist is going to make it.

---------------- **N** ----------------

NAMES

Professional golfer Karen Permezel hails from Yackandandah, Australia. Finding that name to be a mouthful, writers sometimes ask Permezel where the town is located. Permezel is happy to be of assistance. "It's near Mount Murramurra-bong, not far from Tangambalanga," she replies.

— Sports Illustrated

Heintz Loeffler, a successful businessman, was a Rear Admiral during World War II, and he is so listed in various directories. One day he received a letter from a respected charity that began, "Dear Rear . . ."

NATIVE AMERICANS

When NASA was preparing for the Apollo project, they did some astronaut training on a Navajo reservation. One day, a Navajo elder and his son were herding sheep and came across the space crew. The old man, who spoke only Navajo, asked a question which his son translated. "What are these guys in the big suits doing?" A member of the crew said they were practicing for their trip to the moon. The old man got all excited and asked if he could send a message to the moon with the astronauts. Recognizing a promotional opportunity for the spin-doctors, the NASA folks found a tape recorder. After the old man recorded his message, they asked the son to translate it. He refused. So the NASA reps brought the tape to the reservation where the rest of the tribe listened and laughed but refused to translate the elder's message to the moon. Finally, the NASA crew called in an official government translator. He reported that the moon message said, "Watch out for these guys; they have come to steal your land."

When asked by an anthropologist what the Native Americans called America before the white man came, one of them said simply, "Ours."

NATURE

One day recently our five-year-old daughter, Roberta, was sitting very quietly in the kitchen, staring out the window. I thought she was wrestling with a very serious problem, so I asked her what was on her mind. "Dad," she replied, "is Mother Nature God's wife?" —*Irish Grit*

NEIGHBORHOODS

My neighborhood is so dangerous, AOL can't even deliver e-mail here. —Bill Jones

NEIGHBORS

The Bible tells us to love our neighbors, and also to love our enemies; probably because they are generally the same people. —G. K. Chesterton

Nothing makes you more tolerant of a neighbor's noisy party than being there. —Franklin P. Jones

The only thing more disturbing than a neighbor with a noisy old car is a neighbor with a quiet new one. Don't be jealous if your neighbor has a nicer house than you do; it may help when you go to sell. —Richard C. Miller

NEW YEAR

May all your troubles last as long as your New Year's resolutions.

NEW YORK

Question: How many polite, considerate New Yorkers does it take to screw in a light bulb?
Answer: Both of them.

"Night Heat," a CBS detective series, is filmed in Toronto, Canada, and the city's much-vaunted cleanliness sometimes presents a problem for co-producers Sonny Grosso and Larry Jacobson. Being New Yorkers, "we thought an alley we were shooting in was too clean," says Jacobson. "So we sprayed some graffiti on it. We took a lunch break, and when we got back it was all cleaned up." —Ben Yagoda in *TV Guide*

New York City's former mayor David N. Dinkins, when urged by Manhattan officials to buy some property thought to be an "extraordinary opportunity for the city," said: "If they're selling elephants two for a quarter, that's a great bargain. But only if you have a quarter—and only if you need elephants."

NEWLYWEDS

My niece Charlotte after ten months of marriage exclaimed: "I have my husband eating out of my hand." My reply: "Beats washing dishes, doesn't it?"

A word to new brides: if you want to be remembered forever, don't write a thank-you note for a wedding gift.

—Edward L. Rankin, Jr.

NEWSPAPERS

News article: "A hole has been found in the fence surrounding the Happydale Nudist Colony. Police are looking into it."

In my opinion the nightly news on television is a big waste of time. It's the same news every night. It just happens to different people.   —Ron Dentinger

Headline on a Utica, N.Y., *Observer-Dispatch* report of a docking accident: "Staten Island Ferry Hits Pie, 18 Injured."

In a North Platte, Neb., *Telegraph* story about Croatia: "The restaurants serve fresh Adriatic octopus and bars serve just about any alcoholic drunk you can think of."

Item from the Cincinnati *Post:* "Representatives of teachers' organizations appeared before the board to ask for a further cost-of-loving adjustment in wages."

The widow phoned the newspaper and asked how much they charged for running obituaries. "A dollar an inch," she was told. "Oh dear," she said, "It will be far too expensive. My husband was six feet tall."

Fred Abernathy was a devoted reader of the obituary column of his local paper. All of Fred's friends knew of this habit, so one day they decided to play a trick on him by placing his name and picture in the obituaries. The following morning Fred picked up his newspaper, turned to the obituary page, and there he saw his name, his biography and his photo. Startled, he went to the telephone and rang up his pal, George. "Listen," he said. "Do you have the morning paper? You do? Please turn to the obituary page. You have? What do you see in the second column?" There was a pause, then George said, "Holy smoke! It's you, Fred! It's you all right! Listen, where are you calling from?"

The fact that a man is a newspaper reporter is evidence of some flaw of character.   —Lyndon Johnson

The Boston Globe ran a story on the Ford/Volvo deal. The headline was "Have You Driven a Fjord Lately?"

In an item about a pet tattoo clinic, the West Bend, Wisconsin Daily News reported: "The fee for the tattooing is $5 per dog and is $3 for senior citizens age 55 and over."

NOISE

The worst wheel of the cart makes the most noise.
                    —Benjamin Franklin

Noise proves nothing. Often a hen who has merely laid an egg cackles as if she has laid an asteroid.   —Mark Twain

NOTHING

When you have nothing to say, say nothing.
                    —Charles Caleb Colton

The trouble with doing nothing is that you never know when you are finished.   —Edna Wolf

NOVEMBER

November is nature's way of giving you time to eat up the leftover Halloween candy before you have to start eating up the leftover turkey.   — Bill Tammeus

OLD AGE

"What are you so happy about?" I asked my 101-year old great-aunt one day. "I broke a mirror," she replied. "But that means seven years of bad luck." "I know," she said, beaming. "Isn't it wonderful?"

The doctor asked the weather-beaten mountaineer how he was feeling. "It's like this," drawled the man from the hills after a few seconds of silence, "I'm still kickin', but I ain't raising any dust."
— Ed Steiner

Why can't we build orphanages next to homes for the aged? If someone's sitting in a rocker, it won't be long before a kid will be in his lap.
— Cloris Leachman

You know you're getting older when in the morning you hear snap, crackle, pop, and it isn't your breakfast cereal.

In Cape Coral, Florida, two elderly women were out driving in a large car, both could barely see over the dashboard. As they were cruising along they came to an intersection. The stoplight was red but they just went on through the red light. The woman in the passenger seat thought to herself,  "I must be losing my mind, I swear we just went through a red light." After a few more minutes they came to another intersection and the light was red again, and again they went right through. This time Bessie in the passenger seat was almost sure that the light had been red, but was really concerned that she was mistaken. She was getting nervous and decided to pay very close attention to the road and the next intersection to see what was going on. At the next intersection, sure enough, the light was definitely red and they went right through. She turned to the woman driving and said, "Shirley! Did you know we just ran through three red lights in a row! You could have killed us!" Shirley turned to her and said, "Oh, am I driving?"

A man once counseled his son that if he wanted to live a long life, the secret was to sprinkle a little gunpowder on his cornflakes every morning. The son did this religiously, and he lived to the age of 93. When he died, he left 14 children, 28 grandchildren, 35 great-grandchildren, and a 15-foot hole in the wall of the crematorium.

William Mann tells about the old-timer talking with his grandson. "If you were 16 years old, Granddaddy, what would you wish for most of all?" the lad questioned. The elderly gentleman thought only a moment before answering, "I reckon nothin' else, son."

OOPS!

Herb Uttley walked into the Cottonwood Drugstore and asked the pharmacist if he had a cure for hiccups. The pharmacist walked around the corner and approached Herb. He reached out and slapped Herb soundly in the back. The pharmacist then hopefully asked, "Do you have the hiccups now?" As Herb composed himself after such a sudden blow, he answered the pharmacist, "No, I do not! But I'll just bet you that my wife out in the car still does."

The following was written on the program of the New Mexico Arts and Crafts Fair: "Graduating with a B.F.A. from Northern Arizona University in 1976, Ernest Wilmeth turned to clay in 1982."

A family spent the night in a motel and the wife had awakened early. She packed the bags and carried them to the car. Returning after one load she accidentally went into the wrong room. Seeing a sleeping man and assuming it was her husband, she shook the headboard and shouted as loud as she could, "Get out of that bed!" Suddenly she realized her mistake, and she turned and ran out. As she ran she heard the man exclaim, "Boy, that sure is some wake-up service."

From Illinois State University's *Daily Vidette:* "Correction: It was incorrectly reported that today is T-shirt Appreciation Day. In fact, it is Teacher Appreciation Day."

From the Prescott, Ariz., *Daily Courier:* "Arizona's fifth-largest bank is seeking experienced bankers to stuff a downtown office."

The Peoria, Ill., *Journal Star* reported that after an accident a man was ticketed for driving while expired.

From a card in a Moroccan hotel room: "Males and snacks may be served in your room at any time. Please call room service."

From the Haverford, Pa., Main Line Art Center class-registration booklet: "Advanced Life Painting Studio. This group grows out of a need for professional artists to have an opportunity to paint from the model. Tuition includes model feel."

The dosage on a doctor's prescription for a congested Bremerton, Wash., four-year-old: "Give half teaspoon four times daily for funny nose."

From a hospital cafeteria menu, printed in the Moscow Pullman, Idaho, *Daily News:* "Wednesday lunch—Grilled Pastrami and Swill on Dark Rye."

In the Houston, Texas, *Chronicle* classified-ad section for farms and ranches: "Deer, turkey, wild wife."

In the Sterling, Kan., *Bulletin:* "Promotion exercises will be held Thursday for 53 eighth-graders. The choir will sing 'I Am But a Small Vice.'"

From a wedding announcement: "Following a trip to Mexico, the couple, who met on a blind date set up by a fiend, will live in Waco."

In a restaurant review: "If prime rib is your thing, they have a dull dinner with salad, potato, dessert and beverage."

Classified ad in the Edina, Minn., *Star Tribune:* "String of perils, 30 years old, with box."

Help-wanted ad in *The Blowing Rocket,* Blowing Rock, N.C.: "Part-time youth director wanted. Salary confiscated with experience."

Elisabeth Shoemaker Linscott, one of the first women to enlist in the Marine Corps in 1918, tells about the dispersal of her unit when the war ended: "The Secretary of the Navy dismissed us at a big press-covered ceremony. He said the Corps would miss us, and finished, in ringing tones, with, 'We will not forget you. As we embraced you in uniform yesterday, we will embrace you without uniforms tomorrow.'"
                                        —Modern Maturity

Realty ad in Ishpeming, Mich., *Action Shopper:* "Starter home, large kitchen with mice eating area."

Classified ad for drivers in the Harrisburg, Pa., *Sunday Patriot News:* "Taking applications for experienced dumb truck drivers."

From a Lenexa, Kan., church bulletin's Order of Service: "We present our thighs and offerings."

In a Pittsburgh *Post-Gazette* brief about the Pittsburgh Zoo seeking historical items: "The zoo will use the material for marketing and public relations porpoises."

The Columbus, Ohio, *Dispatch* reported that country singer Garth Brooks was worried whether his new album would sell: "Perhaps he's trying to lower expectations in case it doesn't go plutonium."

Mother to daughter: "Did your girlfriends admire your engagement ring?" The daughter says, "More than that. Two of them recognized it."

A correction in the Yuma, Arizona, *Daily Sun* still needs work. It reads: "Terri K is not a Marine sergeant, as reported in Thursday's 'Yuma Roundup.' He is the wife of one."

The first mistake that Scott Reyst made was breaking into the home of James Bannon, Detroit's executive deputy police Chief. The 18-year-old's second mistake was showing up at the preliminary hearing wearing the deputy chief's boots.

—*Punch*

From a department-store ad in the Elmira, N.Y., *Star-Gazette:* "Whatever type your father is, we know we can help you choose a gift to make him grim all over."

—Antony B. Lake, *A Pleasury of Witticisms and Word Play*

From a classified ad in the Fairmont, W. Va., *Times West Virginian:* "Siding and roofing crews needed. Must have own fools and trucks."

In the Bellingham, Wash., *Herald:* "The recipe for Chewy Oatmeal Surprise Cookies in yesterday's food section omitted the three cups of oatmeal. The rest of the ingredients are correct."

From the Webster, Mass., *Times:* "The letter to the editor that objected to a dog in Dudley should have read 'the owner should be fined and warned,' not 'fixed and wormed.'"

O

Before you send out your next résumé, weed out the goofs, cautions recruiting executive Robert Half, who has been collecting examples of "resumania" for years. Some of his favorites:

1. "Please call after 5:30 P.M. because I am self-employed and my employer does not know I am looking for another job."
2. "I am very conscientious and accurite."
3. "I am also a notary republic."
4. "The firm currently employs 20 odd people."
5. "My consideration will be given to relocation anywhere in the English-speaking world and/or Washington, D.C."
6. Under physical disabilities: "Minor allergies to house cats and Mongolian sheep."

7. Reasons given for leaving the last job: "The company made me a scapegoat—just like my previous three employers did."

Business Times

From the Placerville, California, *Mountain Democrat:* "Actor Jimmy Stewart's name was incorrectly spelled in Wednesday's 'Beyond the Beat' column as H-e-n-r-y F-o-n-d-a."

From *Focus,* an AT&T employee magazine: "Our Feb. 9 issue reported our 1987 earnings per share as $1.88 billion. The addition of 'billion' was a typesetter's error, and we apologize for any ecstasy the error may have caused."

In the Oxford, Ohio, *Press:* "Gourmets of any religious persuasion can register to attend the class entitled 'Fundamental Gourmet Cooking Methods and Techniques.' A typographical error in last week's paper was not intended to limit the class to Methodists only."

OPPORTUNITY

The wolves were decimating the farmers' sheep. So the farmers' association raised the bounty on them to a hundred dollars a pelt. Two hunters, Sam and Ed, decided they could use the money. So they got their gear together and headed out to the wide open spaces to shoot some wolves and make themselves rich. They had just fallen asleep out under the stars when a noise woke Ed. By the light of the campfire he saw the eyes of a hundred wolves—teeth gleaming. He shook his friend and whispered hoarsely, "Sam! Sam! Wake up! We're rich!"

I was seldom able to see an opportunity until it had ceased to be one.
—Mark Twain

Lots of people know a good thing the minute the other fellow sees it first.
—Job E. Hedges

You miss 100 percent of the shots you never take.
—Wayne Gretzky

Dig where the gold is . . . unless you just need some exercise.
—John M. Capozzi, *Why Climb the Corporate Ladder When You can Take the Elevator?*

OPTIMISM

The sports reporter asked the football coach, "How do you keep your spirits up when your team is losing?" He shrugged and replied, "I'm the kind of guy who, if I fell in a mud puddle, would get up and feel in my pockets for fish."

Charlie Pell, Clemson football coach, said it best. "I expect my players to think as positively as the eighty-five-year-old man who married a twenty-five-year-old woman and ordered a five-bedroom house near an elementary school."

——————————— **P** ———————————

PACIFICISM

No man can tame a tiger into a kitten by stroking it.
—Franklin D. Roosevelt

P

PARENTS

Before I got married I had six theories about bringing up children. Now I have six children and no theories.
—Lord Rochester

Miss Swenson's fifth grade class was assigned to write a short essay on parents. Samantha Peters' essay read: "The trouble with parents is that when we get them they are so old it is very hard to change their habits."

Setting a good example for children takes all the fun out of middle age.   —William Feather

Wrinkles are hereditary. Parents get them from their children.   —Doris Day

Parenthood remains the greatest single preserve of the amateur.
— Alvin Toffler

If parents would only realize how they bore their children.
— George Bernard Shaw

Parent: Something so simple even a child can operate it.

One of the college grad's first big discoveries is that jobs are handed out by some person who thinks and acts a lot like his or her parents.
— Bob Talbert

PARKING

A distinguished-looking man entered a Geneva bank and inquired about taking out a loan for 1000 Swiss francs. "What security can you offer?" the banker asked. "My Rolls-Royce is parked out front," he said. "I will be away for a few weeks. Here are the keys." A month later, the man returned to the bank and paid off the loan, 1017 francs with interest. "Pardon me for asking," the banker said, "but why a one-thousand franc loan for a man of your obvious means?" "Very simple," he replied. "Where else can you store a Rolls for a month for seventeen francs?"

Don't park a mobile home on top of a hill. It can leave you if it is so inclined.
— Frank Tyger

One of life's simple pleasures is parking on someone else's dime.

PEACE

Ramsay MacDonald, one-time Prime Minister of England, was discussing with another government official the possibility of lasting peace. The latter, an expert on foreign affairs, was unimpressed by the Prime Minister's idealistic viewpoint. He remarked cynically, "The desire for peace does not necessarily ensure it." This MacDonald admitted, saying, "Quite true. But neither does the desire for food satisfy your hunger. However it at least gets you started towards a restaurant."

PERFECTION

If it wasn't for my faults, I'd be perfect.

PERSISTENCE

If your ship doesn't come in, swim out to it—Jonathan Winters

Don't worry if your job is small
And your rewards are few,
Remember that the mighty oak
Was once a nut like you!

PERSPECTIVE

During a hard period in Soviet history, the government showed the film version of Steinbeck's *The Grapes of Wrath*, on the state-run television network. The government wanted to show how much worse off people were in the United States. All that the Soviet citizens noticed was that even the poorest Americans owned cars!

Never mistake motion for action.   —Ernest Hemingway

The average person thinks he isn't.—Father Larry Lorenzoni

PESSIMISM

A young man entered a jewelry store and purchased an expensive engagement ring. The jeweler asked, "What names do you wish it engraved in it?" he asked. "From Lance to Cindy," the young man whispered, red-faced. The jeweler looked from the ring to the young man and smiled. "Take my advice, young fellow," he said. "Have it engraved simply, 'From Lance.'"

The pessimist sees the difficulty in every opportunity; the optimist, the opportunity in every difficulty.   —L. P. Jacks

PETS

I have fish for pets. That's what I have. Goldfish. It was originally for the stress thing. They say if you watch fish, it helps you relax, to fall asleep, which explains why I always doze off while I'm snorkeling. —Ellen DeGeneres

I've got a sheep dog. He doesn't have fleas—he's got moths. —Joey Adams

Dogs come when they're called; cats take a message and get back to you.
—Mary Bly

A dog doesn't want much and is happy to get it. A cat doesn't know what it wants and wants more of it.
—Richard Hexem

What do you call a parrot wearing a raincoat? Polly unsaturated.

PHILOSOPHY

Being a philosopher, I have a problem for every solution.
—Robert Zend

Tonight we're going to consider one of the great questions of our time: Why the people who forget to turn off their car headlights always remember to lock the doors.
—Robert Orben, *2500 Jokes To Start 'Em Laughing*

PLASTIC

Nowadays, when you get right down to brass tacks, they're plastic. —Gil Stern

PLAY

As Plato remarked, "You can discover more about a person in an hour of play than in a year of conversation."

POETS

After a dinner party, poet Robert Frost and the other guests went out onto the veranda to watch the sunset. "Oh, Mr. Frost, isn't it a lovely sunset?" exclaimed a young guest. "I never discuss business after dinner," Frost replied.

—*Little, Brown Book of Anecdotes*

POLICE

A rookie police officer was asked in an examination what he would do to break up a crowd. His answer indicated a deep knowledge of human nature. He replied, "I would take up a collection."

A women went to the police station with her next door neighbor to report that her husband was missing. The police officer asked for a description. She said, "He's 35 years old, 6 foot 2, has dark eyes, dark wavy hair, an athletic build, weighs 185 pounds, is soft-spoken, and is good to the children." The next-door neighbor protested, "Wait a minute! Your husband is 5 foot 4, chubby, bald, has a big mouth, and is mean to your children." The wife replied, "Sure, but who wants him back?"

My stepson Todd, who is a sheriff's deputy, pulled over a speeding motorist and asked, "Do you have any ID?" The motorist replied, "About what?"

Officer Mark Blank stopped George Goodman driving the wrong way on a one-way street. At the court hearing, the traffic judge asked Goodman, "Didn't you see the arrow?" "Arrow? Honest, your honor, I didn't even see the Indians."

The police in Worcester, Massachusetts, were able to put out unusually specific information about a robbery suspect. The suspect had decided to rob a tailor, Philip Smith, only after the tailor had measured him completely for a new suit.

My cousin Sandy is a highway patrol officer. Recently she pulled over a driver for speeding. The irate speeder confronted Officer Sandy and said: "Why don't you people get organized? First you take away my driver's license and the next day you ask to see it."

Policeman: "Why didn't you report the robbery right away? Didn't you suspect something when you came home and discovered all the drawers opened and the contents scattered about?"

Woman: "No, I didn't suspect a thing. I just thought my husband was looking for a clean shirt."   *— Quote*

When our son Todd was a police officer in training, he and his trainer found three hand grenades in an abandoned cabin and decided to take them to the police station. "What if one of them explodes?" asked Todd. "It doesn't matter," reassured the experienced officer. "We'll say we only found two."

A man was driving along in his beat up old Dodge, when suddenly it broke down. He was parked on the side of the road trying to fix it, when a Jaguar pulled up in front of him and offered to help. After a few minutes the two men obviously weren't going to get the old car going again, so the Jaguar driver offered to tow the Dodge to the nearest garage. A few minutes later the two had hitched up the old Dodge to the Jaguar, and they agreed that if the Jaguar driver was going too fast, the man should blow his horn and flash his lights to get him to slow down. With that the two men got into their cars and the Jaguar driver started to pull away with the Dodge behind it. At the first traffic light, a Ferrari pulled up beside the Jaguar and started to rev his engine. As soon as the light turned green the Ferrari and the Jaguar hit their accelerators and took off. Before long the cars were racing at over 120 mph. As the cars sped along, they passed through a police speed trap. The officer couldn't believe his eyes when he saw the three cars go by, and he decided that he couldn't catch them all by himself, so he decided to radio for help: "You won't believe what I just saw! I saw a Ferrari and a Jaguar doing 120 mph side by side, and a beat up old Dodge behind them flashing his lights and blowing his horn trying to get by!"

Police in Los Angeles had good luck with a robbery suspect who just couldn't control himself during a lineup. When detectives asked each man in the lineup to repeat the words, "Give me all your money or I'll shoot," the man shouted, "That's not what I said!"

If you're stopped by the police, shut off your engine and put your mouth in neutral.   —Newspaper Enterprise Assn.

A speeding driver was signaled to the side of the highway by a motorcycle officer. "I'm a good friend of the mayor," the speeder told him. "Great," said the officer as he wrote the ticket. "Now he'll know I'm on the job."

The police sent out mug shots of an escaped convict in six different poses. A constable from a town nearby sent the following telegram two days later: "Have captured five of them and am on the trail of the sixth."

POLITICS

A bishop advised a politician to go out into the rain and lift his head toward heaven. It will bring a revelation to you, he said. The next day the politician reported: "I followed your advice and no revelation came. The water poured down my neck and I felt like a fool." "Well," replied the bishop, "isn't that quite a revelation for the first try?"

A candidate for office can have no greater advantage than muddled syntax; no greater liability than a command of the language.   —Marya Mannes

Former Senator Eugene McCarthy once said, "Being in politics is like being a football coach. You have to be smart enough to understand the game and dumb enough to think it's important."

He is the kind of politician who would cut down a redwood tree, then mount the stump and make a speech for conservation.
—Adlai Stevenson

I am not a member of any organized party. I am a Democrat.
—Will Rogers

I know a politician who believes that there are two sides to every question—and takes them both.
—Ken Murray

I like political jokes, unless they get elected.

I once said cynically of a politician, "He'll double-cross that bridge when he comes to it."
—Oscar Levant

I think the next four years we should try it with no President.
—Dana Fradon

I voted for the Democrats because I didn't like the way the Republicans were running the country, which is turning out to be like shooting yourself in the head to stop your headache.
—Jack Mayberry

"I wouldn't vote for you if you were St. Peter himself," I told one candidate with whom I was in particular disagreement. "Don't worry," he replied. "If I were St. Peter, you wouldn't be in my district."

If you can't convince them, confuse them.—Harry S Truman

In politics, it's a good rule to follow the first law of holes. If you are in one, stop digging.
—Denis Healey

It is dangerous for a national candidate to say things that people might remember.
—Eugene McCarthy

The politician began his speech like this. "Ladies and gentlemen, please let me tax your memories for a moment." Someone in the crowd immediately spoke up, "Well, you've tried to tax everything else."

Henry Cabot Lodge, Jr.'s, advice to then novice political campaigner, Dwight D. Eisenhower: "Meet the sun every day as if it could cast a ballot."

Perhaps the greatest compliment ever paid President Grover Cleveland was when he was put in nomination before the Democratic Convention. The orator who presented his name said, "We love him for the enemies he has made."

Political success is the ability, when the inevitable occurs, to get credit for it.   —Laurence J. Peter

Politics is the ability to foretell what is going to happen tomorrow, next week, next month and next year. And to have the ability afterwards to explain why it didn't happen.
                                                    —Winston Churchill

Politics is the gentle art of getting votes from the poor and campaign funds from the rich by promising to protect each from the other.   —Oscar Ameringer

Politics is the art of the possible.
                                    —Otto von Bismarck (1815–1898)

When you're leading, don't talk.   —Thomas E. Dewey

Winston Churchill once noted that the nation will find it hard to look up to leaders who keep their ears to the ground.

You campaign in poetry. You govern in prose.
                                                    —Mario Cuomo

You really have to be careful of politicians who have no further ambitions. They may run for president.
                                                    —Harry S Truman

The 1980 Presidential campaign contained a heavy emphasis on economic issues. Candidate Ronald Reagan warned of the coming of another depression if America continued in its present path. President Jimmy Carter responded, "That shows how much he knows. Mr. Reagan clearly does not know the difference between a depression and a recession." That reaction gave Reagan, the communicator, a platform comment to build his campaign on. Reagan responded, "If Mr. Carter wants a definition, I'll give him one. Recession is when your neighbor loses his job, depression is when you lose yours, and recovery will be when Jimmy Carter loses his."

In an article on Northern Ireland, the political party Sinn Fein was described as the political wing of the IRA. I guess that makes the U.S. Democratic Party the political wing of the IRS.

State legislators are merely politicians whose darkest secrets prohibit them from running for higher office.
—Dennis Miller

The only way to combat criminals is by not voting for them.
—Dayton Allen

There are three types of politicians: those that cannot lie, those that cannot tell the truth, and those that cannot tell the difference.

There is a story about a gubernatorial candidate in Texas who got an urgent call from the manager of his campaign in Houston. "Jim, you should get over here right away," the manager said. "The opposition is telling a lot of lies about you around the city." "Can't come today," the candidate told him. "I've got to go to Dallas." "But, Jim, this is important. They're telling lies about you in Houston," the manager protested. "Dallas is even more important," said Jim. "They're telling the truth about me there."

There were so many candidates on the platform that there were not enough promises to go around.   —Ronald Reagan

Two elderly women were walking around a typical over-crowded English country churchyard and came upon a tombstone on which was the inscription, "Here lies John Smith, a politician and an honest man." "Good heavens," said one woman to the other, "isn't it awful that they had to put two people in the same grave!"

Vote for the man who promises least. He'll be the least disappointing.
—Bernard Baruch

Question asked of actor Jimmy Stewart: "Why did you never think of running for President?" Answer: "I can't talk fast enough to be a politician."

I used to say that politics was the second oldest profession. I have come to know that it bears a gross similarity to the first.—Ronald Reagan

During his stint as governor of Georgia, Lester Maddox explained why his state should not create a consumer protection agency as follows: "Honest businessmen should be protected from the unscrupulous consumer."

I think that the undecideds could go one way or the other.
—George Bush in 1988

I believe we are on an irreversible trend toward more freedom and democracy. But that could change.
—Vice-President Dan Quayle

The trouble with politicians is they always put our money where their mouths are.   —Baloo in *Forbes*

Political debates are sort of like stock-car races—no one really cares who wins; they just want to see the crashes.
—Molly Ivins

Any man who is under 30, and is not a liberal, has no heart; and any man who is over 30, and is not a conservative, has no brains.   —Winston Churchill

You have all the characteristics of a popular politician: a horrible voice, bad breeding, and a vulgar manner.
—Aristophanes

"Can you believe a candidate dropped out of the race because of a lack of campaign funds?" asks comedian Kevin Nealon. "Any politician who stops spending just because he's out of money doesn't belong in Washington anyway!"

Politicians, are people who, when they see light at the end of the tunnel, go out and buy some more tunnel.

—John Quinton

Politics is perhaps the only profession for which no preparation is thought necessary.   —Robert Louis Stevenson

A group of politicians, shortly before an oncoming election, were busily engaged in a Texas cemetery, copying names from gravestones, in order to vote for them, fraudulently. They came to one stone that was overgrown with moss, the name hard to decipher, so they decided to skip that one, and go on to the next. At this, the leader of the group registered a vehement protest: "No! No! No! Go right back and get that name! That fellow has just as much right to vote as anybody in this cemetery!"   —Hugh Harrison

A banker, an electrician, and a politician were taking an IQ test. One of the questions was "What term best describes the problem when outflow exceeds inflow?" The banker wrote, "Overdraft." The electrician answered, "Overload." The politician scratched his head and wrote, "What problem?"

Grandma Jones disagrees with the view that someday there may be a woman President. "I'll tell you why," she says. "If the woman who runs for that high office is homely, the men won't vote for her. And if she's good looking, the women won't."   —*Ozarks Mountaineer*

POSITIVE THINKING

I was going to buy a copy of *The Power of Positive Thinking*, and then I thought: What good would that do?

—Ronnie Shakes

POST OFFICE

In 1984, 500 postal workers received their paychecks three days late—because their original checks were lost in the mail.   —AP

In the post office: "I don't want to say the mail is slow, but last week my flower seeds arrived as a bouquet."

—Joey Adams

PRAISE

Praise does wonders for the sense of hearing.

—*Bits & Pieces*

PRAYER

My brother Scott says the country is in far worse shape than most people suspect. His evidence: "Every time I call Dial-a-Prayer I get a busy signal."

Little Darlene surprised her mother with the postscript to her bedtime prayer: "And, dear Lord, please send the beautiful snow to keep the little flowers warm through the winter." Climbing into her bed, she confided to her mother: "That time I fooled him. I want the snow so I can go sledding with my new sled." —*Capper's Weekly*

The object of most prayers is to wangle an advance on good intentions.   —Robert Brault

Susanna, age eight, was reprimanded by her mother for laughing while saying her bedtime prayers. "It's okay, Mom," she replied, "I was just sharing a joke with God."

May those that love, love universities and those that don't love us, may God turn their hearts; and if He doesn't turn their hearts, may He turn their ankles so we'll know them by their limping.

—An Irish Prayer

Jean had been troublesome and had been sent into the den to think things over. After a while she came out all smiles and said, "I thought and I prayed." "Fine," said her mother. "That will help you to be good." "Oh, I didn't ask God to help me to be good, I just told him to help you put up with me," she said.   — *Grit*

The 8-year-old didn't exactly dislike going to church; it was the excruciatingly long pastoral prayer which seemed especially tiresome to him. So he was naturally a little apprehensive when his father asked the visiting minister to say grace at dinner. Surprisingly, the prayer was brief and to the point. Pleased, the child looked up and observed: "You don't pray so long when you're hungry, do you?"   — *Grit*

PREACHERS/PREACHING

Prison Chaplain Larry Swenson said to a soon-to-be ex-convict, "As you make your way in the world, son, remember the sermons you heard while you were here." Replied the about-to-be-released prisoner: "Chaplain, no one who's heard you preach would ever want to come back here."

What I meant to say was, "Let us bind ourselves with willing bonds to our covenant with God. The way it came out was, Let us bind ourselves with willing blondes . . ."

The average man's idea of a good sermon is one that goes over his head and hits a neighbor.

The preacher was wired for sound with a lapel mike, and as he preached, he moved briskly about the platform, jerking the mike cord as he went. Then he moved to one side, getting wound up in the cord and nearly tripping before jerking it again. After several circles and jerks, a little girl in the third pew leaned toward her mother and whispered, "If he gets loose, will he hurt us?"

As a visiting preacher, D. L. Moody was warned that some of the congregation usually left before the end of the sermon. When he rose to begin his sermon, he announced, "I am going to speak to two classes of people this morning; first to the sinners, then to the saints." He proceeded to address the "sinners" for awhile, and then said they could leave. For once, every member of the congregation stayed to the end of the sermon.   —Viola Walden

Our pastor delivered a compelling sermon describing the plight of the poor, reminding everyone in strong terms that it is a charitable duty of the rich to share their wealth. After Mass a friend asked our pastor if he thought he had persuaded the parishioners. "Well, I'm sure it was at least a partial success," he answered with a smile. "I'm sure I convinced the poor!"

PREDICTIONS

We all make mistakes. Consider the following judgments:

- There is no reason anyone would want a computer in their home.—Ken Olson, president, chairman and founder of Digital Equipment Corp., 1977
- 640K ought to be enough for anybody.—Bill Gates in 1981
- The concept is interesting and well-formed, but in order to earn better than a 'C,' the idea must be feasible.—A Yale University management professor in response to student Fred Smith's paper proposing reliable overnight delivery service (Smith went on to found Federal Express Corp.)
- Who the heck wants to hear actors talk?—H. M. Warner (1881–1958), founder of Warner Brothers, in 1927
- We don't like their sound, and guitar music is on the way out.—Decca Recording Co. rejecting the Beatles, 1962
- Everything that can be invented has been invented.—Charles H. Duell, Commissioner, U.S. Office of Patents, 1899

PREGNANT

A friend who was eight months pregnant went to visit a sick relative in Memphis and took a wrong turn. Stopping at a filling station for directions, she said, "I don't know where I went wrong, but I'm trying to get to Baptist Hospital." The attendant, who couldn't help but notice her condition, smiled and replied, "I don't know where you went wrong either, but if you drive four blocks straight ahead you'll get there."
—Jessye Lee Alexander

PREJUDICE

Thinking is what a great many people think they are doing when they are merely rearranging their prejudices.
—William James

PRESIDENTS

Jimmy Carter's promise of amnesty to the Haitian generals had the White House very upset. "We don't care what Carter promised. If President Clinton wanted to grant pardons, he would have sent Gerald Ford."

Mr. Coolidge is the best Democrat we ever had in the White House. He didn't do nothin', but that's what we wanted done.
—Will Rogers

President Wilson's mind, as has been the custom, will be closed all day Sunday.
—George S. Kaufman

Former President Jimmy Carter spoke at the Economic Club luncheon and told the joke about three envelopes that each incoming president should have for guidance. "If the going gets tough during the first year, the president should open the first envelope that says: 'Blame the past president!' After the second year, if there is no improvement, he should open the second envelope that declares: 'Blame Congress!' If things continue to get progressively worse, the President should open the third envelope. This one advises: 'Prepare three envelopes.'"

—How the Platform Professionals Keep 'em Laughin'

When Franklin D. Roosevelt was President, the pastor of the church he attended in Washington was asked over the phone, "Is the President expected to attend church this Sunday?" "I don't know," replied the minister. "But I can assure you that God will be there, which should be incentive enough."

When asked what his favorite song was, John F. Kennedy replied, "I think 'Hail to the Chief' has a nice ring to it."

Preparing for a citizenship test, a lady was shown a photo of Abraham Lincoln by her son and asked to identify it. "That's Abe Lincoln," she said confidently. The he showed her a picture of bewigged George Washington. She looked at the picture perplexedly and then answered, "That's his wife."

—R & R Magazine

PRESS

Wooing the press is an exercise roughly akin to picnicking with a tiger. You might enjoy the meal, but the tiger always eats last.

—Maureen Dowd

PRICES

After eating a meal in a first-class restaurant nowadays, you need an after-dinner mint—such as the one in Denver.

—Irving Lazar

PRIDE

Early to bed and early to rise makes a man healthy, wealthy, and hell-bent to talk about it.   *—Franklin P. Jones*

To hide the shameful fact that his father had been hanged for cattle stealing, a lawyer rewrote his own family history thus: Father died while taking part in a public ceremony when the platform gave way.

—Msgr. Arthur Tonne, Jokes Priests Can Tell, vol. 6

He was as shy as a newspaper is when referring to its own merits.
—Mark Twain

Did you ever have one of those nights where you didn't want to go out . . . but your hair looked too good to stay home?
—Jack Simmons

PRIESTS

Father O'Brien, the new parish priest was making a visit to my nephew's home. He knocked on the door, and Tad, their little 4-year-old boy went to the door and saw the priest. He called to his father, "Hey, Dad! That guy that works for God is here!"

I was visiting my friend Father Miles at his office in the city. As I entered, he instructed his secretary, "Unless it's the archbishop or the pope, don't put any calls through." In the middle of our meeting, the phone rang. Annoyed, Father Miles answered it. Then his eyes widened. "Yes," he said, "that's right. I told her not to let any calls through unless they came from the archbishop, the pope or you, Mom."

While I was visiting Father Miles, the UPS guy came by with a large package. He had a very strange look on his face. "I have a package for the Father," he explained and had Miles sign for it. I clearly understood the delivery man's chagrin when I saw what was stamped on the box: Contents: FULL COLOR MADONNA CALENDARS.

When I first met Father Miles, he had just come from the Catholic church across from his office, where he had been celebrating mass. He looked odd to me in his cassock and to cover my discomfort I quipped,, "I didn't know you wore dresses!" Without losing a beat, Father Miles replied, "Oh, this old thing?"

PRIORITIES

One Sunday, my then eight-year-old daughter Susie was given two quarters as she left for church, one for the collection plate and one for herself to spend as she wished. As she walked to Sunday school she was playing with the quarters in her hand, and one dropped on the street and rolled through the grates of a sewer. Susie looked down into the watery depths and said sadly, "There goes God's quarter."

PRISON

In his youth, my friend Ralph was a prison chaplain. His first day on the job, he visited a man on death row. Ralph established a good rapport with the condemned felon, visited him daily for several weeks, and when it came time for the criminal to be executed by the electric chair, Ralph was asked to be there and console the man on the way to his death. When the day arrived, Ralph walked the last mile with the convict, but was very anxious about what to say. "Good-bye" seemed trite, "See you later" seemed inappropriate, and he became desperate for the right words. Just as they got to the electric chair, Ralph blurted out, "More power to you!!"

The warden was very upset that his daughter married one of the convicts. Partially because the guy was a lifer, but mostly because they eloped.
                                          —Ron Dentinger

PROBLEMS

I don't have a solution, but I admire your problem.

PROCRASTINATION

She said procrastination was the cause of all my sorrow.
I don't know what that big word means . . . I'll look it up tomorrow.   —Mary Alice Sherman

Procrastinators suffer from hardening of the oughteries.
  —*The Pundit,* The International Save the Pun Foundation.

PROFESSIONS

All professions are conspiracies against the laity.
                                          —George Bernard Shaw

A doctor can bury his mistakes, but an architect can only advise his clients to plant vines. —Frank Lloyd Wright

PROGRESS

Progress is man's ability to complicate simplicity.

—Thor Heyerdahl

PROMISES

And all of my free programs come with a money-back guarantee. —Jim Butterfield, early Commodore software superstar, 1983

PROVERBS

Rolling Stones gather an audience —Ray Przybysz

A stitch in time saves embarrassment.

—Al Frisbie in *Omaha World-Herald*

Where there's life there's cope. —Lane Olinghouse

PRUDENCE

I believe in practicing prudence at least once every two or three years. —Molly Ivins

PSYCHIATRISTS

Psychiatrists tell us that most women tend to marry men who are like their fathers. My brother-in-law's wife adds: "That's why the mothers always cry at weddings."

—Ron Dentinger

Julia Winton explained to a psychiatrist that her husband Fred thought he was the Lone Ranger. The psychiatrist asked, "How long has this been going on?" "About twenty years." "Bring him in. I'll cure him." The woman nodded and said, "I guess it's the right thing to do. But Tonto is so good with the children!"

You know how everyone wants a second opinion these days? Well, this lady had been going to a psychiatrist for years and

finally she decided she'd had enough of it. "Doctor," she announced, walking into his office, "I've been seeing you every week for five years now. I don't feel any better, I don't feel any worse. What's the story? I want you to level with me. What's wrong with me?" "All right," said the doctor, "I'll tell you. You're crazy." "Now wait just a minute," she protested. "I think I'm entitled to a second opinion." "Fine," he responded. "You're ugly, too."
— Mel Calman

And then there was the psychiatrist who showed very poor taste when he equipped his waiting room with a cuckoo clock.
— Ron Dentinger

"I can't imagine," Betty James said indignantly to Harvey Nuxall, the prominent psychiatrist, "why my family has insisted upon dragging me to see you. What's wrong with loving pancakes?" "Nothing at all," agreed the psychiatrist in a tone of obvious surprised. "I like pancakes myself." "Wonderful," said the Mrs. James. "You must come to my house and let me show you my collection. I've got display case after display case full of them."

My cousin Ed is a psychiatrist. He firmly believes in shock treatment. He gives his clients their bills in advance.

I told my psychiatrist, "I sometimes feel so inferior that I don't think anyone notices me at all." He said, "Next."

Our guide on a tour bus pointed to a mansion as we drove by. "This place was built by a psychiatrist. You'll notice the porch is done completely in over-wrought iron."
— Ohio Motorist

In Russia, three patients in a mental institution prepare for an examination given by the chief psychiatrist. If the patients pass the exam, they will be free to leave the hospital.

However, if they fail, the institution will detain them for five years. The doctor takes the three patients to the top of a diving board looking over an empty swimming pool, and asks each patient in turn to jump. The first patient jumps head first into the pool and breaks both arms. The second patient jumps and breaks both legs. The third patient looks over the side and refuses to jump. "Congratulations! You're a free man. Just tell me why didn't you jump?" asked the doctor. "Well, Doc," replied the patient, "I can't swim!"

A guy wearing a beret, a smock, and a goatee, goes to see a psychiatrist. The psychiatrist says, "You fantasize you're an artist." The guy says, "No." The psychiatrist says, "Then you really are an artist?" The guy says, "No." The psychiatrist says, "Then why are you wearing a beret and that smock?" The guy says, "That's what I came here to find out."

PSYCHOLOGY

The psychology instructor had just finished a lecture on mental health and was giving an oral test. Speaking specifically about manic depression, she asked, "How would you diagnose a patient who walks back and forth screaming at the top of his lungs one minute, then sits in a chair weeping uncontrollably the next?" A young man in the rear raised his hand and answered, "A basketball coach?"

PUNCTUALITY

The trouble with being punctual is that nobody's there to appreciate it.
— Franklin P. Jones

PUNISHMENT

An old-fashioned, hell-and damnation preacher was scolding his congregation for their terrible misdeeds. "Remember what it says in the Bible," he thundered. "Jesus told us that for those who do evil there shall be weeping and gnashing of teeth." [Matthew 22:13] At this point the preacher saw a very old parishioner grinning up at him, unconcerned, toothless. He accepted the challenge and pointed at the grinning gums, "Don't worry, James Lippincott. Teeth will be provided!"

PUNS

Three animals were having a huge argument over who was the best: The first, a hawk, claimed that because of his ability to fly, he could attack anything repeatedly from above, and his prey had nary a chance. The second, a lion, based his claim on his strength—none in the forest dared to challenge him. The third, a skunk, insisted he needed neither flight nor strength to frighten off any creature. As the trio debated the issue, a grizzly bear came along and swallowed them all: hawk, lion and stinker!

Fifty years ago, my Uncle Marty, then a photographer for *National Geographic,* gained considerable notoriety when he made a two-week trek, completely alone, through some of the most forbidding and unmapped wilds of the Gobi Desert, and did it without a compass! "Nothing to it!" he airily told reporters. "You've just got to mark every jog in the route, so you can go back the way you came. Every time I changed direction, I just built a little cairn of rocks, so I'd know one way from another. It's a snap if you just leave no turn unstoned."

Presidio Little League's Sefton Field in Mission Valley, Calif., has been devastated by floods for years. When the water receded last year, attorney Terry Lehr, a reclamation volunteer, reported that they found exposed electrical wiring, several hundred golf balls from the Stardust course next door, and a 15-pound carp. This led, ineluctably, to Lehr's pun: "For a while, we were the only Little League in the country with its own electric golf carp."

—Tom Blair

Among the runners finishing last in a marathon was an older man wearing a T-shirt that proclaimed: "Abominably Slow Man."

Because his trip to North America took so long, Leif Ericson returned home only to learn that his name had been crossed from the list of village inhabitants. He complained to the village chief, who relayed the adventurer's displeasure to the village statistician. "I'm so sorry," said the census keeper. "I must have taken Leif off my census."

The game show contestant was only 200 points behind the leader and about to answer the final question—worth 500 points! "To be today's champion," the show's smiling host intoned, "name two of Santa's reindeer." The contestant, a man in his early thirties, gave a sigh of relief, gratified that he had drawn such an easy question. "Rudolph!" he said confidently, "and, . . . Olive!" The studio audience started to applaud (like the little sign above their heads said to do,) but the clapping quickly faded into mumbling, and the confused host replied, "Yes, we'll accept Rudolph, but could you please explain . . . 'Olive?!?'" "You know," the man circled his hand forward impatiently and began to sing, "Rudolph the Red Nosed Reindeer—had a very shiny nose. And if you ever saw it, you would even say it glows. Olive, the other reindeer. . . ."

I was driving down a lonely country road one cold winter day when it began to sleet pretty heavily. My windows were getting icy and my wiper blades were badly worn and quickly fell apart under the strain. Unable to drive any further because of the ice building up on my front window I suddenly had a great idea. I stopped and began to overturn large rocks until I located two very lethargic hibernating rattle snakes. I grabbed them up, straightened them out flat and installed them on my blades and they worked just fine. What! You've never heard of . . . wind chilled vipers?

Many years ago, in the South Pacific, there was a small island kingdom that was ruled by a kind and benevolent King. Each year, on the King's birthday, the residents of the island gave the King a new throne as token of their love and respect for him. And each year, the King would put last year's gift up in the attic of his small house. After many years of ruling the island, the weight of the large number of birthday presents stored up in the attic became too heavy and caused the house to fall down. The moral of the story is: People in grass houses shouldn't stow thrones.

The bad and ugly king had a beautiful girl as a captive. Though her beauty shone like a thousand moons, the dress she was forced to wear was very unbecoming. She waited day and night, looking with hope out the dungeon window, searching for the knight who would free her. However, every knight was scared away by her dress, as I've said before, was very ugly. She was crying in hopelessness when the evil king jeered, . . . "See, I told you no knight would rescue a damsel in this dress!!!"

--------------------------------- **Q** ---------------------------------

QUOTATIONS

It is better to be quotable than to be honest.—Tom Stoppard

She had a pretty gift for quotation, which is a serviceable substitute for wit.　　　　　—W. Somerset Maugham

Fine words! I wonder where you stole them.

　　　　　　　　　　　　　　　—Jonathan Swift

--------------------------------- **R** ---------------------------------

RACE

Isaac Asimov loved the following, possibly apocryphal, story about Thurgood Marshall, the first black member of the Supreme Court: He was mowing the lawn at his posh residence in a Washington suburb when a car stopped in the street. The woman driving the car noted a black man mowing a lawn and called out, "How much do you charge for mowing a lawn, my good man?" Marshall hesitated, and the woman

said, "Well, what does the lady of the house pay you?" And Marshall said, "She doesn't pay me anything ma'am. She just lets me sleep with her every night."
—Isaac Asimov, *Asimov Laughs Again*

RADIO

Then coming through Iowa I heard a Des Moines radio announcer warn: "Drivers, if you are going north or south on I-80, be extremely cautious because I-80 runs east and west."
—Ron Dentinger

Sportscaster Vin Scully once received a letter from a Los Angeles woman whose spouse was a dedicated Scully listener. "My husband falls asleep at night listening to the Dodgers game. The radio is on his side of the bed, and to turn it off, I have to crawl across him. I want you to be the first to know that we're expecting a baby in about six months."

RAILROADS

People may complain about the railroads but I never spent three hours on one circling the station.
—Robert Orben, *2500 Jokes To Start 'Em Laughing*

RAIN

Question: What normally follows two days of rain?
Answer: Monday. —Ron Dentinger

Rain was trouble enough when it contained only water.

READING

The man who does not read good books has no advantage over the man who cannot read them. —Mark Twain

REAL ESTATE

Real-estate agent to prospective home buyers: "Yes, we have a house in your price range. Its present owner is a German Shepherd named Prince."

At a neighborhood cocktail party, a new Coronado, California, resident who'd just paid $300,000 for a tiny house on a little lot on an alley was seeking reassurance. "Do you think I paid too much?" she asked her host. "Nah, you can't lose in Coronado," the neighbor replied. "But $300,000, and it's so small," she persisted. "If you don't trust me, ask this guy," the neighbor said. "He's one of our top brokers." "I just bought a house near here, and I'm worried," she blurted out to the real-estate salesman. "You can't lose in Coronado," he interrupted. "Look, some idiot just paid $300,000 for a tiny house on a little lot fronting on an alley."

—Tom Blair in *San Diego Union*

Whoever uses the term "dirt cheap" probably hasn't bought any real estate lately.   —D. O. Flynn in *On the Upbeat*

RECOGNITION

See that fellow over there? Well—he's gotten so bald and so fat he didn't even recognize me!

I don't recognize you—I've changed a lot.   —Oscar Wilde

REFORMS

Every abuse ought to be reformed unless the reform is more dangerous than the abuse itself.   —Voltaire

REJECTION

It was hard for me to leave my hometown . . . covered in tar and feathers as I was.   —Gene Perret

I was so ugly when I was a kid, my imaginary playmate was ashamed to hang around with me.

You have to know how to accept rejection and reject acceptance.   —Ray Bradbury, advice to writers.

It is better to be looked over than overlooked.
—Mae West, in *Belle of the Nineties* (1934)

RELATIVES

Wanda and Millard Prufrock's happy married life almost went on the rocks because of the presence in the household of old Aunt Flora. For eighteen long years she lived with the Prufrocks. Aunt Flora was always crotchety, always demanding, never satisfied, always the first one at the table at mealtimes even though she complained about every meal set before her. Finally, the old woman caught double pneumonia and died. On the way back from the cemetery, Mr. Prufrock told his wife that he had a confession to make. "Darling," he said, "if I didn't love you so much, I don't think I ever could have stood having your Aunt Flora in the house all that time." His wife looked at him, aghast. "My Aunt Flora!" she cried. "I thought she was your Aunt Flora!"

My wife's Aunt Beverly is famous for her green thumb. The last time I visited her, my Uncle Dick warned me as I drove up to their house: "Keep your car doors locked! This is zucchini season!"

My wife's Aunt Aggie is looking for an older man with a strong will—made out to her.

My Uncle Will was an angry man. In his will, he instructed my Aunt Celia to put on his tombstone: "What are you lookin' at?"

Uncle Sid says, "My brother-in-law works at the same company I do—he's our anchor man. We call him that because he keeps us from moving forward."

RELATIVITY

Asked to explain this theory of relativity in layman's terms, Albert Einstein replied: "When a man sits with a pretty girl for an hour, it seems like a minute. But let him sit on a hot stove for a minute—and it's longer than any hour."

RELAXATION

The time to relax is when you don't have time for it.

—Sydney J. Harris

RELIGION

Most people have some sort of religion; at least they know which church they're staying away from.   —John Erskine

Following the Vatican declaration that women cannot become priests because they do not resemble Christ, sources reported that Colonel Sanders declared that he would not employ anyone who didn't resemble a chicken. —Jane Curtin

A man going into church was stopped cold by a huge sign the janitor had placed in front of the area of the floor that he just washed. It read: "PLEASE DON'T WALK ON THE WATER."

Somebody put it rightly: Almost everybody believes in tithing—a few even practice it.

An aging church custodian once said: "I've seen 12 preachers come and go and I STILL believe in God."—Larry Eisenberg

Notice on a church bulletin board: "Work for the Lord. The pay is not much but the retirement plan is out of this world."

Two fellows are talking religion. One says to the other, "Sometimes I'd like to ask God why he allows poverty, famine and injustice when he could do something about it." "What's stopping you?" asks the second. And the first replies, "I'm afraid God might ask me the same question."

Sister Serafina was on a much desired mission assignment to the Apache Indians. She was so excited that she drove past the last gas station without noticing that she needed gas. She ran out of gas about a mile down the road, and had to walk back to the station. The attendant told her that he would like to help her, but he had no container to hold the gas. Sympathetic to her plight, he agreed to search through an old shed in the back for something that might suffice. The only container that would hold fuel was an old bedpan. He was doubtful, but the grateful nun told him that the bedpan would work just fine. She carried the gasoline back to her car, taking care not to drop an ounce. When she got to her car, she carefully poured the contents of the bed pan into the tank. A truck driver pulled alongside the car as the nun was emptying the container into the tank. He rolled down his window and yelled to her, "I wish I had your faith, Sister!"

Many folks want to serve God, but only as advisers.
— Sr. Monique Rysavy

It is easier to preach ten sermons than it is to live one.
— Rev. Robert E. Harris

There are ten church members by inheritance for one by conviction.
— Eugene O'Neill

If your religion does not change you, then you should change your religion.
— Elbert Hubbard

It is a test of a good religion whether you can make a joke about it.
— G. K. Chesterton

When a rural Kansas preacher returned after visiting New England, a parishioner met him at the train station. "How are things out our way, Hiram?" the preacher asked. "Sad, sir. A cyclone came and wiped out my house." "Dear, dear," cried the parson. "Well, I'm not surprised, Hiram. You remember I warned you about the way you had been living. Punishment for sin is inevitable." "It also destroyed your house, sir," said Hiram. "It did?" The pastor was horrified. "Ah me, the ways of the Lord are past human understanding."
— Oren Arnold, *Snappy Steeple Stories*

REPAIRS

No one can make you feel more humble than the repairman who discovers you've been trying to fix it yourself.
— Savannah, Ga., *Pennysaver*

REPUTATION

Reputation is character minus what you've been caught doing.

RESEARCH

LAWS OF RESEARCH:

1st Law of Research: If you think of something new, it's been done.

2nd Law of Research: If you think something is important, no one else will.

3rd Law of Research: If you throw it away, someone else will publish it, obtain a grant, write a book, and get on the Oprah Winfrey show.

Research is what I'm doing when I don't know what I'm doing.
—Wernher Von Braun

Bacteriologist Robert Koch discovered the causes for Cholera, TB and Bubonic Plague, but not one of his peers, not even his wife, shook his hand to congratulate him. In fact, every night before she'd let him get into bed she sprayed him with Lysol.

RESPECT

Boris Yeltsin is being driven from his dacha to Moscow and is in a hurry. He is getting irritated with the slowness of his driver. "Can't you go any faster?" he says angrily. "I have to obey the speed limits," says the driver. Finally Yeltsin orders the driver into the back and takes the wheel. Sure enough a patrol car soon pulls them over. The senior officer orders the junior to go write up the ticket. But the junior officer comes back and says he can't give them a ticket, the person in the car is too important. "Well, who is it?" the senior officer asks. "I didn't recognize him," says the junior officer, "but Boris Yeltsin is his chauffeur."

RESPONSIBILITY

Donna, the minister's eight-year-old daughter, ran into the house, crying as though her heart would break. "What's wrong, dear?" asked the pastor. "My doll! Jeffrey broke it!"

she sobbed. "How did he break it, Donna?" "I hit him over the head with it."

REST

Nothing wilts faster than laurels that have been rested on.

RESTAURANTS

Connie Wilson, a successful real estate broker, stopped at a coffee shop and ordered a cup of coffee. The waitress grudgingly delivered it and asked, "Anything else?" "Yes," said the businesswoman, "I'd like some sugar, cream, a spoon, a napkin, and a saucer for the cup." "Well, aren't you the demanding one?" snapped the waitress. "Look at it from my point of view," said Connie. "You served a cup of coffee and made five mistakes."

I went into an authentic Mexican restaurant. The waiter poured the water and warned me not to drink it.

—Brad Garrett

Last night my father ordered a whole meal in French and even the waiter was surprised. It was a Chinese restaurant.

A mountaineer happened to get to Boston where he entered a seafood restaurant. "Bring me the best meal you have," he told the waiter. "I want to find out what you Bostonians eat." The waiter brought a bowl of clam chowder. The hillbilly eyed it suspiciously but ate it. He also ate a shredded cabbage salad. Finally, the waiter brought in the main course, a fine broiled lobster. The man stared at it for a moment, then jumped to his feet and cried:" I drunk your dishwater and I et your weeds, but I'm not touching your big red bug!"

—Msgr. Arthur Tonne, *Jokes Priests Can Tell,* vol. 6

Going out to eat is expensive. I was out at one restaurant and they didn't have prices on the menu. Just faces with different expressions of horror.   —Rita Rudner

When a group of us entered a delicatessen that I frequent in Minneapolis, the owner came up to take our order. A friend of mine, in a playful mood, ordered the following: "Ron, I want 140 knockwursts on pumpernickel buns, 100 with the works and 40 with just hot mustard. Then give me 27 pints of coleslaw, about 40 of baked beans. And could you toss in about six dozen kosher dills and 37 pieces of cheesecake and hold the cherries on seven of them?" Ron looked at my friend, cupped his hand to his mouth, turned toward the kitchen and hollered: "Number 3."   —Dave Wood

The difference between eating out and dining out is about twenty dollars per person.

Buffet. A French word that means "Get up and get it yourself!"

Once I was in a French restaurant that had enough stars to qualify as a minor constellation. The wine came cradled in the tuxedoed arms of a waiter who looked down his considerable nose and presented the bottle with a condescending, "Monsieur?" My host, a cosmopolitanite who was immune to the hauteur of waiters with accents, ignored the proffered dollop and requested the cork. I half-expected him to sniff it, but with a bold look at the wine steward, he raised the cork and put it in his ear. "Sounds good," he said, nodding sagely. "Pour it."   —Ben Blackburn

RESUMES

How bad a mistake can you make on your resume? Here are some real-life examples:

- "My intensity and focus are at inordinately high levels, and my ability to complete projects on time is unspeakable."

- "Education: Curses in liberal arts, curses in computer science, curses in accounting."
- "Instrumental in ruining entire operation for a Midwest chain store."
- "Personal: Married, 1992 Chevrolet."
- "I have an excellent track record, although I am not a horse."
- "I am a rabid typist."
- "Created a new market for pigs by processing, advertising and selling a gourmet pig mail order service on the side."
- "Exposure to German for two years, but many words are not appropriate for business."
- "Proven ability to track down and correct erors."
- "Personal interests: Donating blood. 15 gallons so far."
- "I have become completely paranoid, trusting completely nothing and no one."
- "References: None, I've left a path of destruction behind me."
- "Strengths: Ability to meet deadlines while maintaining composer."
- "Don't take the comments of my former employer too seriously, they were unappreciative beggars and slave drivers."
- "My goal is to be a meteorologist. But since I possess no training in meteorology, I suppose I should try stock brokerage."
- "I procrastinate—especially when the task is unpleasant."
- "I am loyal to my employer at all costs. Please feel free to respond to my resume on my office voice-mail."
- "Qualifications: No education or experience."
- "Disposed of $2.5 billion in assets."
- "Accomplishments: Oversight of entire department."
- "Extensive background in accounting. I can also stand on my head!"
- Cover letter: "Thank you for your consideration. Hope to hear from you shorty!"

RETIREMENT

A recently retired man came into the house after a morning of gardening and said, "One of the greatest joys of retirement is using my neckties to tie up tomato plants."

—*Capper's Weekly*

It is time I stepped aside for a less experienced and less able man. —Professor Scott Elledge on his retirement from Cornell

REUNIONS

Two women overheard at a class reunion:

"Did you ever look at a guy and kind of wish you were single again?"

"Yes."

"Who was it?"

"My husband." —Ron Dentinger

RIGHT

It is better to be approximately right than precisely wrong. —Warren Buffett

Being right half the time beats being half-right all the time. —Macolm S. Forbes

RONALD REAGAN

Our family didn't exactly come from the wrong sides of the tracks, but we were certainly always within the sound of the train whistles. —Ronald Reagan

Ronald Reagan has held the two most demeaning jobs in the country—President of the United States and radio broadcaster for the Chicago Cubs. —George Will

Ronald Reagan is not a typical politician because he doesn't know how to lie, cheat, and steal. He's always had an agent for that. —Bob Hope

Speaking at the 1992 Republican National Convention, former president Ronald Reagan observed, "When we see all that rhetorical smoke billowing out from the Democrats, ladies and gentlemen, I'd follow the example of their nominee. Don't inhale."

Ronald Reagan was beyond the age at which most Americans retire when he ran for the presidency in 1980. At age 69, he conducted a vigorous campaign, never passing up the chance to defuse the issue of his age with humor. On one occasion, he remarked, "I want to say that I don't mind at all any of the jokes or remarks about my age. Thomas Jefferson made a comment about the Presidency and age. He said that one should not worry about one's exact chronological age in reference to his ability to perform one's task. And ever since he told me that, I stopped worrying."

RUDENESS

Rudeness is a weak man's imitation of strength.

—Eric Hoffer

RUSSIA

A Russian man loses his pet parrot. He looks everywhere, all around the neighborhood, in the park, everywhere. He just can't find the parrot. Finally, he goes around to the local KGB office, and tells the desk officer his problem. The desk officer is a little puzzled. " Look comrade, I'm sorry you lost your pet, but this is the KGB. We don't handle missing animal reports." "Oh, I know that," says the man. "I just wanted you to know, if you do happen to find my parrot—I don't know where he could have picked up his political ideas."

In a Moscow café, a man asks the waiter for a cup of coffee and a copy of *Pravda*. "Here is your coffee, sir," says the waiter, "but *Pravda* is not available anymore." "Waiter," says the man, "I asked for a cup of coffee and *Pravda*." "I'm sorry but *Pravda* is no longer published." "Bring me coffee and *Pravda*!" the man insists. "I told you, sir, there is no *Pravda*!"

says the waiter, losing patience. "Why do you persist in asking for it?" "Because," smiles the man, "I like to hear it again, and again, and again."   —Vladimir Bukovsky

— S —

SAFETY

SAFETY TIP: Wait one hour before going into the water after eating. Three days if you had sponge cake.
                                        —Ron Dentinger

When Billy was in kindergarten his class visited the local fire station to watch a film on fire safety. In the film, children were told that if their clothes ever caught fire they should "Stop, drop, and roll" on the ground to extinguish the flames. After the film ended a fireman quizzed the children about what they had learned. "What would you do if your clothes were on fire?" he asked Billy, who answered matter-of-factly, "I wouldn't put them on."   —Catholic Workman

SALES

A businessman was having trouble with his sales. So he called in a consultant to give him an objective view and some good advice. After he had explained all of his plans and problems, he showed the consultant a map into which he had stuck brightly colored pins wherever he had a salesman. Then he said, "O.K., for a starter, what is the first thing we should do?" "Well," said the consultant, "the first thing is to take those pins out of the map and stick them in the salesmen."   —Eric W. Johnson, A Treasury of Humor II

My father's cousin Josh was a fantastic salesman. He actually made a handsome living going door to door selling signs that read, "No salespeople allowed."

The salesman was showing his prospect through a house. Everything was fine until the prospect glanced up at the ceiling and found unmistakably obvious signs of water damage. "It's a bit damp, isn't it?" he asked. "Damp!" the sales-man enthused. "Of course it's damp. Just think what an advantage that would be in case of fire!"   *—Good Reading*

SANITY

Show me a sane man and I will cure him for you.
                                —Carl Gustav Jung

Sanity is a madness put to good uses.   —George Santayana

SCHOOL

I will never forget my first day of school. My mom woke me up, got me dressed, made my bed, and fed me. Man, did the guys in the dorm tease me.   —Michael Aronin

Mrs. Hildrick, the third grade teacher was quizzing her pupils on natural history. "Now, Jason, tell me where the elephant is found." Jason struggled for the answer. Finally a look of pride lit up his face as he replied, "The elephant is so big that he's never lost."

Teacher: Give me a sentence with antidotes in it.
Pupil: My uncle kinda likes me, but auntie dotes on me.

Mrs. Hilton, the kindergarten teacher, was suddenly taken ill and a replacement was hastily found. The substitute teacher had a degree in computer science and was at a loss as to what to do with the children. She decided to tell them stories. And always, at the end of each story, she would say, "And the moral of that story is. . . ." Hearing dozens of stories, the children had sat through dozens of morals. In a few days, Mrs. Hilton recovered from her illness and returned to her class. One of her students greeted her with a smile and said, "Teacher, I'm glad you're back. I like you better than that other teacher." Mrs. Hilton was flattered by the child, but was curious. "Why do you like me better than the other teacher?" The child looked into the teacher's eyes and said, "Because you don't have any morals."

School is never the same after you get your driver's license. A teenager got back home from his first day at school as a driver. His mother asked him what he learned at school today. "I learned," said the son, "that if I don't get to school early, I don't get a good parking place."

When the power failed at the elementary school, the cook couldn't serve a hot meal in the cafeteria, so at the last minute she whipped up great stacks of peanut-butter-and jelly sandwiches. As one little boy filled his plate, he said, "It's about time. At last—a home-cooked meal."

Gregory, a second-grader came home from school and asked his mother for a dollar. His explanation: "Our principal's leaving, so we're all chipping in to give her a little momentum."

A teacher was asking her class: "What is the difference between 'unlawful' and 'illegal'"? Only one hand shot up. "OK, answer, Joan," said the teacher. "'Unlawful' is when you do something the law doesn't allow and 'Illegal' is a sick eagle."

SCHOOL BLOOPERS

Probably the most pirated, photocopied, e-mailed, and otherwise reproduced humor material of the past few decades is Richard Lederer's compilation of bloopers and blunders found in student history exams. Extensive excerpts from Lederer's book, *Anguished English,* are found throughout the Internet under such titles as "History of the World" and "The World According to Student Bloopers." Rarely is Lederer given credit. I contacted him directly and asked him for an authorized selection. His reply follows:

Dear Lowell: Here's my approximately 329-word version of "The World According to Student Bloopers"—as much humor per square syllable as I can possibly muster.

All Good Luck With Your Humor Projects,
Rich Lederer

Excerpted and adapted from Richard Lederer, *Anguished English* (Wyrick, Dell), this condensed version of the opening is composed entirely of genuine, certified, authentic student fluffs and flubs and goofs and gaffes.

- Ancient Egypt was inhabited by mummies, and they all wrote in hydraulics. They lived in the Sarah Dessert, which they cultivated by irritation.
- Ancient Egyptian women wore a loose-fitting garment which began just below the breasts which hung to the floor.
- The Bible is full of many interesting caricatures.
- Noah's wife was called Joan of Ark.
- Lot's wife was a pillar of salt by day and a ball of fire by night.
- Moses went up on Mt. Cyanide to get the ten commandments, but he died before he ever reached Canada.
- Solomon had 300 wives and 700 porcupines.
- Jesus was born because Mary had an immaculate contraption.
- An epistle is the wife of an apostle.
- The Greeks were a highly sculptured people, and without them we wouldn't have history.
- The Greeks invented three kinds of columns: corinthian, ironic, and dorc. They also invented myths.
- A myth is a female moth. One myth tells us that the mother of Achilles dipped him in the river Stinks until he became intolerable.
- The Romans conquered the Geeks. Their leader, Julius Caesar, extinguished himself on the battlefields of Gaul and when the Ides of March murdered him, he expired with these immortal words upon his dying lips: "Tee hee, Brutus"! Then came the Middle Ages, when everyone was middle aged. King Ar-

thur lived in the Age of Shivery, with brave knights on prancing horses and beautiful women. Magna Carta ensured that no free man should be hanged twice for the same offense. Joan of Arc was burnt to a steak. People contracted the blue-bonnet plague, which caused them to grow boobs on their necks. They also put on morality plays about ghosts, goblins, virgins, and other mythical creatures.

- Then came the Renaissance, a time of a great many discoveries and inventions. Gutenberg invented the Bible and removable type. Sir Walter Raleigh discovered cigarettes and started smoking. And Sir Francis Drake circumcised the world with a 100-foot clipper.

A heavy snowstorm closed the schools in one town. When the children returned to school a few days later, one grade-school teacher asked her students whether they had used the time away from school constructively. "I sure did, teacher," one little girl replied. "I just prayed for more snow."

—Catherine Hall

The old pastor made it a practice to visit the parish school one day a week. He walked into the fourth-grade class, where the children were studying the states, and asked them how many states they could name. They came up with about 40 names. He jokingly told them that in his day students knew the names of all the states. One lad raised his hand and said, "Yes, but in those days there were only 13."

—Msgr. Charles Dollen

It's Elementary! A first-grader had just been given an introduction to vowels. "Which is correct," his teacher asked, "an egg or a egg?" "An egg," he replied, "because egg starts with a fowl." —*NEA Journal*

The teacher had asked her pupils to list, in their opinions, the 11 greatest Americans. As they were writing, she stopped at one desk. "Have you finished your list, Bobby?" she asked.

"Not quite," answered the boy. "I can't decide on the full-back."
—Dan Bennett

Dad tells his fourth grader, "If your grades are B+ or better, I'll give you twenty dollars." It starts the kid thinking. The next day the kid walks up to his teacher and says, "How'd you like to make yourself an easy ten bucks?"

"Just to establish some parameters," said the professor, "Mr. Nichols, what is the opposite of joy?" "Sadness," said the student. "And the opposite of depression, Ms. Biggs?" "Elation." "And you Mr. Johnson, how about the opposite of woe?" "I believe that would be 'giddy up.'"

The teacher was giving her class of seven-year-olds a natural-history lesson. "Worker ants," she told them, "can carry pieces of food five times their own weight. What do you conclude from that?" One child was ready with the answer: "They don't have a union."
—Peterborough in *Daily Telegraph,* London

As long as there are tests, there will be prayer in public schools.
—*Evenstar's Extensive Collection of One-Liners* website

Upon seeing the same pupil again, the annoyed principal said, "This is the fifth time this week you've been sent to my office. What do you have to say for yourself?" Small boy: "Thank heaven it's Friday."
—*Carolina Country*

SCIENCE

From Lloyd Smith, MD, during his address at the graduation ceremony for the University of Texas Medical School at Galveston: "Then there was the man who was so imbued with the scientific method that he sent two of his children to Sunday school and kept the other two at home as controls."

This isn't right. It isn't even wrong.
—Wolfgang Pauli, on a paper submitted by a physicist colleague

My uncle Leo once crossed a chicken with a silkworm. He got a hen that lays eggs with a pantyhose in them!

———◼———

FOUND IN STUDENT SCIENCE TEST ANSWERS:

- One horsepower is the amount of energy it takes to drag a horse 500 feet in one second.
- You can listen to thunder after lightening and tell how close you came to getting hit. If you don't hear it, you got hit, so never mind.
- Talc is found on rocks and on babies.
- The law of gravity says no fair jumping up without coming back down.
- When they broke open molecules, they found they were only stuffed with atoms. But when they broke open atoms, they found them stuffed with explosions.
- When people run around and around in circles we say they are crazy. When planets do it we say they are orbiting.
- Rainbows are just to look at, not to really understand.
- While the earth seems to be knowingly keeping its distance from the sun, it is really only centrificating.
- Someday we may discover how to make magnets that can point in any direction.
- South America has cold summers and hot winters, but somehow they still manage.
- Most books now say our sun is a star. But it still knows how to change back into a sun in the daytime.
- Water freezes at 32 degrees and boils at 212 degrees. There are 180 degrees between freezing and boiling because there are 180 degrees between north and south.
- A vibration is a motion that cannot make up its mind which way it wants to go.
- There are 26 vitamins in all, but some of the letters are yet to be discovered. Finding them all means living forever.

S

- There is a tremendous weight pushing down on the center of the Earth because of so much population stomping around up there these days.
- Lime is a green-tasting rock.
- Many dead animals in the past changed to fossils while others preferred to be oil.
- Genetics explain why you look like your father and if you don't why you should.
- Vacuums are nothings. We only mention them to let them know we know they're there.
- Some oxygen molecules help fires burn while others help make water, so sometimes it's brother against brother.
- Some people can tell what time it is by looking at the sun. But I have never been able to make out the numbers.
- We say the cause of perfume disappearing is evaporation. Evaporation gets blamed for a lot of things people forget to put the top on.
- To most people solutions mean finding the answers. But to chemists solutions are things that are still all mixed up.
- In looking at a drop of water under a microscope, we find there are twice as many H's as O's.
- Clouds are high flying fogs. I am not sure how clouds get formed. But the clouds know how to do it, and that is the important thing. Clouds just keep circling the earth around and around. And around. There is not much else to do. Water vapor gets together in a cloud. When it is big enough to be called a drop, it does.
- Humidity is the experience of looking for air and finding water. We keep track of the humidity in the air so we won't drown when we breathe.
- Rain is often known as soft water, oppositely known as hail. Rain is saved up in cloud banks.
- In some rocks you can find the fossil footprints of fishes.
- Cyanide is so poisonous that one drop of it on a dogs tongue will kill the strongest man.
- A blizzard is when it snows sideways.
- A hurricane is a breeze of a bigly size.

- A monsoon is a French gentleman.
- Thunder is a rich source of loudness.
- Isotherms and isobars are even more important than their names sound.
- It is so hot in some places that the people there have to live in other places.
- The wind is like the air, only pushier.

Why do scientists call it research when they're looking for something new that's never been searched?

Scientist to Colleague: "I'm not afraid of the unknown. The stuff we already know is what scares us!"
—Bob Goddard in *St. Louis Globe-Democrat*

SCREAM

Sometimes a scream is better than a thesis.
—Ralph Waldo Emerson

SECRETARIES

If you really want a job done, give it to a busy, important man. He'll have his secretary do it.   —Calvin Coolidge

SELF

Know thyself? If I knew myself, I'd run away.
—Johann Wolfgang von Goethe

SELF-CENTERED

If you are all wrapped up in yourself, you are overdressed.

SELF-DEFENSE

Aunt Aggie reports: "My 9-year-old grandson Donny, who had taken several judo lessons, was very impressed with Billy, a boy in his class at public school, who held a blue belt in judo. Donny came home from school one day and excitedly told his mother that Billy had given the class bully a bloody nose. When asked which judo technique Billy had used, Donny replied, 'He stuck out his foot and tripped him!'"

SENSITIVITY

At a parent-teacher conference, a mother told the teacher, "My son Paul is a very sensitive boy." "Yes," said the teacher, "I've noticed that. Is there anything we should do about it?" "Well," said the mother, "if Paul misbehaves, please spank the boy next to him."

—Eric W. Johnson, *A Treasury of Humor*

SERIOUS

They that are serious in ridiculous things will be ridiculous in serious affairs. —Cato the Elder (234–149 B.C., AKA Marcus Porcius Cato)

SERVICE

A man dropped into a bank on business and found the customer-service clerk chatting on the phone, discussing new restaurants with her friend. After three minutes of exchanging dark glances with the man, she told her caller, "Hold on a minute? I'm being interrupted by a customer." —Jim Allen

SEX

Seventeen-year-old Tony and his grandfather Al went fishing one day. Al began expostulating about how times have changed. The teenager added a few thoughts of his own about lax sexual mores and the dangerous diseases that had emerged. The following conversation ensued:

Tony: "Grandpa, they didn't have a whole lot of problems with herpes and AIDS when you were young did they?"

Grandpa: "Nope."

Tony: "Well, what did you guys use for safe sex?"

Grandpa: "A wedding ring."

Nine-year-old Heather quizzed her mother as to her origin, and was given the traditional answer, "God sent you." "And how did you get here, Mother? Did God send you, too?" "Yes, dear." "And grandma?" "Yes, dear." "And great-grandma?" "Yes, dear." "Do you mean to say, Mother, that there have been no normal births in this family for over a hundred years?"

Literature is mostly about having sex and not much about having children. Life is the other way round.

—David Lodge

The wonderful thing about celibacy is that you don't have to bother reading the manual. —Sheldon Keller

Men reach their sexual peak at eighteen. Women reach their sexual peak at thirty-five. Do you get the feeling God is into practical jokes? We're reaching out sexual peak right around the same time they're discovering they have a favorite chair.

—Rita Rudner

SHOPPING

Heard at the mall: "I'd like a pair of stockings for my wife." "Sheer?" "No, she's at home."

A lot of antique dealers charge you extra if they have to stand there and listen to you tell them about what your mother used to have. —Ron Dentinger

My aunt loves to watch the Home Shopping Channel and QVC. She says that television used to exhibit bad taste. Now, thanks to home shopping, you can have it delivered.

My favorite contact sports—football and Christmas shopping.

My wife will buy anything marked down. Yesterday, she tried to buy an escalator. —Joey Bishop

Pat Schwab notes, "For the past few years, my watch word has been: I came, I saw, I bought! Or, as they say in Latin, 'Veni, Vidi, VISA'!"

Recent studies claim there are millions of adults who can't read or count—and if you don't believe it, take a look at the folks in front of you at the express checkout.—Jay Trachman

Spend each day as if it were your last . . . and you'll be broke by sunset.   —Los Angeles Times Syndicate

Supermarket carts carry a lot of wait.   —Steve Keuchel

A middle-aged couple were shopping . . . that is, she was shopping and he was questioning the need for each item she selected. When she chose an expensive brand of hair color, he asked plaintively, "When are you going to let your hair go gray like Barbara Bush's?" "On your Inauguration Day, dear," she sweetly replied.   —Joni Cagle

SHYNESS

The following letter is self-explanatory:

Mrs. Ladybird Johnson
The White House, Washington

Dear Mrs. Johnson: I like the idea of beautifying American cities and I want to help you in your project, so I am enclosing my check for $8. You'll pardon me for not signing it, but I want to remain anonymous.

Scientists have found the gene for shyness. They would have found it years ago, but it was hiding behind a couple of other genes.   —Jonathan Katz

SIGNS OF THE TIMES

In a supermarket in Westchester, a sign informs the shopper: "THIS IS THE EXPRESS LANE. YOU ARE LIMITED TO FIFTEEN ITEMS OR LESS. THE NUMBER FIFTEEN IS NOT SUBJECT TO NEGOTIATION."

The sign on the desk of an airline executive in Chicago reads: "Don't bother to agree with me, I've already changed my mind."

In a store this anti-shoplifting message: "God helps those who help themselves. We prosecute them."

———————————————◼———————————————

SIGNS CURRENTLY ON DISPLAY:

- On a real estate agent's car: Site-seeing bus
- On the sales lot for mobile homes: Wheel Estate
- In a public utilities office: We're Pleased to Meter You!
- In a TV repair shop: Do it yourself—then call us.
- In a doctor's office: The doctor is very busy—please have your symptoms ready.
- Sign on a college bulletin board: "Books for sale. Like new. Hardly used."
- Sign seen by the entrance to a maternity shop: "Clothes for the wait conscious."
- Sign seen in an obstetrician's office: "Pay as You Grow."
- Sign in a Minneapolis toy store: "No eating, drinking, or whining."
- Sign in front of a Colonie, N.Y., church: "We have a prophet-sharing plan for you."
- Sign in a science-fiction bookstore: "Warning—shoplifters will be disintegrated."
- Notice posted for the All Seasons Resorts in Lake Delton, Wisconsin: "Closed for the winter."
- Sign in a veterinarian's office: "The doctor is in. Sit. Stay."
- A bumper sticker on a Rabbit convertible: "I'm not a brat. Am not, am not, am not!"

On the desk of a plumbing supply manufacturer: "Don't tell me what I mean. Let me figure it out myself."

Sign in a cemetery: "Persons are prohibited from picking flowers from any but their own graves."

Signspotter Sheila Gould caught this in the cafe of Borders Books at Union Square: "Do not leave tables unattended. We are not responsible for articles left while browsing and we must keep tables available for eating customers." Forget the table, I'll have mine to go.   —Herb Caen

On the door at the U.S. Patent Office: "This patent office is a government agency. Should you decide to patent your invention, copies of all documentation must be stored in triplicate for a minimum of 20 years, costing hundreds, if not thousands of dollars. Should a commercial interest decide to implement your invention on a commercial scale, tens of millions of dollars could be required in tooling and production costs. Should your invention have military applications, it could be responsible for hundreds if not thousands of deaths. Should your invention turn out to be a new destructive force far in excess of anything known and potentially deadly in the wrong hands, it could be responsible for the end of life as we know it on this planet. Are you sure that you want to do this?"

Sign in the hallway of a railroad division office, above a row of hooks: "For supervisory personnel only." Underneath someone had added: "May also be used for coats and hats."
          —Capper's Weekly

On an outdoor sign at Northway Christian Church (Disciples of Christ) in Dallas, Texas: "Premarital Workshop 8 hours May 17 and 18. Grief Recovery Starts Tuesday May 21."

Sign outside a Philadelphia business: "Open most days about 9 or 10, occasionally as early as 7, but some days as late as

12 or 1. We close about 4 or 5, but sometimes as late as 11 or 12. Some days we aren't here at all, and lately I've been here just about all the time, except when I'm someplace else."

SIGNS AND BLUNDERS

On October 13, 1944, the Durham N.C. *Sun* reported that a local resident had been brought before a Judge Wison in traffic court for having parked his car on a restricted street right in front of a sign that read "No Stoping." Rather than pleading guilty, the defendant argued that the missing letter in the sign meant that he had not violated the letter of the law. Brandishing a Webster's dictionary, he noted that stoping means: "extracting ore from a stope or, loosely, underground." "Your Honor," said the man, "I am a law-abiding citizen and I didn't extract any ore from the area of the sign. I move that the case be dismissed." Acknowledging that the defendant hadn't done any illegal mining, the judge declared the man not guilty and commented, "since this is Friday, the 13th, anything can happen, so I'll turn you loose."

"No Stoping" is a blunderful example of the suspect signs and botched billboards that dot the American landscape. Here are some others that need to be re-signed:

- At restaurant-gas stations throughout the nation: "Eat here and get gas."
- At a Sante Fe gas station: "We will sell gasoline to anyone in a glass container."
- In a New Hampshire jewelry store: "Ears pierced while you wait."
- In an New York restaurant: "Customers who consider our waitresses uncivil ought to see the manager."
- In a Michigan restaurant: "The early bird gets the worm! Special shoppers' luncheon before 11:00 A.M."
- On a delicatessen wall: "Our best is none too good."
- On the wall of a Baltimore estate: "Trespassers will be prosecuted to the full extent of the law."—Sisters of Mercy

- On a long-established New Mexico dry cleaning store: "Thirty-eight years on the same spot."
- In a Los Angeles dance hall: "Good clean dancing every night but Sunday."
- On a movie theater: "Children's matinee today. Adults not admitted unless with child."
- In a Florida maternity ward: "No children allowed!"
- In a New York drugstore: "We dispense with accuracy."
- On a New York loft building: "Wanted: Woman to sew buttons on the fourth floor."
- In the office of a loan company: "Ask about our plans for owning your home."
- In a New York medical building: "Mental health prevention center."
- In a toy department: "Five Santa Clauses—no waiting."
- On a New York convalescent home: "For the sick and tired of the Episcopal Church."
- On a Maine shop: "Our motto is to give our customers the lowest possible prices and workmanship."
- At a number of military bases: "Restricted to unauthorized personnel."
- In a number of parking areas: "Violators will be enforced and Trespassers will be violated."
- On a display of "I Love You Only" Valentine cards: "Now available in multi-packs."
- In the window of a Kentucky appliance store: "Don't kill your wife. Let our washing machines do the dirty work."
- In a funeral parlor: "Ask about our layaway plan."
- On a window of a New Hampshire hamburger restaurant: "Yes, we are open. Sorry for the inconvenience."
- In a clothing store: "Wonderful bargains for men with 16 and 17 necks."
- In a Tacoma, Washington men's clothing store: "15 men's wool suits—$10.00—They won't last an hour!"
- On an Indiana shopping mall marquee: "Archery tournament. Ears pierced."
- Outside a country shop: "We buy junk and sell antiques."

- On a North Carolina highway: "EAT 300 FEET."
- On an Ohio highway: "Drive Slower When Wet."
- On a New Hampshire highway: "You are speeding when flashing."
- On a Pennsylvania highway: "Drive carefully: Auto accidents kill most people from 15 to 19."
- In downtown Boston: "Calahan Tunnel/No. End."
- In a Massachusetts parking area reserved for birdwatchers: "Parking for birds only."
- In a New Jersey restaurant: "Open 11:00 A.M. to 11:00 P.M. Midnight."
- In front of a New Hampshire restaurant: "Now serving live lobsters."
- In front of a New Hampshire store: "Endurable floors."
- On a radiator repair garage: "Best place to take a leak."
- On a movie marquee: "Now Playing: Adam and Eve with a cast of thousands!"
- In the vestry of a New England church: "Will the last person to leave please see that the perpetual light is extinguished."
- On a roller coaster: "Watch your head."
- On a New Hampshire road: "Will build to suit Emory A. Tuttle"
- On the grounds of a private school: "No trespassing without permission."
- In a library: "Blotter paper will no longer be available until the public stops taking it away."
- On a Tennessee highway: "Take Notice: When this sign is under water the road is impassable."
- Similarly in a New Hampshire car wash: "If you can't read this, it's time to wash your car."

Posted at an Arizona church at the beginning of August every year: "You think it's hot here?"   —Thomas LaMance

In a German hotel room: "If you wish for breakfast in your bedroom, just lift your telephone and speak to the receptionist. This will be enough to bring your food up."

—San Francisco Examiner

At a watch-repair shop in Providence, R.I.: "Come in and see us when you haven't got the time." —Ludlow Mahan

At a reducing salon: "Thinner Sanctum."—Thomas LaMance

At a credit union in New Brunswick, Canada: "A Loan Again? See Us." —Susan Osborne

On the top of a mountain in Idaho: "Skiing Beyond This Point May Result in Death And/Or Loss Of Skiing Privileges." —*St. Paul Pioneer Press*

At a repair shop: "Cuckoo Clocks Psychoanalyzed." —Thomas La Mance

In front of a Cleveland restaurant: "T-Bones 85 cents. With meat $5.95." —Ed Szalkowski

In a plant nursery: "We will sell no vine before its time." —Shelby Friedman

In the office of a marriage counselor: "Lead us not into tempertation." —Jacqueline Schiff

In Highland Park, Ill.: "Parks will not issue parking permits to fish." —Jack Eppolito

At a tax office: "It is more deductible to give than to receive." —Hal Evans

From the Costa Mesa, Calif., *Orange Coast Pilot:* "Free: One owner, low-mileage used cat. Answers to Tabitha or electric can opener."

Sign in Dillard's department store in Omaha, Neb.: "For your convenience the elevator is located in China."

Ben and Carol Stowell live beside a dirt road in New Hampshire that becomes practically impassible during mud season. For eight years, people came knocking at their door at all hours, asking to be towed out. Stowell finally posted a sign: "Mud! Pass at your own risk! If you pass, the following charges will apply: To use the phone—$5; to be towed out—$25; to have me come out and say, 'I TOLD YOU SO'—free of charge!" The end of mud season came, and not one person had stopped for help. — *Yankee*

A Phoenix, Ariz., hardware store that sells propane had this sign out front: "Tank heaven for little grills."

A dentist in Southern Pines, N.C., posted this sign in his office: "Floss that bridge when you come to it."

Sign on a newspaper reporter's desk: "The strongest desire is neither love nor hate. It is one person's need to change another person's copy." —Gilbert Cranberg

MORE SIGNS

- Posted outside a furniture refinishing shop in Lawrenceville, Ga.: "Male stripper on duty."
- At a plumber's: "We repair what your husband fixed."
- On the trucks of a local plumbing company in Pennsylvania: "Don't sleep with a drip; call your plumber."
- At a tire shop in Milwaukee: "Invite us to your next blowout."
- Door of a plastic surgeon's office: "Hello, can we pick your nose?"
- At a dry cleaner's: "How about we refund your money, send you a new one at no charge, close the store and have the manager shot. Would that be satisfactory?"
- At a towing company: "We don't charge an arm and a leg. We want tows."
- Billboard on the side of the road: "Keep your eyes on the road and stop reading these signs."
- On an electrician's truck: "Let us remove your shorts."
- In a nonsmoking area: "If we see smoking we will assume you are on fire and take appropriate action."
- At an optometrist's office "If you don't see what you're looking for you've come to the right place."
- On a taxidermist's window: "We really know our stuff."
- In a podiatrist's office: "Time wounds all heels."
- On a butcher's window: "Let me meat your needs."

- On a fence: "Salesman Welcome. Dog food is expensive."
- At a car dealership : "The best way to get back on your feet—miss a car payment."
- Outside a muffler shop: "No appointment Necessary, we hear you coming."
- Outside a hotel: "Help! We need inn-experienced people."
- On a desk in a reception room: "We shoot every 3rd salesman, and the 2nd one just left."
- At the electric company: "We would be de-lighted if you send in your bill. However, if you don't you will be."
- On the door of a computer store: "Out for a quick byte."
- In a restaurant window: "Don't stand there and be hungry, come on in and get fed up."
- Sign in a gas station: "Coke—49 cents. Two for a dollar."

Billboard promoting Boston's Charles Hayden Planetarium at the Museum of Science: "Visit Our Planetarium, You Tiny, Insignificant Speck in the Universe."   —Herm Albright

Cheese shop: "Our Swiss has 22-percent fewer cavities."

Delicatessen: "Some people come in just for the smell of it."
—Norma Levi

Health-food store: "Our hamburger is something else."
—Marge Bernsen

Hot-dog stand: "Franks for the memory."
—Irene Hannigan

Bakery: "Our ryes have seen the glory."

Sign in store window: "Any faulty merchandise will be cheerfully replaced with merchandise of equal quality."

Art museum: "Come In and Browse to Your Art's Content."
—Shelby Friedman

Allergist's office: "Wheeze Be Seated."

Poultry farm: "Quiet! May They Roost in Peace."
— Jane Hunt Clark

Diet salon: "No Amnesty for Deserters."   — Lois Lindauer

Building-supply store: "Planks to You, We're Lumber One."

Sign in the window of a florist shop: "End-of-season clearance sale! Catch us with our plants down."

On a community bulletin board: "Wanted—a set of golf clubs that shoot in the low 80s."   — Rudy Joe Mano

In a Greek tailor shop window, recommending that customers order summer suits early: "In big rush we will execute customers in strict rotation."   — *Wall Street Journal*

On a billboard for the Niagara Falls Aquarium in Niagara Falls, Ontario: "Everyone welcome—except Mrs. Paul!"
— Mary Ann Janda

On Marks & Spencer Bread Pudding: "Product will be hot after heating."   — Good Clean Fun Web site

On Nytol (a sleep aid): "Warning: may cause drowsiness."
— Good Clean Fun Web site

On Sainsbury's Peanuts: "Warning: contains nuts."
— Good Clean Fun Web site

On a bag of Fritos: "You could be a winner! No purchase necessary. Details inside."   — Good Clean Fun Web site

On a hotel-provided shower cap: "Fits one head."
— Good Clean Fun Web site

For a sale on hammocks: "We can support you the rest of your life."   — Pauline C. Bartel

BUMPER SNICKERS

- I've taken a vow of poverty. To annoy me, send money.
- A waist is a terrible thing to mind.

- Support Your Local Lawyer. Send Your Kid To Medical School.
- Energizer bunny arrested, charged with battery.
- Santa's elves are just a bunch of subordinate clauses.
- Editing is a rewording activity.
- My life has a superb cast, but I can't figure out the plot.
- Out of my mind. Back in five minutes.
- Gene Police: YOU!! Out of the pool!
- I used to be indecisive; now I'm not sure.
- My reality check just bounced.
- What if there were no hypothetical questions?
- No sense being pessimistic. It wouldn't work anyway.
- 43.3% of statistics are meaningless!
- I used to have a handle on life, but it broke.
- You're just jealous because the voices only talk to me.
- I'm not a complete idiot, some parts are missing.
- The more you complain, the longer God lets you live.
- Help wanted, telepathy: you know where to apply.
- Hang up and drive.
- I took an IQ test and the results were negative.
- Always remember you're unique, just like everyone else.
- Consciousness: that annoying time between naps.
- Ever stop to think, and forget to start again?
- If you try to fail, and succeed, which have you done?
- Be nice to your kids. They'll choose your nursing home.
- Stupidity does not qualify as a handicap, park elsewhere!
- Very funny, Scotty. Now beam down my clothes.
- The gene pool could use a little chlorine.
- I don't suffer from insanity. I enjoy every minute of it.
- Okay, who put a "stop payment" on my reality check?
- Air Pollution is a mist-demeaner.
- Anything free is worth what you pay for it
- Everyone is entitled to my opinion.
- Don't take life too seriously, you won't get out alive.
- Hard work has a future payoff, laziness pays off now.
- Warning: Dates in Calendar are closer than they appear.
- Lottery: A tax on people who are bad at math.

- Age is a very high price to pay for maturity.
- I doubt, therefore I might be.
- Procrastination is the art of keeping up with yesterday.
- If all the world is a stage, where is the audience sitting?
- Where are we going, and what am I doing in this hand-basket?

In a real-estate office: "For rent. Four-story beach house—five stories when the tide is out."

—California Highway Patrolman

At a bank promoting vacation loans: "Bye now, pay later."
—James Alexander Thom in *Nuggets*

At the entrance to a one-lane bridge in Sonoma, California: "When this sign is underwater, this road is impassable."
—Jeffrey Freiberg

Sign on the road from an Arkansas farm: For Sale. 1962 Ford Smokes, but is old enough. $135

Sign at church parking lot: We forgive those who trespass against us, but they'll be towed just the same.
—St. Olaf Catholic Church, Minneapolis

SILENCE

Drawing on my fine command of language, I said nothing.
—D. E. Knuth

It's better to remain silent and be thought stupid than to open your mouth and forever remove all doubt.

He didn't utter a word, but he exuded mute blasphemy from every pore. —Mark Twain

Few slanders can stand the wear of silence. —Mark Twain

Folks who think they must always speak the truth overlook another good choice—silence. —C. L. Null

To keep your marriage brimming

With love in the loving cup
Whenever you're wrong, admit it
Whenever you're right, shut up!

—Ogden Nash

Silence is argument carried out by other means.

—Ernesto "Che" Guevara

SIMPLICITY

Simple pleasures . . . are the last refuge of the complex.
—Oscar Wilde

SIN

Once Margaret Denton, an elderly church member, was discussing with me an uncle of hers who had repented of his sins and joined a Southern Baptist church after a lifetime of riotous living. "Will my converted uncle's sins be forgiven, Pastor?" she asked. "Oh, certainly, yes!" I replied. "Remember, the greater the sins, the greater the saint." Margaret thought silently for a time. Then she said, "Oh, Pastor, I wish I'd known this fifty years ago."

Poverty is reflected in many places, even in the hearts of men, according to a Maryknoll missionary in Bolivia. The missionary, hearing confessions at a badly run-down ranch here, asked the penitent: "Do you have any sins?" The penitent replied: "Padre, we are so poor in our house that we don't even have sins." —*Maryknoll News*

Most of us spend the first six days of each week sowing wild oats, then we go to church on Sunday and pray for a crop failure. —Fred Allen

SINCERITY

It is dangerous to be sincere unless you are also stupid.
—George Bernard Shaw

SINGING

One pastor was trying to encourage better participation in singing the new hymns. "Remember," he said, "if the Lord gave you a good singing voice, this is the way to thank Him. If He didn't, this is also a good way to get even."

—Catholic Digest

A Milwaukee couple called a neighbor to extend birthday greetings. They dialed his number and then sang Happy Birthday into the telephone. But when they had finished their off-key rendition, they discovered they had the wrong number. "Don't let that bother you," said the stranger. "You folks sure can use the practice!"   *—Milwaukee Journal*

Son: "Dad, why do you always make me sing every time Mrs. Burmally comes?"
Dad: "It's not as rude as telling her to leave."   *—Irish Grit*

SINGLE

I'm 33, single . . . Don't you think it's a generalization you should be married at 33? That's like looking at somebody who's 70 and saying, hey, when are you gonna break your hip? All your friends are breaking their hip—what are you waiting for?   —Sue Kolinsky

I don't think of myself as single. I'm romantically challenged.
    —Stephanie Piro

SLEEP

Overheard: "My insomnia is worse. Now I can't even sleep when it's time to get up."   —Ron Dentinger

SMALL TOWNS

Small Town: Where people go to church on Sunday to see who didn't.

I moved recently to Cottonwood, California, a town so small it only has two streets in it—Main Street and Non-Main Street.

I live in a town so dull that our local newspaper doesn't even have a front page.

Nothing ever happens in our town. Our town gossip had to hire a writing staff.

Tourist: "What's the speed limit through this one-horse town of yours?"

Native: "Ain't any. You folks cain't go through here fast enough to suit us." —*Modern Maturity*

You can't walk for exercise in a little town. It takes too long to explain what you're doing to all the neighbors who honk, stop, and offer you a ride.

—*The Milwaukee Journal*

A public-relations man on assignment in tiny Beatty, Nev., stopped at a local store for high-speed film. "I need two rolls of 35-millimeter, 1000 ASA film," he told the shopkeeper. "Honey," she drawled, "nobody needs 1000 ASA film in Beatty, Nevada. There's nothin' here moves that fast."

—Dick Licciardi

The manager of a touring theatrical company wired to the proprietor of the theater in a small town where his company was due to appear. "Would like to hold rehearsal next Monday afternoon at three. Have your stage manager, property man, carpenter, electrician, and all stage hands present at that hour." Four hours later he received the following reply: "All right. He'll be there." —C. Kennedy

SMILING

She would smile, and all her wrinkles would rearrange themselves into pleasure. —Irene Mortenson Burnside

SMOKING

A friend said, "I quit smoking cold turkey." I said, "What do you smoke now? Ham?" —Yakov Smirnoff

Pipe smokers are almost always model citizens. They're so busy cleaning, filling, and relighting their pipes, they just haven't time to get into trouble.   —William Vaughan

The FCC came along and it said no more cigarette commercials on television . . . I'd much rather watch a pretty girl offer me a cigarette than an old lady ask if I'm constipated.
                                                            —Mark Russell

A rebel leader was finally apprehended by the military police and summarily sentenced to death. The generalissimo watched as the blindfolded man was led before the firing squad, then magnanimously came over to offer him a last cigarette. "No, thanks," was the condemned man's answer. "I'm trying to quit."

My Uncle Irv smoked unfiltered cigarettes for forty years. He would take one puff from a cigarette, throw it down and step on it. He did this hour after hour, day in day out. Last week he came down with cancer of the shoe.

It's easy to give up smoking. All you need are willpower, determination, and wet matches.   —*Funny Funny World*

SNOBBERY

The stuffy but elegant matriarch of a prominent family asked the dog breeder, "Is this a dog of which my family and I can be proud? Does he have a good pedigree?" "Indeed, he does," declared the breeder. "If he could talk, he wouldn't speak to either of us!"

Aunt Laura is such a snob that her automobile sports the following sign: "Private bumper sticker. Do not read."

Snobs talk as if they had begotten their own ancestors.
                                                            —Herbert Agar

He's so snobbish he has an unlisted zip-code. —Earl Wilson

SNORING

Dinner was over and Grandpa retreated to his easy chair to relax. Pretty soon the rafters were shaking with his resounding snores. Mother came in just in time to see Junior twisting one of Grandpa's vest buttons. "Don't disturb Grandpa," she said. "I'm not," protested Junior. "I'm just trying to get another station." —*Capper's Weekly*

SNOW

This should be an interesting winter. My neighbor and I have parallel driveways—and we both bought snow blowers.
—Robert Orben, *2500 Jokes To Start 'Em Laughing*

SOLITUDE

In Genesis it says that it is not good for a man to be alone, but sometimes it is a great relief. —John Barrymore

SONS

Somewhat skeptical of his son's newfound determination to become Charles Atlas, the father nevertheless followed the teenager over to the weight-lifting department. "Please, Dad," wheedled the boy, "I promise I'll use 'em every day . . ." "I dunno. It's really a commitment on your part," the father pointed out. "Please, Dad?" "They're not cheap either." "I'll use 'em Dad, I promise. You'll see." Finally won over, the father paid for the equipment and headed for the door. From the corner of the store he heard his son yelp, "What! You mean I have to carry them to the car?"

I still vividly remember the little talks I had with my son. One time I said, "When I was your age, I never thought of doing any of the things you do." To which he replied, "And that's the only reason you didn't do them."

SPACE

Black holes are where God divided by zero. —Steven Wright

SPEAKING

Back in 1955, Uncle Jack made the following speech to a large conference of sales representatives: "I dictated my talk to my secretary and told her to cross out anything she thought was dull and uninteresting. 'And so, in conclusion?'"

The banquet speaker droned on and on, apparently hypnotized by the sound of his own voice. Finally, one trapped listener who could tolerate no more without falling asleep, put his napkin over his left arm, picked up a pitcher of water, and slipped out—as one more waiter.

—Msgr. Arthur Tonne, *Jokes Priests Can Tell*, vol. 6

Douglas Fairbanks, Jr., began a speech with one of the all-time best opening lines: "I feel like a mosquito in a nudist colony. I look around and I know it's wonderful to be here, but I don't know where to begin."

In a talk to the Louisiana Trial Lawyers Association, speech professor Waldo Braden began by noting that all the other speakers had highly technical backgrounds related to the practice of law. Then he analogized his position to William Howard Taft's great granddaughter. "When she was asked to write her autobiography in the third grade, the young lady responded: 'My great grandfather was president of the United States, my grandfather was a United States senator, my father was an ambassador, and I am a Brownie.' On this morning, at this elegant hotel here in the French Quarter in this distinguished company, I feel like a Brownie."

Commencement speakers have a good deal in common with grandfather clocks: standing usually some six feet tall, typically ponderous in construction, more traditional than functional, their distinction is largely their noisy communication of essential commonplace information.　　—Willard Wirtz

Gen. John W. Vessey, Jr., Chairman of the Joint Chiefs of Staff, was telling an audience about the best speech he had ever heard. It was delivered by Gen. Curtis LeMay, then Chief of Staff of the Air Force. "'I have a speech,' he quoted General LeMay as saying. 'It's a good speech. It was written by a smart lieutenant colonel who works for me, and I read it on the way here. Now I'm going to put it in the library, and you can read it, too.'"

SPEEDING

"What am I supposed to do with this?" inquired the motorist when the clerk handed him a receipt for his traffic fine. "Keep it," advised the clerk. "When you get four of them, you get a bicycle." —*Catholic Digest*

SPELLING

It is a poor mind indeed that can't think of at least two ways of spelling any word. —Andrew Jackson

SPILLS

A spilled drink flows in the direction of the most expensive object. —Judye Briggs

SPORTS

Question asked of Bob Uecker, actor, sportscaster, and former major leaguer: "How did you handle pressure as a player?" Answer: "It was easy. I'd strike out and put the pressure on the guy behind me."

Whoever invented bungee jumping must have watched a lot of Road Runner cartoons. —Nick Arnette

Chicago Bulls rookie forward Stacy King scored one point in a basketball game in which Michael Jordan scored sixty-nine points. His analysis of the game was: "I'll always remember this as the night that Michael Jordan and I combined to score seventy points."

One night at a basketball banquet the president of our local junior college was congratulating the coach and the team profusely. The beaming coach asked the president, "Would you still like me as much if we didn't win?" "I'd like you as much," the president replied. "I'd just miss having you around."

The difference between soccer and baseball is that in baseball you have a father taking his son and explaining the strategy, and in soccer you have the son taking his father and explaining it to him.
   —Danny Villanueva

If sports are supposed to be good for you, how come athletes are over the hill at 31?   —Bill Vaughan

Do you know why mountain climbers rope themselves together? To prevent the sensible ones from going home.

A Hampshire, England, cricketer who had his hand injured in a match had to complete an accident insurance claim form. Under "Witnesses" he put: "2891 spectators, 21 players, two reserves, two umpires, two groundsmen, three gatekeepers and one schoolboy up a tree." —Reginald Mitchell, *Amusing Tales From Hampshire and Dorset*

ESPN sportscaster Dave Campbell on the quickness of Toronto Blue Jays second baseman Roberto Alomar: "He gets to the ball quicker than Cinderella's sisters."

Dan Shaughnessy in the *Boston Globe:* "Defensively the Red Sox are a lot like Stonehenge. They are old, they don't move, and no one is certain why they are positioned the way they are."

In-line skating provides thrills, cardiovascular conditioning and muscle tone. It can also introduce you to a whole new set of friends—ambulance drivers, emergency room technicians and physical therapists, as well as those nice neighbors on the next block who called the rescue squad. —Chuck Moss

We're going to turn this team around 360 degrees.
—Jason Kidd, upon his drafting to the Dallas Mavericks

Sports historians pretty much agree that we may never know what made Babe Ruth, Ty Cobb and Lou Gehrig so great. There's absolutely no record of what brand of shoes they wore.

Remember sports fans, if you can't control your emotions, it can be costly. It cost my neighbor $300 because he threw a full can of beer at the umpire. And it could have cost more, but he was watching on their old television.

Pro Bowler Mark Williams was once asked, "Why do you travel the PBA tour in a van instead of flying?" "I'd sure like to fly," Williams replied. "But did you ever try to check 20 bowling balls?" —*Sports Illustrated*

Basketball coach Bill Jones of Alabama's Jacksonville State University was asked if his team's 37-point win over Kentucky Wesleyan in the NCAA Division II tournament was beyond his wildest dreams. "My wildest dreams," Jones replied, "don't include basketball." —*Sports Illustrated*

When the TV movie "A Love Affair: The Eleanor and Lou Gehrig Story" premiered on Greek TV last year, the film lost its subtitle but gained a racy subplot. Next to a scene from the film showing the Yankees' legendary Lou Gehrig and Babe Ruth locked in warm embrace, the blurb in Greece's TV magazine reported: "'A Love Affair' is the title of a dramatic adventure that really happened. The film is about the love link between baseball player Lou Gehrig and the beautiful 'Babe' Ruth. The idyll of the two young people ended up in marriage. But their happiness didn't last long. Mrs. Babe became very ill and . . ."   —*Sports Illustrated*

A college swimming coach was summarizing his team's achievements at the annual athletic banquet. "Well, we didn't win any meets," he conceded, "but we all had a good time, and nobody drowned."   —*Washington Post*

STEALING

Finishing their shopping at the mall, a couple discovers that their brand-new car has been stolen. They file a report at the police station, and a detective drives them back to the parking lot to look for evidence. To their amazement, the car has been returned and there's a note in it that says, "I apologize for taking your car. My wife was having a baby and I had to hot-wire your ignition to rush her to the hospital. Please forgive the inconvenience. Here are two tickets for tonight's Shania Twain concert." Their faith in humanity restored, the couple attends the concert. But when they return home, they find their house has been ransacked. On the bathroom mirror is another note: "I have to put my kid through college somehow, don't I?"   —*Playboy*

STOCK MARKET

A broker is a man who takes your fortune and runs it into a shoestring.   —Alexander Woollcott

The Bible says that we came into this world without riches and that we shall take no riches with us into the next. So, in a sense, stockbrokers are just doing the Lord's work.
                    —Florence Berglund

STORIES

During my graduate school days, Meyer Peller, my maternal grandfather, had a massive heart attack and was not expected to live. I sent him a letter telling him that my son often asked me what I did when I was his age. I told Grampa that I would tell him about the many days I spent with him and about the time when I was helping him in the garden. Grampa couldn't figure out why the onions which I had planted took so long to emerge. When he finally harvested them he said that they were the longest onions he had ever seen. I had planted all the bulbs upside-down! My letter was read to the old man, the resignation that had gripped his spirits lifted, and he rallied. Never doubt the power of a good family story!

To make a long story short, don't tell it.   —Tal Bonham

STRESS

Not long ago a prominent lawyer called upon his doctor for an annual check-up. The examination indicated signs of hypertension and stress. The doctor warned him to slow down, to take up a hobby—perhaps painting—to relax. He readily agreed and left his physician's office. The next day, the doctor phoned to check on his patient's progress. "Doc," the lawyer responded enthusiastically, "this painting stuff is wonderful. I've already finished ten of them!"

Talk about stress. I'll tell you how much stress there is in my life. You know those coin changers that hang on your belt? I got one that dispenses Rolaids.   —Ron Dentinger

STUDENTS

Student answers to test questions:

- Matrimony is a place where souls suffer for a time on account of their sins.
- Where was the Declaration of Independence signed? At the bottom.
- Where is Cincinnati? First place in the American Football League.
- Denver is located just below the O in Colorado.

- The soil of Prussia was so poor, the people had to work hard just to stay on top of it.
- The climate of Bombay is such that its inhabitants have to live elsewhere.

STUPIDITY

Only two things are infinite, the universe and human stupidity, and I'm not sure about the former.   —Albert Einstein

There is more stupidity than hydrogen in the universe, and it has a longer shelf life.   —Frank Zappa

If stupidity got us into this mess, then why can't it get us out?   —Will Rogers

He was born stupid, and greatly increased his birthright.
—Samuel Butler

He was distinguished for ignorance; for he had only one idea and that was wrong.   —Benjamin Disraeli

His mind is so open—so open that ideas simply pass through it.   —F. H. Bradley

No more sense of direction than a bunch of firecrackers.
—Rob Wagner

They never open their mouths without subtracting from the sum of human knowledge.   —Thomas Brackett Reed

While he was not dumber than an ox he was not any smarter either.   —James Thurber

Ordinarily he is insane. But he has lucid moments when he is only stupid.   —Heinrich Heine

She never lets ideas interrupt the easy flow of her conversation.   —Jean Webster

STYLE

A new convict is sitting in his cell at the state prison. Suddenly someone yells out, "419." The whole cellblock starts laughing. Someone yells, "78." Everyone laughs. "642." Hysteria. And this goes on every afternoon between two and three o'clock. The new guy can't figure it out. He asks his cell mate. "What's so funny?" "There's only one book in the prison library," the cell mate explains. "It's a joke book. We've all heard it so many times we memorized all the jokes. All we have to hear are the numbers." So the new guy goes to the library and studies the book. A few weeks later he's ready. Two o'clock arrives. Someone yells, "316." Everyone's howling. "56." Gales of laughter. The new guy yells, "237." There's dead silence. He asks his cell mate what happened. The cell mate says, "Some people can tell a joke and some people can't."

SUCCESS

Jim Fixx, author of a best-selling book on running, was asked if fame and fortune had changed his life. He said yes, and explained, "One day I took a check for $100,000 to deposit in the bank, and the female teller said to me, 'Are you married?'"
—"Good Morning America" (ABC)

The only thing that ever sat its way to success was a hen.
—Sarah Brown

SUMMER

A perfect summer day is when the sun is shining, the breeze is blowing, the birds are singing, and the lawn mower is broken.
—James Dent

SUNDAY SCHOOL

The Sunday before Christmas, Melissa James asked her Sunday school students at Holy Trinity Lutheran Church to draw a picture of the Holy Family. When the pictures were handed in, she saw that some of the youngsters had drawn the conventional pictures—the Holy Family in the manger, the Holy Family riding on the mule, and so forth. But she was confused by the drawing made by little Joshua, so she called him up and asked him to explain his picture, which showed an airplane with four heads sticking out of the plane windows. She said, "I can understand why you drew three of the heads to show Joseph, Mary, and Jesus. But who's the fourth head?" "Oh," answered Joshua, "that's Pontius the Pilot!"

Ruth Troutman, the Sunday school teacher, was very keen on religious ceremonies and had spent an entire session talking to the class about the correct way to pray. "Now," she said finally, "suppose we want to pray to God for forgiveness. What must we do first of all?" "Sin?" suggested one little boy.

Austin Markle, the Sunday School teacher, asked his class: "What are sins of omission?" After some thought one little fellow said: "They're the sins we should have committed but didn't get around to."

A Sunday School teacher asked a group of children in her class. "Why do you believe in God?" In reporting some of the answers the teacher confessed that the one she liked best came from a boy who said, "I don't know, unless it's something that runs in the family."   —King Duncan

Little Johnny came home from Sunday School and told his mother that if he missed three Sundays in a row, the teacher would throw him into the furnace. The horrified mother telephoned the teacher at once. "What I said was," the calm teacher explained, "that if any child missed three Sundays in a row, he would be dropped from the register."

—Presbyterian Life

The children were invited to participate in the groundbreaking ceremony for the new Sunday school building. Each child turned over a small shovelful of dirt. Later in the day, Granddad asked his little granddaughter what they did at church

that morning. "Well," she said sadly, "we dug for a new Sunday school, but we didn't find it."
— *Liguorian*

One Sunday late in Lent a Sunday School teacher decided to ask her class what they remembered about Easter. The first little fellow suggested that Easter was when "all the family comes to the house and they eat a big turkey and watch football." The teacher suggested that perhaps he was thinking of Thanksgiving, not Easter, so she let a pretty young girl answer. She said Easter was the day "when as you come down the stairs in the morning you see all the beautiful presents under the tree." At this point, the teacher was really feeling discouraged. But after explaining that the girl was probably thinking about Christmas, she called on a lad with his hand tentatively raised in the air. Her spirits immediately perk up as the boy says that Easter is the time "when Jesus was crucified and buried." She felt she had gotten through to at least one child until he added, "And then He comes out of the grave and if He sees His shadow we have six more weeks of winter."

A little boy in Sunday School gave the explanation as to why Mary and Joseph took baby Jesus to Egypt. He claimed: "They couldn't get a sitter."

At Sunday school the topic was Elijah and the prophets of Baal. The teacher explained that Elijah built an altar, placed wood upon it, cut the sacrificial bullock in pieces and laid them on the wood. He then commanded that the people fill four jars with water and pour the water over the sacrifice. "Why do you think they did that?" asked the teacher. A little girl raised her hand and said, "To make gravy." —Bill Dana

Nine-year-old Joey, was asked by his mother what he had learned in Sunday school. "Well, Mom, our teacher told us how God sent Moses behind enemy lines on a rescue mission to lead the Israelites out of Egypt. When he got to the Red Sea, he had his engineers build a pontoon bridge and all the people walked across safely. Then he used his walkie—talkie to radio headquarters for reinforcements. They sent bombers to blow up the bridge and all the Israelites were saved." "Now, Joey, is that really what your teacher taught you?" his mother asked. "Well, no, Mom. But if I told it the way the teacher did, you'd never believe it!"

A Sunday school teacher asked her little children as they were on the way to church service, "And why is it necessary to be quiet in church?" One bright little girl replied, "Because people are sleeping."

SWISS

Swiss Army Knives got their names because it takes the entire Swiss army just to carry one.   —Nick Arnette

---------------------- **T** ----------------------

TACT

Tact is the art of making guests feel at home when that's really where you wish they were.   —George E. Bergman

TATTOOS

Tattoo: Permanent proof of temporary insanity.
                                                —Wise & Aldrich

TAXES

Of the two classic certainties, death and taxes, death is preferable. At least you're not called in six months later for an audit.   —Bill Vaughan

They say that everybody should pay their taxes with a smile. Well, I tried it, but they wanted cash.

I'm not sure what I should do about my taxes this year. The way I've got it figured . . . if I use the short form, the government gets my money. And if I use the long form, the accountant gets my money.   —Ron Dentinger

Internal Revenue service auditor to nervous taxpayer: "Let's begin with where you claim depreciation on your wife."

Around April 15 we discover that America is the land of untold wealth.

INCOME TAX FORMS are a test of the power of deduction.

Last April, Stephen Sprenger, who owns the H&R Block on Denny Way in Seattle, commented, "It's that time of year: the time for ceiling deductions." "Ceiling deductions?" I asked. Sprenger explains, "You ask how many miles the client drove and he looks at the ceiling and says, 'About 8,000.'"

A decade ago, Tom Lehrer remarked: "On my income tax form 1040 it says 'Check this box if you are blind.' I wanted to put a check mark about three inches away."

The botanical name for the American yew tree, used extensively for shrubbery around Washington government buildings, is *Taxus taxus*. —David Gordon

IRS agent to taxpayer: "Just because your mother-in-law lives in the suburbs and you have two teen-agers at home, you cannot list the telephone company as a dependent." —George E. Bergman

A government bureau is where they keep the taxpayer's *Graffiti*

Noel Coward, on leaving England to take up residence in Switzerland for the obvious purpose of avoiding taxes, was met by the press at the airport. Why, asked a reporter, was he moving to Switzerland? "Devoted to chocolates," was Coward's reply. —William F. Buckley, Jr., *Four Reforms*

IRS Auditor to taxpayer: "The trick is to stop thinking of it as your money." —Serrano

TEACHERS

A teacher, asked why she preferred working in an elementary school, explained: "Well, I love children of all ages, but at the grade school I'm always sure of finding a parking space." —*Capper's Weekly*

When a teacher calls a boy by his entire name it means
trouble.   —Mark Twain

An elderly woman strolled calmly out
into the street after a policeman had
flagged her to stay on the sidewalk.
"Lady," he bellowed, "don't you know
what it means when I holdup my
hand?" "I ought to," she snapped, "I
was a schoolteacher for 40 years."

TEACHING

Good teaching is one-fourth preparation and three-fourths
theater.   —Gail Godwin

TEAMWORK

On his way to give a talk at a rural high school a speaker
slipped into the ditch. He walked to the nearest house to
find that the farmer's tractor wouldn't work. The only power
was an old, blind mule. They hitched the mule to the car and
the farmer shouted: "Giddap, Frankie; Giddap, Bessie." The
mule didn't move. "Giddap, Ben; Giddap, Mabel: shouted
the farmer. The mule didn't budge. Then the farmer shouted:
"Giddap, Mike!" The mule leaned into the harness and
pulled the car out. "How come?" asked the traveler, "he
didn't move until you called him 'Mike?'" "Well," explained
the farmer, "Mike's his name. Blind Mike, cuz he can't see.
When I call out those other names, he things there are a lot
of other mules pulling too. But he won't start until I call his
name. If he thought he was the only one he would never even
try."   —Ed Steiner

TECHNOLOGY

These days it's absolutely in to know how to use word processors and computers. But the manager of an aerospace company was a cyberphobic (one who is afraid of electronic
devices). One day he entered his office and found a computer

terminal set up next to his desk. "What's this?" asked the manager. An engineer replied vigorously, "It's your new terminal, and it's just waiting for you to give it a command." The manager glared at the computer and said, "Go away!"

A hot trend these days is computers, word processors, and all sorts of cybernetic devices. Perhaps we should have a sense of perspective about this. Consider a rod of graphite encased in wood, first used in the 16th century. It's called a pencil. Here are some of the marvels about it: It can write underwater. It can write in outer space. A standard 7¼-inch pencil can draw a line 35 miles long. It can write 45,000 words. It can scratch your back. It can lubricate a stuck zipper. It can pin up long hair. Pencils can be bought for three dollars a dozen.

TEENAGERS

Telling a teenager the facts of life is like giving a fish a bath.
— Arnold H. Glasow.

Remember that as a teenager you are at the last stage in your life when you will be happy to hear that the phone is for you.
— Fran Lebowitz

After listening to a lengthy lecture from his father about his sloppy appearance, shaved head, Van Dyke beard, numerous body piercing, earrings, and general attitude, the teenager blurted out: "But, Dad, I gotta be a nonconformist . . . How else can I be like the other kids?"

Four men at the office were discussing what they hoped to get out of their new cars. "Economy," said one man. "Dependability," said another. "Styling," added the third. They all turned to the fourth fellow, who was standing there with a grim expression on his face. "What I'd most like to get out of my new car," he said, "is my teenage son." — *Liguorian*

Dennis Miller's definition of body piercing: "A powerful compelling visual statement that says, 'Gee, in today's competitive job market, what can I do to make myself less employable?'"

There's nothing wrong with teenagers that reasoning with them won't aggravate.

Commuter to seatmate: "We're equipped three ways to have all the answers—we've got an encyclopedia, a home computer, and a teenager." —Laurence J. Peter, *Peter's Almanac*

Adolescence is not so much a period as it is an exclamation point. —*Chicago Tribune*

A 14-year-old girl got her own phone for her room. Her father ventured into no man's land one day and found his daughter sobbing amid the sea of debris. "The telephone just rang," she cried. "I heard it, but I couldn't find it."

It isn't what a teenager knows that worries his parents. It's how he found out. —Ann Landers

They say teenagers are smarter than ever so I asked mine to do something about the snow on the front walk. Well, sir— that vacuum cleaner will never be the same!
—Robert Orben, *2500 Jokes To Start 'Em Laughing*

Following dialogue was overheard between teenage son and parent: "I'm off to the party." "Well, have a good time." "Look, Pop, don't tell me what to do." —*The Railway Clerk*

Smart Son: "Dad, I just siphoned a couple of gallons of gas out of your car for my old bus. It's okay, isn't it?"
Smarter Father: "Sure, it's okay, son. I bought the gas with your allowance for next week. So run along and have a good time." —*Sunshine Magazine*

The mother of a teenage boy was going on holiday, leaving him alone for the first time. Concerned about his eating habits, she wanted to make sure he ate balanced, nutritious meals in her absence. She phoned him a few days after her departure and thinking of vegetables, asked anxiously: "Have you been eating anything green?" "Only the bread," he replied. —*Rosary*

TELEVISION

Husband to wife: "I'll say this for television. The more unsuitable the program, the quieter it keeps the children!"

Imitation is the sincerest form of television. —Fred Allen

When the politicians complain that TV turns the proceedings into a circus, it should be made clear that the circus was already there, and that TV has merely demonstrated that not all the performers are well trained. —Edward R. Murrow

It is difficult to produce a television documentary that is both incisive and probing when every twelve minutes one is interrupted by dancing rabbits singing about toilet paper. —Rod Serling

Television—a medium. So called because it is neither rare nor well-done. —Ernie Kovacs

Television remote controls encourage couch potatoes to exercise their options while broadening their base. —William Arthur Ward

Why do they report power outages on TV?

During intermission at the Metropolitan Opera in New York, I saw a familiar face. Thinking it was someone I knew, I said, "Hi, where have we met before?" He shook my hand, smiled and said, "I'm Edwin Newman, and you've been watching too much television." —Lea K. Bleyman

Television news is like a lightning flash. It makes a loud noise, lights up everything around it, leaves everything else in darkness and then is suddenly gone. —Hodding Carter

TEMPER

Ever notice, it's easier to control your temper if the other guy is bigger?

TEMPTATION

Lately it seems like I don't have to worry about avoiding temptation. At my age temptation is avoiding me.

—Ron Dentinger

Those who flee temptation generally leave a forwarding address. —Lane Olinghouse

TENSION

Americans are so tense and keyed up that it's impossible even to put them to sleep with a sermon.

—Norman Vincent Peale

TEXANS

Did you hear about the wealthy Dallas oil man who went on vacation to Hawaii? He went out to the beach one afternoon to discover that his wife had just been rescued from the surf, and was being revived by the lifeguards. "What are you doing?" he asked. The lifeguards replied, "We are giving her artificial respiration." "Artificial nothing," the oil man shouted, "Give her the real thing. We can afford it."

An Easterner was riding with a rancher across a blistering hot stretch of Texas. Equally warm was the glowing praise of the rancher for the glories of his home state. Suddenly a beautiful plumed bird dashed across the road. "What kind of bird is that?" asked the easterner. "Bird of Paradise," said the Texan. The easterner rode in silence for a few more bumps, then remarked, "Long way from home, isn't he?" —*Woodchuckles*

THEORY

In theory, there is no difference between theory and practice. But, in practice, there is. —Jan L. A. van de Snepscheut

THIEVES

As through this world I've traveled, I've seen lots of funny men. Some will rob you with a six-gun. And some with a fountain pen.
—Woody Guthrie

Ludlow Bean was arrested the other day for stealing a woman's change purse. He told the judge that he hadn't been feeling well, and he thought the change would do him good.
—Charley Weaver (Cliff Arquette)

My grandfather invented the burglar alarm but someone stole it from him.
—Victor Borge

There's one good thing about kleptomania—you can always take something for it.

This guy was a terrible burglar. He didn't even take our TV. He just took our remote control. Now he drives by once in a while and changes channels on us.
—Brian Kile

She could carry off anything; and some people said that she did.
—Ada Leverson

TIME

An Air Force lieutenant with a terrible cough went to see a doctor. "This cough is serious," diagnosed the doctor. "Do you smoke?" "No," answered the lieutenant, "I gave up smoking." The physician was not convinced. "When did you give it up?" The lieutenant's response was immediate: "Nineteen fifty-nine." "That long ago?" questioned the surprised doctor, "I don't think that is possible." "What's the big deal," asked the annoyed lieutenant as he looked at his watch. "It's only twenty-one sixteen now."

Last year, when daylight savings time ended, I realized that you cannot turn a digital watch backwards one hour to get back to standard time. My wife said, "All you have to do is turn it ahead twenty-three hours. I did . . . and for six months I was a day early for all my appointments."

—Ron Dentinger

There is no distance on this earth as far away as yesterday.

—Robert Nathan, *So Love Returns*

While proudly showing off his new apartment to friends, a college student led the way into the den. "What is the big brass gong and hammer for?" one of his friends asked. "That is the talking clock," the man replied. "How's it work?" the friend asked. "Watch," the man said, then proceeded to give the gong an ear shattering pound with the hammer. Suddenly, someone screamed from the other side of the wall "KNOCK IT OFF, YOU IDIOT! It's two o'clock in the morning!

Three o'clock is always too late or too early for anything you want to do.   —Jean-Paul Sartre

Unaware that Indianapolis is on Eastern Standard Time and Chicago on Central Standard Time, a man inquired at the Indianapolis airport about a plane to Chicago. "One leaves at 1 P.M.," a ticket agent said, "and arrives in Chicago at 1:01 P.M." "Would you repeat that, please?" the man asked. The agent did so and then inquired, "Do you want a reservation?" "No," said the man. "But I think I'll hang around and watch that thing take off."   —*United Methodists Today*

TRAFFIC

The first one to see the light turn green is the driver of the second car back.   —Terry Marchal

One time a cop pulled me over for running a stop sign. "Didn't you see the stop sign?" the officer asked. "Yeah," I said. "But I don't believe everything I read."

—Steven Wright

TRAGEDY

"In this world there are only two tragedies. One is not getting what one wants, and the other is getting it." —Oscar Wilde

TRANSLATIONS

English translation printed on a sign inside a ferry in San Juan Harbor: "In case of emergency, the lifeguards are under the seats in the center of the vessels."

TRAVEL

A long sea-voyage not only brings out all the mean traits one has, and exaggerates them, but raises up others which he never suspected he possessed, and even creates new ones.
—Mark Twain

In the Dominican Republic, a tour guide pointed out the tomb of Christopher Columbus. "That's interesting," said a tourist. "In Spain, a few years ago, I was shown the tomb of Columbus in Seville." "Ah," replied the Dominican guide, "the one in Seville is the tomb of the old Christopher Columbus. This is the tomb of the young Christopher Columbus."

Thanks to the interstate highway system, it is now possible to travel across the country from coast to coast without seeing anything.
—Charles Kuralt

The following are actual stories provided by travel agents:

- I had someone ask for an aisle seat so that his hair wouldn't get messed up by being near the window.
- A client called in inquiring about a package to Hawaii. After going over all the cost info, she asked, "Would it be cheaper to fly to California and then take the train to Hawaii?"
- A man called, furious about a Florida package we did. I asked what was wrong with the vacation in Orlando. He said he was expecting an ocean-view room. I tried to explain

that is not possible, since Orlando is in the middle of the state. He replied, "Don't lie to me. I looked on the map and Florida is a very thin state."

- I got a call from a man who asked, "Is it possible to see England from Canada?" I said, "No." He said, "But they look so close on the map."

- A nice lady just called. She needed to know how it was possible that her flight from Detroit left at 8:20 A.M. and got into Chicago at 8:33 A.M. I tried to explain that Michigan was an hour ahead of Illinois, but she could not understand the concept of time zones. Finally I told her that the plane went very fast, and she bought that!

- I just got off the phone with a man who asked, "How do I know which plane to get on?" I asked him what exactly he meant, which he replied, "I was told my flight number is 823, but none of these darn planes have numbers on them."

- A businessman called and had a question about the documents he needed in order to fly to China. After a lengthy discussion about passports, I reminded him he needed a visa. "Oh no I don't, I've been to China many times and never had to have one of those." I double checked and sure enough, his stay required a visa. When I told him this he said, "Look, I've been to China four times and every time they have accepted my American Express."

T

Columbus headed for India and wound up in Santo Domingo. Today, if you head for India, you get to India. It's your baggage that winds up in Santo Domingo.

When Executive Travel invited readers to relate their worst flying experience of the year, the winner was a businessman who described the following: "Officials, after discovering a domestic West African flight had been grossly overbooked, asked all passengers with boarding cards to run twice around the plane. The fastest ones got the seats."   —AP

Woman to travel agents: "We've already seen the world. What else do you have?"
                                                                              —E. A. Harris

TROUBLE

Borrow trouble for yourself if that's your nature, but don't lend it to your neighbors.
                                              —Rudyard Kipling, *Rewards and Fairies*

If a husband has troubles, he should tell his wife, and if he hasn't he should tell the world how he does it.

T-SHIRTS

SUGGESTED SAYINGS FOR T-SHIRTS:

- Well, this day was a total waste of makeup.
- Make yourself at home! Clean my kitchen.
- Who are these kids and why are they calling me Mom?
- I thought I wanted a career, turns out I just wanted paychecks.
- Don't bother me. I'm living happily ever after.
- Do I look like a people person?
- Is it time for your medication or mine?
- I started out with nothing and still have most of it left.
- I pretend to work. They pretend to pay me.
- If I throw a stick, will you leave?
- Therapy is expensive, poppin' bubble wrap is cheap! You choose.
- I like cats, too. Let's exchange recipes.
- Everyone thinks I'm psychotic, except for my friends deep inside the earth.
- Ambivalent? Well, yes and no.
- If only you'd use your powers for good instead of evil . . .

- Allow me to introduce my selves.
- Sarcasm is just one more service we offer.
- Whatever kind of look you were going for, you missed.
- Suburbia: where they tear out the trees and then name streets after them.
- Do they ever shut up on your planet?
- I'm just working here till a good fast-food job opens up.
- A woman's favorite position is CEO.
- Chaos, panic, and disorder—my work here is done.
- I'm trying to imagine you with a personality.
- A cubicle is just a padded cell without a door.
- Stress is when you wake up screaming and you realize you haven't fallen asleep yet.
- Here I am! Now what are your other two wishes?
- Don't worry. I forgot your name, too!
- Adults are just kids who owe money.
- I have a computer, an ice cream maker, and pizza delivery. Why should I leave the house?
- Nice perfume. Must you marinate in it?
- I'm not tense, just terribly, terribly alert.
- Can I trade this job for what's behind door #2?

At the coin laundry, a little gray-haired woman was wearing a T-shirt that read: "I finally got it all together and now I forgot where I put it."

—Contributed by Nadine Saunders Saundwes

TWINS

I grew up with Jonathan and Gene Katz, who were twin brothers. One became a minister and the other a physician. It was almost impossible to tell the twins apart. A man approached one of them on the street and asked, "Are you the twin who preaches?" "No," came the answer, "I'm the one who practices."

Know why the Siamese twins moved to London? So the other one could drive.

My neighbor told me his girlfriend is a twin. I asked him if he ever kissed the wrong twin. He said, "No, her brother won't even come near me." —Ron Dentinger

TYPOS

LOVE THOSE TYPOS . . .

- For sale—one executive desk, one secretarial desk with chains.—Classified ad in Jefferson, *Wisconsin Advertiser*
- Personal Coping Machine With Paper Supply—Montrose, Pennsylvania, *Shopping Guide*
- Hall of Fame To Indict Nine New Members.—Headline in Pleasanton, California, *Tri-Valley Herald*
- Hot tub, seats eight, rearly used.—Classified ad spotted in Pittsburgh Pennysaver
- Appalling two-story home in quiet neighborhood.—Classified ad in Ionia County, Michigan, *Shopper's Guide*
- Do's and Don'ts for Hormonious Honeymoon.—Headline on advice article for brides in Cedar Park, Texas, *Hill Country News*
- 1981 Citation, goof transportation.—In Bay City, Michigan, *Times*

U

UNFULFILLED PROPHECIES

"The place will be crawling with great-looking girls."

"When it says empty, there are always a couple of gallons left."

"Counting drinks and tip, you'll pay thirty dollars tops."

"They'll feel wonderful once you break them in."

"We're bringing it in right under budget."
"You can assemble it yourself in minutes."
"It won't feel cold once you dive in."
"You'll housebreak him in no time."

—————————— **V** ——————————

VACATIONS

Talk about your unbelievable coincidences: Every year I go on vacation at the very same time the fish do.
—Ron Dentinger

A family vacation is one where you arrive with five bags, four kids and seven I-thought-you packed-its. —Ivern Ball

Wife to husband: "Our vacation isn't a total loss, dear. Most people go a lifetime without ever seeing icicles on palm trees."
—Franklin Folger

Take a vacation to get away from it all, and you run into a lot of people who want to get it all away from you.
—Lane Olinghouse

Real charity is the ability to hope that the guy whose work you are doing while he vacations in the sun is having a wonderful time.
—Bill Vaughan

You know that summer camp is going to be expensive when it lists the weenie roast as a "frankfurter flambé"
—Arch Napier

Woman to friend: "Our neighbor's vacation was over three months ago, and would you believe were still suffering from slide effects?"
—Ivern Ball

VEGETARIANS

I was a vegetarian until I started leaning toward sunlight.
—Rita Rudner

VICE PRESIDENTS

Women are being considered as candidates for Vice President of the United States because it is the worst job in America. It's amazing that anyone will take it. A job with real power is first lady. I'd be willing to run for that. As far as the men who are running for President are concerned, they aren't even people I would date.
                                                —Nora Ephron

The man with the best job in the country is the Vice President. All he has to do is get up every morning and say, "How is the President?"
                                                —Will Rogers

The Vice-Presidency is sort of like the last cookie on the plate. Everybody insists he won't take it, but somebody always does.
                                                —Bill Vaughan

VIRTUE

An unprincipled businessman who liked to appear full of virtue, told Mark Twain, "Before I die, I'm going to make a pilgrimage to the Holy Land. I shall climb to the top of Mount Sinai and read the Ten Commandments aloud." "I have a better idea," said Mark Twain. "You do?" said the businessman. "I'd like to hear it." "About the Ten Commandments," Twain replied, "why don't you stay right at home in Boston and keep them."

VISITING

Santa Claus has the right idea. Visit people once a year.
                                                —Victor Borge

---

W

WAITERS/WAITRESSES

Waiter to diner: "I'm sorry. My lawyer suggested that I don't make any more recommendations."

The worst new dining trend is hearing the waiter exclaim, "Good choice!" immediately after a person at your table selects a dish. It was bad enough in the old days, when waiters introduced themselves to us. Now they're reviewing us.

—Alan Richman

WAITING

Being on the tightrope is living; everything else is waiting.

—Karl Wallenda

The man who goes alone can start today; but he who travels with another must wait till that other is ready.

—Henry David Thoreau

WASHING

The three-year-old boy was ordered by his mother to carry all those cloth animals in his room to the washing machine in the basement so that she could give them the cleaning they badly needed. While she was busy in the laundry room, the telephone rang and her son ran back upstairs to answer it. A man's voice inquired, "Is your mother home?" "Yes, she is," the youngster said, "but she can't come to the phone right now. She's busy putting an elephant into the washing machine." There was a long silence on the other end of the line. "I guess I have the wrong number," the man stammered and quickly hung up.   —*American Weekly*

WASHINGTON

A Princeton graduate applied for a job with the State Department in Washington. The personnel director called one of the fellow's references to ask about him, and received a lengthy response detailing the applicant's fine social standing and family background from Pilgrim stock. "Sir," the personnel director responded, "I think you misunderstood. We want to employ the young man for diplomatic purposes, not breeding purposes."

W

How on earth did we expect to know who the good guys were in Kosovo when we can't even figure out who the good guys are in Washington?

WEALTH

Every day I get up and look through the Forbes list of the richest people in America. If I'm not there, I go to work.

—Robert Orben

WEATHER

Heard on National Weather Service radio in Memphis: "The weather warning alarm system will be activated today for test purposes between 11 and 11:30 A.M., weather permitting."

═══════════════ ■ ═══════════════

TEMPERATURE (DEGREES FAHRENHEIT):

- +60 Californians put on sweaters.
- +50 Miami residents turn on the heat.
- +45 Vermont residents go to outdoor concert.
- +40 You can see your breath. Californians shiver uncontrollably. Minnesotans go swimming.
- +35 Italians cars don't start.
- +32 Water freezes.
- +30 You plan your vacation in Australia.
- +25 Ohio water freezes. Californians weep pitiably. Minnesotans eat ice cream. Canadians go swimming.
- +20 Politicians begin to talk about the homeless. New York City water freezes. Miami residents plan vacation further south.
- +15 French cars don't start. Cat insists on sleeping with you.
- +10 You need jumper cables to get the car going.
- −5 American cars don't start.
- −10 Alaskans put on T-shirts.
- −10 German cars don't start. Eyes freeze shut when you blink.
- −5 You can cut your breath and use it to build an igloo. Arkansans stick tongues on metal objects. Miami residents cease to exist.

- −20 Cat insists on sleeping in pajamas with you. Politicians actually do something about the homeless. Minnesotans shovel snow off roof. Japanese cars don't start.
- −25 Too cold to think. You need jumper cables to get the driver going.
- −30 You plan a two week hot bath. Swedish cars don't start.
- −40 Californians disappear. Minnesotans button top button. Canadians put on sweater. Your car helps you plan your trip south.
- −50 Congressional hot air freezes. Alaskans close the bathroom window.
- −80 Hell freezes over. Polar bears move south. Green Bay Packer fans order hot cocoa at the game.
- −90 Lawyers put their hands in their own pockets.
- −100 Canadian buildings turn off air conditioning.

WEDDINGS

Late one Saturday afternoon, Pastor Harold returned home. "How did the wedding go?" his wife asked. "Fine, my dear, until I asked the bride if she would obey," and she said, 'Do you think I'm crazy?' and the bridegroom, who was in sort of a stupor, mumbled, 'I do,'—then things began to happen!"

A Midwest preacher received this thank you note from a bridegroom he had married: "Dear Reverend, I want to thank you for the beautiful way you brought my happiness to a conclusion."

At a wedding reception attended by four pairs of the divorced and remarried parents and stepparents of the bride and groom, one father rose

W

and gave the following toast to the newlyweds: "I wish you the joy and humor of Jesus, good health, longevity, and only one Christmas every year."

WHY DID THE CHICKEN CROSS THE ROAD?

Stay tuned as a panel of chickens reveals the shocking truth!
—Geraldo Rivera

Whether the chicken crossed the road or the road crossed the chicken depends upon your frame of reference.   —Albert Einstein

To boldly go where no chicken has gone before.   —Gene Roddenberry

Give me ten minutes with the chicken and I'll find out.

—Tomas de Torquemada, Grand Inquisitor of the Spanish Inquisition

You tell me.   —The Sphinx

Whaddaya want, it should just stand there? —Jackie Mason

To die. In the rain.   —Ernest Hemingway

To prove to the 'possum it could be done.

What? I missed one?   —Colonel Sanders

And the No. 1 reason? Fricassee!   —David Letterman

WHY IS IT

That the same guy who has a $1000 treadmill has a $2000 riding mower?

WILLS

Where there's a will there's a wail.   —Arnold H. Glasow

The old man on his deathbed made the final adjustments to his will. "And to each employee who has been with me 20

years or more," he said to the attorney, "I bequeath $10,000."
"Very generous of you," said the lawyer. "I wouldn't say so,"
said the dying man. "None of them has been with me that
long. But it will look pretty good in the papers, don't you
think?"
— *The Malabar Herald*

WINNING

An older gentleman won millions in the state lottery. Since
he had a weak heart, his wife enlisted the pastor's help to
gently break the good news. The priest did a fine job, and
the winner was jubilant indeed. "Father," he exclaimed, "I
want to give half of it to our parish!" And the pastor dropped
dead.
— *The Priest*

WISDOM

Wisdom is the ability to keep your mouth shut while your
mind continues to talk to itself.

Conrad Hilton, the hotel mogul, had a droll sense of humor.
Once he was on the Johnny Carson show, and he was asked
if he had a message for the American people. He looked
straight into the camera and said, slowly and distinctly to
about 30 million listeners. "Please put the shower curtain
inside the tub."

The difference between a smart man and a wise man is that
a smart man knows what to say, and a wise man knows
whether or not to say it.
— Frank M. Garafola

Some folks are wise and some are otherwise.
— Tobias George Smolett

W

WISHES

Wife: "You're always wishing for something you haven't
got."
Husband: "What else is there to wish for?"

When you reach for the stars, you may not quite get one, but you won't come up with a handful of mud either.

—Leo Burnett

WIT

Wit is educated insolence. —Aristotle

You can pretend to be serious; you can't pretend to be witty.

—Sacha Guitry

Wit ought to be a glorious treat, like caviar. Never spread it about like marmalade. —Noel Coward

WIVES

A bridge table is the only place I've seen where a wife is usually eager to do her husband's bidding. —Charles Goren

 My father's cousin, the respected Judge Louis Streiker, had a wife, forty years his junior, who was just a bit too fond of the grape. At a party one afternoon at the governor's mansion, he reproved her, "My dear, that's the seventh time you've gone up to the bar and asked for another whiskey sour. Doesn't it embarrass you? Don't you worry about what the people at the bar think?" "Why should it?" she chirped merrily. "I just explain I'm getting them for you."

Rob: "My wife is very touchy. The smallest thing will set her off."
Stan: "You're fortunate. Mine is a self-starter."

There is no use arguing with the inevitable. Do what your wife says in the first place. —O. Battista

My wife thinks I'm too nosy. At least that's what she scribbles in her diary. —Drake Sather

When a man steals your wife, there is no better revenge than to let him keep her.   —Sacha Guitry

Aunt Roz explains, "Uncle Albert and I have managed to be happy together for forty years. I guess this is because we're both in love with the same man."

When it comes to preaching, my wife is my severest critic. One Sunday after church, she whispered in my ear: "Lowell, dear, I believe Jesus wanted us to CLOTHE the naked, not VISIT them as you said in your sermon today!"

My wife makes the budget work. We do without a lot of things I don't need.   —Milton Berle

My VISA card was stolen two months ago, but I don't want to report it. The guy who took it is using it less than my wife.

The easiest way to get your wife's attention is by looking comfortable.

My Aunt Mindy told her fellow bridge club members: "I have the most marvelous recipe for goulash—all I have to do is mention it to my husband and he says, 'Let's eat out.'"

If you want to be sure you'll always remember your wife's birthday, just try forgetting it once.

WOMEN

High heels were invented by a woman who has been kissed on the forehead.   —Christopher Morley

In politics, if you want anything said, ask a man. If you want anything done, ask a woman.   —Margaret Thatcher

When women kiss, it always reminds me of prize fighters shaking hands.   —H. L. Mencken

Woman begins by resisting a man's advances and ends by blocking his retreat.   —Oscar Wilde

Women are like elephants to me. I like to look at them but I wouldn't want to own one.   —W. C. Fields

W

Women's styles may change, but their designs remain the same. —Oscar Wilde

There's a difference between beauty and charm. A beautiful woman is one I notice. A charming woman is one who notices me. —John Erskine

You'd be surprised how much it costs to look this cheap. —Dolly Parton

Any girl can be glamorous. All you have to do is stand still and look stupid. —Hedy Lamarr

A woman's mind is cleaner than a man's. She changes it more often. —Oliver Herford

A reader writes: "Who originated the custom of the man giving the woman a diamond engagement ring?" We're not sure, but we think it was a woman.

One young woman about another: "She's never really cared for a man's company—unless he owns it."
—Quipster, in Odessa, Texas, *American*

They keep trying to tell us that women are smarter than men, but did you ever see a man wearing a shirt that buttoned in the back?

WORDS

The difference between the right word and the almost right word is the difference between lightning and the lightning bug. —Mark Twain

Recreational wordplayers wonder why we drive on a parkway and park on a driveway. And in what other language do people play at a recital and recite at a play?
—Richard Lederer in *Crazy English*

Ever notice that PRICE and WORTH mean the same thing, but priceless and worthless are opposites? —Jay Trachman

When ideas fail, words come in very handy. —Goethe

Metaphors are apt to do a speaker in unless they are carefully crafted. Columnist William Safire recounted a story about the late Sen. Everett Dirksen, who rose in the Senate to say, "Around the world there is a feeling that there is a firm hand on the rudder of the ship of state." Explains Safire: "As Dirksen's speechwriter, I was chagrined later to learn that the man with the hand on the rudder would be drowning, and nobody would be minding the tiller."

—Jack Valenti, *Speak Up With Confidence*

WORK

Millions of people in this country aren't working, and that is scary. However, the real problem is that so many of these people are employed.   —Ron Dentinger

The virtues of hard work are extolled most loudly by people without calluses.

John came home flushed with pride. "I've been promoted," he announced. "I have a new job! They've made me an expediter." "What's an expediter?" asked his wife. "Well, it's hard to explain but if you did what I'm supposed to do, it would be called nagging."

Wife: "You look tired dear. Did you have a bad day at the office?"

Husband: "I'll say. I took an aptitude test, and believe me, it's a good thing I own the company!"

Two exasperated company executives were discussing a scatterbrained office boy who had a habit of fouling up important errands. "How long has he been with us, anyway?" asked one of the executives. "He's never been with us," replied the other. "He's been against us from the start."   —*Quote*

Receptionist to salesman: You can either wait till the boss comes back or I can give you the old runaround myself.

In the words of Robert Frost, the great American poet, "The brain is a wonderful organ. It starts working the moment you get up in the morning and does not stop until you get to the office."

I used to work in a fire hydrant factory. You couldn't park anywhere near the place.   —Steven Wright

My Uncle Irv always contended: "The trouble with getting to work on time is that it makes the day so long."

Man to co-worker: "I learn more from originals left in the copier than I do from the employee newsletter."
                    —Litzler in *The Wall Street Journal*

Employee: "The stress my boss puts me under is killing me. I have migraines, my blood pressure is going through the roof, I can't sleep at night, I just found out I have an ulcer, and as long as I stay in this job, the only question is whether I'll have a stroke or a heart attack."
Friend: "So why don't you quit?"
Employee: "I have a great health plan."
                    —Richard Jerome

Pope John XXIII was a kind man with a marvelous sense of humor. Someone once asked him how many people worked at the Vatican. "Half of them," he said.
        —Theodore M. Hesburgh, *God, Country, Notre Dame*

- When you take a long time, you're slow. When your boss takes a long time, he's thorough.
- When you don't do it, you're lazy. When your boss doesn't do it, he's too busy.
- When you make a mistake, you're an idiot. When your boss makes a mistake, he's only human.
- When doing something without being told, you're overstepping your authority. When your boss does the same thing, that's initiative.
- When you take a stand, you're being bull-headed. When your boss does it, he's being firm.

- When you overlooked a rule of etiquette, you're being rude. When your boss skips a few rules, he's being original.
- When you please your boss, you're apple polishing. When your boss pleases his boss, he's being cooperative.
- When you're out of the office, you're wandering around. When your boss is out of the office, he's on business.
- When you're on a day off sick, you're always sick. When your boss is a day off sick, he must be very ill.
- When you apply for leave, you must be going for an interview. When your boss applies for leave, it's because he's overworked.

At the water cooler: "They gave him a watch when he retired, and in a week it quit working too." —Clyde Moore

Employee: I have been here 11 years doing three men's work for one man's pay. Now I want a raise.

The trend lately is to find some job where you can work out of your home. A reader writes to say, "This is okay if they are working with a computer, but the guy who lives upstairs from me is a blacksmith."

In an employment office: "Confident? Look at his résumé. It's the first time I've seen 'omnipotence' listed under job skills." —*Orben's Current Comedy*

Nobody is sicker than the man who is sick on his day off.

WORRY

Don't sweat the petty things and don't pet the sweaty things. —Jacquelyn Small

When I don't have anything to worry about, I begin to worry about that. —Walter Kelly

WORTH

The real worth of a person is determined by what that person does when there is nothing to do.

W

WRITING

The difference between fiction and reality? Fiction has to make sense.   —Tom Clancy

Said the literary agent to the aspiring novelist, "When did they open up that sidewalk cafe I saw you in last night?" "That wasn't a sidewalk cafe," replied the writer sadly. "That was my furniture."

My father says he can't understand why a person would take a year to write a novel when he can easily buy one for a few dollars.

A good novel tells us the truth about its hero; but a bad novel tells us the truth about its author.
                                    —G. K. Chesterton

Better to write for yourself and have no public, than to write for the public and have no self.   —Cyril Connolly

Author-historian Shelby Foote, upon completion of the third and final volume of his epic narrative *The Civil War,* noted: "In response to complaints that it took me five times longer to write the war than the participants took to fight it, I would point out that there were a good many more of them than there was of me."

Anybody who corrects all his mistakes is probably writing his autobiography.   —*Chicago Tribune*

Clare Boothe Luce comments on writing her memoirs: "I'll never do it. All autobiographies are alibiographies."
                                    —"Dick Cavett Show," PBS

Manuscript: something submitted in haste and returned at leisure.   —Oliver Herford

Everywhere I go I'm asked if I think the university stifles writers. My opinion is that they don't stifle enough of them.
                                    —Flannery O'Connor

Some editors are failed writers, but so are most writers.
—T. S. Eliot

There's many a bestseller that could have been prevented by
a good teacher.   —Flannery O'Connor

A writer is someone for whom writing is more difficult than
is for other people.   —Thomas Merton

A woman writing at a post-office desk was approached by a
man whose hand was in a cast. "Pardon me," said the man,
"but could you please address this post card for me?" The
woman gladly did so, agreeing also to write a short message
and sign for him. "There," said the woman, smiling. "Is there
anything else I can do for you?" "Yes," the man replied. "At
the end could you put, 'P.S.—Please excuse the hand-
writing?'"   —*Leadership*

Y

YOGI BERRA

You got to be careful if you don't know where you're going,
because you might not get there.   —Yogi Berra

Half this game is ninety percent mental.   —Yogi Berra

YOUTH

I'm all for the young taking over and
thank God I won't be here when they
do.   —Arthur Treacher

Youth is a religion from which one
always ends up being converted.
—Andre Malraux

There's only one thing wrong with
the younger generation: a lot of us
don't belong to it any more.
—Bernard Baruch

I am not young enough to know
everything.   —Oscar Wilde

You can only be young once, but you can be immature forever.

Parents often talk about the younger generation as if they didn't have anything to do with it.   —*Funny Funny World*

----------------------------- **Z** -----------------------------

ZOO

In a huff, a woman rushed up to a zoo attendant. "You should see what's going on in the monkey cage!" she exclaimed. "Four chimps are sitting at a table playing cards!" "So what?" answered the attendant, shrugging his shoulders. "They're only playing for peanuts."   —*Good Living*